In the wake of 1989, with boundless confidence and insufficient reflection, we put the 20th century behind us and strode boldly into its successor swaddled in self-serving half-truths: the triumph of the West, the end of History, the unipolar American moment, the ineluctable march of globalization and the free market.

Tony Judt, "What Have We Learned, If Anything?" *New York Review of Books,* May 2008

# Preface

The Harvard Russia scandal of the 1990s, a turning point of a certain sort in the years after the Cold War ended, never achieved a satisfying resolution, despite its extensive trail of litigation. Even people well versed in controversies of that rancorous decade – the savings-and-loan crisis cleanup, Whitewater, the Wen Ho Lee affair, impeachment, Enron – routinely express doubts about the case. "I never knew whom to believe on that one," they say; "I never quite figured it out."

This book aims to resurrect the story, recollect its key events, and elucidate what was once thought to be merely a subplot, thereby casting new light on the affair, in order to shed some light on a much larger business in the present day – the relationship between the United States and the rest of the world. Russia is part of the story, but it is not mainly about Russia. The North Atlantic Treaty Organization is part of it, too, but the story is not mainly about NATO, or US foreign policy in general.

The Harvard-Russia scandal was never about Russia. It was always a story about the United States, its ethical standards and everyday concepts of fair play. When the US Justice Department charged a prominent Harvard professor, his wife, and his deputy, with financial misconduct in Russia while leading a team of experts advising the government of Boris Yeltsin on behalf of the United States, Harvard defended itself and its professor to the hilt. The university lost – was all but laughed out of court by a jury. It returned to the government most of the money it had been paid.

But Harvard's attorneys silenced a second plaintiff with a settlement and nondisclosure agreement, ensuring that what really happened would be less well understood. The part the long, sad story played in Lawrence "Larry" Summers' resignation as president of the university received very little attention as well. Even though the case was concluded long ago, it has renewed relevance in the present day. Harvard didn't lose Russia – but, as we will see, it nearly lost its sense of right and wrong.

Alas, the Harvard venture turns out to have been the least of the folly. Starting in the 1980s, US foreign policy began pursuing an ambitious agenda of expansion – democracy-promotion, regime-change, nation-building, and, especially, the expansion of the alliance that Western nations had formed to fight World War II. Nicaragua, Panama, Kuwait, Kosovo, Iran; and, after 9/11, Afghanistan, Iraq, Georgia, Libya, Ukraine, Syria – this was something more than one thing after another. Ventures in these places were undertaken for high-minded reasons. Seldom, however, was sufficient account taken of the arguments of the other side. The misconduct of the Harvard project, and the muted response it evoked, was only a small part of the pattern, little more than a vignette, but it is a striking illustration of a state of mind widespread among policy-makers in those days.

A peculiar illusion of global omnipotence emerged in the United States after the collapse of the Soviet Union. Relatively cautious policies adopted during the George H. W. Bush administration were amplified and extended during the presidencies of Bill Clinton, George W. Bush and Barack Obama until they threatened to damage long-term American interests. Similarly, the "Washington consensus" markets masquerading as politics, sufficient unto themselves, superior to all other systems of identity and control, are now pretty well understood to have been a fantasy, if only because China proceeded successfully along completely different lines. For a time, though, in realms of politics and expertise, the notion was plausible and held sway.

I began this project in the summer of 2016, when the state of US-Russia relations was already high on the list of problems facing America. It was widely expected then that Hillary Clinton would be elected president. She had been burnishing her hawkish credentials, and I was thinking about who she might nominate as secretary of state. Trump's victory has complicated matters. Clinton had a lengthy public history of engagement with Russia. Trump is a wheelbarrow of smoke. It is difficult to imagine a man less able to speak with any authority to the history of US-Russia relations since the collapse of the Soviet empire in 1991, or otherwise lead in the interpretation of the tensions of those years. In some ways, it doesn't matter. The story begins with the US presidential election in 1992.

I have called my story *Because They Could* because that is the essence of both the Harvard scandal and the story of NATO enlargement. At every juncture, the principals took advantage of their privileged positions and, when brought to account, employed the strategy summarized by the famous adage, ascribed variously to Henry Ford II, Nellie McClung, and Benjamin Jowett: "Never apologize, never explain, get the thing done and let them howl." The Clinton team were pioneers in this strategy, and used it sparingly. With Donald Trump it has become the spirit of the age.

# Table of Contents

Epigraph .................................................... i
Introdction ................................................ vii

## THE HARVARD RUSSIA SCANDAL

1. The Thing's a Mess  *July 7, 2002* ............................ 1
2. Shleifer to Leave Harvard?  *January 12, 2003* ................ 11
3. A High-Stakes Mediation that Failed  *January 26, 2003* ....... 16
4. Judge Finds Against Shleifer, Hay and Harvard  *July 4, 2004* . 19
5. A Walk on the Beach  *September 5, 2004* ...................... 24
6. Meet the *Siloviki*  *September 12, 2004* ..................... 31
7. The "Assigned To" Trial  *November 5, 2004* ................... 35
8. "A Narrow and Technical Issue"  *November 12, 2004* ........... 40
9. Who Is Minding the Store?  *January 16, 2005* ................. 49
10. A Theory of the Harvard Mess  *March 27, 2005* ............... 57
11. A Bigfoot Enters the Harvard Story  *May 15, 2005* ........... 63
12. Adult on Board  *May 29, 2005* ............................... 67
13. Andrei and [the Baseball Star  *August 7, 2005* .............. 71
14. Who Wants to Know? (Or, Why Economic Principals Is Not a Blog)
    *August 14, 2005* ........................................... 76
15. The Tick-Tock  *January 22, 2006* ............................ 81
16. When the Watchdog Doesn't Bark  *January 29, 2006* ........... 88
17. Those Three Weeks in March  *February 26, 2006* .............. 96
18. In Which, At Last, We Meet, Perhaps, Andrei Shleifer's Evil Twin
    *April 16, 2006* ............................................ 102
19. The Light Gray Curse  *November 5, 2006* ..................... 110
20. When the Attorney General Was a Mensch  *March 25, 2007* ..... 119
21. The Un-Marshall Plan  *April 29, 2007* ....................... 123
22. Climate Change?  *February 24, 2008* ......................... 126
23. A Normal Professor  *June 1, 2008* ........................... 130
24. Is Physiognomy Destiny?  *March 22, 2009* .................... 135
25. The Asterisk  *February 27, 2011* ............................ 140
26. Larry Swings for the Fences Again  *July 28, 2013* ........... 145

27. Summers: A (Mildly) Exculpatory Note  *August 25, 2013* ........ 148
28. Toward a Climax  *September 15, 2013* ...................... 153
29. The End of the Saga  *September 22, 2013* .................... 157

## LOOKING BACK

30. Meet John Keffer ....................................... 160

## THE BROKEN PROMISE

31. Two Roads Diverged .................................... 203
32. The Generation of '91 .................................. 227
33. Toward a New History of Russia .......................... 234
34. Sympathy for the Devil ................................. 243
35. The Accidental President ............................... 251
36. The Broken Promise ................................... 253

Appendix I: Andrei Shleifer's Letter to Provost Albert Carnesale ........ 258
Appendix II: The Steyer Memo ............................... 269

Notes ..................................................... 279
Index ..................................................... 280

# Introduction

August 13, 1997, was a typical August day, not much going on in the news. Steve Jobs returned to Apple. A balance-of-payments crisis erupted in Thailand. Special prosecutor Kenneth Starr wound down his investigation of the Whitewater affair. Against this backdrop, the headline on a front-page article in *The Wall Street Journal* stood out:

> Aborted Mission: How an Aid Program Vital to Economy of Russia Collapsed/ Harvard Men Built Market, Allegedly Didn't Steer Sufficiently Clear of It/ A Trailblazing Mutual Fund.

The story featured a woodcut of its central figure, 36-year-old Harvard University professor Andrei Shleifer, who at 15 had emigrated in 1976 with his parents from the USSR to the United States. In 1992, the US Agency for International Development, a semi-autonomous unit of the US State Department, chose Harvard's Institute for International Development (HIID) to advise the Russian government of Boris Yeltsin on "shock therapy," privatization, and the rule of law.

On an inside page were woodcuts of Shleifer's wife, bond trader Nancy Zimmerman, and Elizabeth Hebert, fiancée, later wife, of Shleifer's deputy, former Rhodes Scholar Jonathan Hay. Shleifer and Hay, USAID said, having "gained influence over nascent Russian capital markets," had "abused the trust of the United States government by using personal relationships... for private gain." What made the accusations especially surprising, wrote *WSJ* reporters Carla Anne Robbins and Steve Liesman, "was that the Harvard men had been assigned to promote, among other things, Western ideals of fair play."

Mentioned in the article as well was US Deputy Treasury Secretary Lawrence Summers. As an undergraduate, Shleifer had won a research assistantship with Summers, then an MIT professor, by citing five alleged shortcomings in a Summers research paper. "They became close," the story explained. "Mr. Summers championed Mr. Shleifer's tenure bid at Harvard and sponsored his first trip back to the USSR by including him in a 1990 World Bank Mission to Lithuania."

The story had broken three months earlier, when USAID suspended programs led by Shleifer and Hay, alleging that both men had used their positions for private gain. A week later, Jeffrey Sachs, in his capacity as director, had fired Shleifer and Hay from the USAID team, asserting that HIID had "zero tolerance" for those who invested in countries they were advising. A week after that, Anatoly Chubais, first deputy to Russian prime minister Viktor Chernomyrdin, dismissed the USAID project, explaining, "The investigation… against the Harvard researchers has some kind of political roots… produced by those in the United States who do not support the ideas of Russian radical reforms."

For a time, Russian media took an interest in what had happened. Soon, however, there were bigger problems to worry about: a battle among oligarchs over the privatization of the Russian telephone system; the falling price of oil; the swoon of the Russian stock market. The United States was distracted by a new turn in the long-running Whitewater investigation; the special prosecutor had turned his attention to the newly discovered Lewinsky matter. In August 1998, Russia devalued the ruble, effectively defaulting on its sovereign debt. The same day, Clinton appeared before the grand jury to acknowledge an "inappropriate relationship" with the intern. A month later, an ominous sell-off took place in markets around the world, which finally got Americans' attention. Long-Term Capital Management, a financial trading firm founded five years before by a handful of traders and economic wizards, two Nobel laureates among them, had fetched up on the brink of collapse. Would the crisis spread to the United States? No. Two intense days of meetings at the Federal Reserve Bank of New York were sufficient to arrange a bailout.

As suddenly as it had arisen, the financial crisis seemed to abate. The Russian economy rebounded. Concerns for Brazil lingered, but in time they, too, went away. In February 1999, *Time* magazine put on its cover Federal Reserve chairman Alan Greenspan, Treasury Secretary Robert Rubin, and Deputy

Secretary Summers, as "The Committee to Save the World." Summers replaced his boss in May after Rubin resigned to join banking giant Citigroup in a three-person "Office of the Chairman," with John Reed and Sanford Weill. At 44, the former Harvard professor had become the youngest treasury secretary since Alexander Hamilton. The American Economic Association recognized Shleifer with its John Bates Clark Medal, awarded every other year in those days, as the economist judged to have made the greatest contributions to the science before the age of 40.

Harvard announced in June 2000 that it would dismantled the HIID, a unit bigger than the university's graduate schools of divinity, dentistry, design, and education, explaining that its consulting practice "did not complement teaching and research priorities." Sachs, who would remain a professor, began listening to offers from other universities. Two years later, he would move to Columbia University, in New York, as director of its Earth Institute.

Then, in the waning days of the Clinton administration, in September 2000, the US attorney in Boston, acting on behalf of the Justice Department, brought civil suit against Harvard. Donald Stern explained that he had ended a criminal probe; instead, his office would seek treble damages for fraud. Named as well were Shleifer, Zimmerman, Hay and Hebert. The case against Hebert, by now married to Hay, was quickly dismissed since she had no contractual relationship with USAID. In December, Summers agreed to seek the presidency of Harvard University.

The first half of this book tells the story of what happened next.

\*\*\*

When the story broke, it seemed mainly a matter of human interest: one man betrayed by another, a mentor by his protégé or, conceivably, the other way around. (What sort of advice had Summers given Shleifer, anyway?) I wrote a couple of quick columns for the *Boston Globe*, wrote to Shleifer to ask if he wanted to talk about it (he didn't), and put the matter away. I had begun a book about developments in growth theory that was a more pressing project.

With the government lawsuit, the Harvard Russia scandal became a more complicated affair: now a great university's reputation for probity was on the line. But the *Globe* had been sold and was under new management. This time

I left the story alone. Within a year I had quit the paper for the web. "The column" had become "the weekly," and I was on my way to becoming a reader-supported independent journalist. I had become free – almost obligated – to follow the story. Once depositions were taken and filed, it became clear that it was not just Shleifer who had embarrassed Harvard and the US government, but his old friend Summers as well – and now Summers headed the university. What was that all about? Did Shleifer have his patron over a barrel? And who was in charge at Harvard?

Today, the significance of the story seems different. The recklessness of the leaders of the Harvard team in disregarding both the rules and common sense; the reflex of the university in defending itself and them against serious charges; and the indifference with which news of the case was received in most quarters, no longer seems so surprising. Not even the story of the second lawsuit – the one that Harvard settled and hushed up in order to disguise what really happened – has the capacity to shock. Instead, the whole episode seems an early symptom of a state of mind that developed among leaders and opinion-makers after 1989, an attitude that recognized no serious constraints on American power to set the rules of whatever game as it pleased. So I've added seven new pieces, seeking to reinterpret the story, bring it up to date, and place it in the context of the larger story of US-Russian relations since 1993.

The mood of exhilaration that set in after 1989 had many sources beside the fall of the Berlin Wall. China had entered the world trading system soon after the death of Mao Zedong. By the late '80s, the Soviet empire was collapsing. The innovative finance that enabled the resulting expansion of world trade produced a twenty-year bull market – a cascade of shares, bonds, swaps, futures, options, and securitized debt emanating from Chicago, New York, and London and spreading around the world. The First Gulf War demonstrated the vast superiority of US weaponry to Soviet arms. Then the Internet seemed to come out of nowhere. The dot-com boom even delivered the miracle of a budget surplus in the United States. The '90s had begun with Francis Fukuyama's *The End of History*; they ended with Alan Blinder and Janet Yellen's triumphant benediction, *The Fabulous Decade*.

Success fostered a sense of virtually unlimited authority. America was said to have become a hyper power, policeman to the world, removing a dictator in

Panama and imprisoning him in Miami, bombing Belgrade to force an end to war in Kosovo in the Balkans, invading Afghanistan and Iraq, boycotting Iran, accomplishing regime change in Libya and seeking it in Syria, and threatening to oppose the Russians at nearly every turn in the course of events. Away from the spotlight, the North Atlantic Treaty Organization expanded to the east over Russian objections, admitting one nation after another, all of them former Soviet satellites or dominions.

It may seem like a leap to compare Harvard's mission to Moscow to NATO expansion. One was a small-scale operation undertaken by a university in what was then a distant corner of international finance. The other required multinational negotiations at the highest levels of government. One affected a handful of firms in Moscow, and not very many as it turned out. The military-industrial complexes of a dozen nations vied for new business in the other. One dispute has been resolved by a court of law, filed away, and mostly forgotten. The other has provoked a short-lived war in Georgia and a protracted conflict in Ukraine and thoroughly soured Russian views of the United States.

Yet the high-and-mighty manner in which Harvard responded to US government charges of misconduct had something in common with the nonchalant disregard three US presidents displayed over 24 years towards ever-more forcefully voiced Russian objections to NATO expansion. Nothing about it was foreordained. When East Germany was absorbed by the Federal Republic of Germany in 1990, its armed forces became part of NATO, with the acquiescence of Russia. Mikhail Gorbachev considered that the George H. W. Bush administration had promised there would be no further expansion of NATO to the east. The Clinton administration went ahead anyway, and the rest is history – hotly contested, but little ventilated.

***

This book has three parts. The first, "The Harvard Russia Scandal," about half the pages in the book, contains 29 Sunday columns written as events unfolded. They were published online. I have cleaned these up a little, combined paragraphs originally designed to be read online, changed a headline in one case ("Andrei and [the Baseball Star] instead of "Andrei and Rafael"), but otherwise these articles appear exactly as they did on *EconomicPrincipals.com*. The result, I hope, is a narrative in which a new reader can watch the story unfold even though the outcome is known in advance – it resembles a slow-motion train wreck – and then share, with readers already well familiar with the story, in the pleasure of seeing the final puzzle pieces fall into place (most of them, anyway).

From the beginning, the Harvard Russia scandal was imperfectly understood. After the *WSJ* broke the story, the other important English-language newspapers failed to cover it with vigor or imagination. Books by Moscow correspondents minimized or ignored the episode; later accounts by participants omitted it altogether. Not until 2005 did a painstaking and persuasive reconstruction of the episode, by veteran investigative reporter David McClintick, appear in *Institutional Investor*. Probably the article cost Summers his Harvard job (chapter 30). Even then, a vital part of the story remained out of reach. A second, private lawsuit had been unfolding in Portland, Maine, parallel to the government action. Harvard lawyers had laid down a smokescreen that obscured its significance, and cloaked the identity of the real victim of the Harvard team – until now.

Thus the second part, "Looking Back," consists of a profile written for this book. "Meet John Keffer" tells the story of the banking entrepreneur who was lured onto the Moscow scene by the Harvard team and very nearly fleeced by them for his troubles. Keffer is the hero of this story, a straight-arrow former Peace Corps volunteer who was exactly the sort of businessman USAID had hoped might represent American ways to the Russians. Instead, Harvard sent two callow economists who quickly went native, to the consternation of all concerned.

The third part, "The Broken Promise," contains six last chapters designed to place the episode in a broader context of US-Russia relations since the collapse of the Soviet Union. "Two Roads Diverged" is about the presidential election of 1992 and the gradual enlargement of NATO over 25 years that followed. "Generation of '91" concerns US press coverage of Russia since the end of the Cold War. "Towards a New History of Russia" is a riff on the career of Fred Weir, of the *Christian Science Monitor* – whom I consider to have been the single best North American correspondent in Moscow in those years – and a periodization of the years after the collapse of the Soviet Union that he proposed. "Sympathy for the Devil" is a meditation on the problems Putin faced in 1999, and what economists don't know. "The Accidental President" is a reading of the significance of the Trump presidency. "The Broken Promise" recapitulates.

All these are representative of what goes on every Sunday afternoon at *EconomicPrincipals.com* – or, for those who subscribe to the bulldog edition, first thing Sunday morning. There are two appendices: the key pieces of evidence from the mountains of documents uncovered in United States v. Harvard University et al.

I've written *EP* online for more than 15 years now, almost as long as I wrote twice a week for the *Globe*. I've never regretted my decision to move to the web. I couldn't have done it without newspaper training. Big newsrooms evolve cultures of their own. I spent 20 years at the *Globe*, a wonderful newspaper, vital, well managed, and well loved by its readers. But it was *The Wall Street Journal* where I internalized the norms that served me best in the years thereafter, though I worked there only a short time. Almost all the journalists who most successfully pursued the Harvard Russia story – reporters Steve Liesman, Carla Anne Robbins, Zachary Seward, David McClintick, Jon Hilsenrath, Paul Steiger, and Peter Kann – all but Michael J. Carroll, the *Institutional Investor* editor who commissioned McClintick's story – were steeped in values of the news-side of the *WSJ*. I am proud to have been a part of a great tradition. The *Harvard Crimson* and *Harvard Magazine*, too, cleaved to very high standards in keeping readers abreast of the story, but they could not be expected to take the lead.

Two people, more than any others, aided in the preparation of this book: Mark Feeney, who, against all odds, has faithfully copy-edited *EP* since 1983; and the book's designer, Jennifer Teichman. Beyond them I am indebted to the usual small circle of family and friends and, above all, to the bulldog edition subscribers who have kept *Economic Principals* in business. The book is dedicated to the memory of Janet Ballantyne, 1939-2017, career Foreign Service officer of the US Agency for International Development. As USAID's principal representative in Moscow in 1997, Ballantyne referred the conduct of the leaders of the Harvard advisory team to the USAID inspector general. She shrugged off the wrath of those in power, kept her own counsel, and, in and out of USAID, and in again, soldiered on for 20 years in the service of everyday American ideals.

THE HARVARD RUSSIA SCANDAL

CHAPTER ONE

# "The Thing's a Mess"

*July 7, 2002*

With the breakdown of negotiations for a settlement last month, the Justice Department's complaint against Harvard University in connection with its 1990s mission to Moscow has taken a new and ominous turn.

*The Boston Globe* reported last month that prosecutors had filed a motion for summary judgment, asserting that in a thousand pages of exhibits and depositions, they had proved their case. (To read Thanassis Cambanis's two excellent stories, however, you'll have to search the *Globe* yourself and pay.)

Before long, we're going to find out what the judge thinks of the government's case that Professor Andrei Shleifer and Jonathan Hay illegally speculated in Russian stocks and bonds, even as they directed a US-funded, Harvard-backed project to help the Russian government set up honest and transparent capital markets – a project whose rules expressly forbid them to invest in the host country.

It's hard to imagine that it's going to end happily for Harvard.

The question is, how big a black eye?

The verdict, when it comes, could cost Harvard as much as $102 million — a substantial sum even for the world's richest university. The United States is seeking treble damages under the False Claims Act.

But in some ways, that's the least of it.

Then again, if the judge finds for Harvard, it's always possible the case simply could go away. Someone at university headquarters in Massachusetts Hall apparently thinks he will – otherwise, why not settle now?

But even if Harvard wins, you can expect aftershocks to continue for years to come.

There is no better introduction to the background of the case than a new book, *The Oligarchs: Wealth and Power in the New Russia,* by David Hoffman. Hoffman was chief of the Moscow bureau of *The Washington Post* from 1995 until 2001. His book is a *tour de force*, focusing on the intertwined lives of six powerful men to demonstrate how a relative handful of highly adaptable buccaneers took control of the Russian economy in the 1990s. It was the greatest seizures of power since the Russian Revolution, and a good deal less widely understood.

The reformers around Boris Yeltsin at the beginning of the decade believed they had little time to dismantle state communism, Hoffman writes. So they deliberately "set out to wreck the old system at any cost." They freed prices and property rights first and established rules only later. "Russian capitalism was born in an airless space, a vacuum without effective laws and a state so badly weakened it could not enforce laws that were on the books."

"Time and again, questions arose about the deals made by these six men," he writes. "Were they legal? Were they criminal? But the questions were not easily answered because the players moved about in a world lacking the legal constraints or the moral compass of a mature Western society. ...Lying, cheating, stealing were a part of daily business..."

Given the situation in Russia, the basic facts of the government's case against Harvard are these. Once a last-ditch coup by the old guard failed in 1991 and it became clear that Russia would remain on a liberalizing path, the Bush administration decided to send it a measure of technical help.

The US State Department twice hired Harvard's Institute for International Development (HIID) to advise the Russian government, first under the Bush administration in 1992 and then again under the Clinton administration in 1995. HIID gave the required assurances to the government that its employees would make no investments. It required no less of them itself. Then it named Shleifer project director and designated Jonathan Hay, a Rhodes Scholar and graduate of Harvard Law School, head of its Moscow office.

Under Shleifer, Harvard's Russia Project quickly became the flagship of US aid to Moscow, offering advice on all manner of financial reforms and overseeing the grants of other contractors as well. After all, the project director wasn't just another out-of-town theorist armed with a quick course from Berlitz.

In fact, Shleifer had grown up in what was then the Soviet Union, the child of successful but frustrated engineers. He was 15 when his family was allowed to emigrate, first to Italy, then to the United States, with the help of the Hebrew Immigrant Aid Society. During a couple of years in high school in Rochester, New York, he showed exceptional promise, before being recruited to Harvard College. There he met a rapidly rising assistant professor of economics named Lawrence Summers, who promptly took him under his wing.

A wry and gregarious man, Shleifer turned out to possess terrific economic intuition. His English, on the other hand, he would tell friends, all came from watching "Charlie's Angels." After an MIT PhD and a year at Princeton and three more at the University of Chicago, he returned to Harvard as a full professor, under Summers' sponsorship. Within a decade, he had won the John Bates Clark Medal given every other year to the most promising economist under 40, for his work in finance, corporate governance and transition economics, securing his reputation as one of the most influential contributors to economics of his generation.

And for a time, in the mid-90s, Shleifer cut a dashing figure on his frequent trips to Moscow, a once-despised local boy who returned as Harvard's point man on the US economic mission, a Kissinger for the next century. He befriended the leadership of a generation of technocratic Russian reformers, including Deputy Prime Minister Anatoly Chubais and Dimitry Vasiliev, chairman of the Securities Commission. He basked in the fact that his old mentor Larry Summers now was second-in-command at the Treasury Department, with broad responsibility for monitoring aid to the Russian economy. (Eventually Summers would succeed to the top Treasury job.)

But almost immediately, according to the government, Shleifer and Hay had begun investing in Russian projects, each in connection with his spouse or girlfriend. It wasn't a matter of their engaging in insider trading, the lawsuit asserts; any investment *at all* would be a stark violation of the terms of service.

In 1994, the government says, Shleifer put $200,000 into a company called Renova Invest. Apparently the money came from his well-to-do wife, Nancy Zimmerman. Not long before, she had left Goldman Sachs in order to start a hedge fund; soon she would be investing in Russian securities.

The same year, he and Hay bought $264,000 of Russian oil stocks through a Channel Islands account registered in the name of Zimmerman's father. Hay made a quick $3,000 profit speculating in short-term Russian government bonds.

The pair then traded on their reputations to launch Russia's first licensed mutual fund depository, operated by a former Harvard employee and Hay's girlfriend. They helped plan its drive to market, then invested in it themselves. The gains were potentially enormous.

None of this is in dispute.

At that point, any number of whistles sounded – commercial competitors, subordinates, rival advisers. Harvard investigated and fired Hay. USAID investigated and fired Harvard. Miffed that their friends had been sacked, the Russians in turn fired USAID. Harvard dissolved HIID. Assistant US Attorney in Boston Sara Miron Bloom investigated and, in due course, sued Harvard, charging that its failure to supervise its project ultimately destroyed its credibility and thus constituted fraud.

The particulars of the case seem well established. The government last month filed a compendium of 249 "undisputed material facts," some of them e-mails describing in excruciating detail various investments and the pains taken – or not taken – to disguise them. Harvard's defense apparently rests on its contention that Shleifer and Hay never disclosed to the university that they were investing. Shleifer apparently contends that he was a consultant rather than an employee under the contract and therefore not covered by conflict-of-interest provisions. Hay, having long ago been fired by Harvard, is working as a consultant in Moscow. His rejoinder, like that of the other defendants, will come later.

There is no point in arguing about it in advance. US District Judge Douglas P. Woodlock will decide the case soon enough. So incendiary are the issues that it wants the closest possible determination. That's what legal proceedings are all about. A civil case against Harvard, brought by competitors for mutual fund licenses who lost out to the Harvard-backed firm, is slowly making its way as well.

But there are two other constituencies here besides the courts. One is Harvard itself – not just the Harvard that is actively managed from Massachusetts Hall, but the larger community that is loosely cared for by faculty and alumni who are concerned for its sensibility and reputation over time. For this constituency the role of Harvard Management is another issue. The highly sophisticated money management firm, which oversees Harvard's $18 billion endowment, apparently invested directly in the Russian economy throughout the '90s.

The other expert community is the economics profession. No matter what happens next, lingering questions will remain in both quarters.

Perhaps the chief surprise so far has been the position of former treasury secretary Larry Summers. In 1996, when he cautioned both Shleifer and his wife about the potential for scandal if she tried to invest in Russia, neither had disclosed to him their personal investments. The assumption had been that he would distance himself after the government case was filed.

But Summers is understood to have regularly stayed at the Shleifers' home in Newton while interviewing for the presidency. And in his deposition last March, he came as close as anyone yet has to defending his friend. "Post this thing coming to light," Summers allowed in his testimony, "there probably were conversations that the thing's a mess; it's a mess."

But, he noted, "I had enough knowledge of Russian mores and Russian practices and Russian views... to be confident that the set of issues contained in the allegations were not issues that were consequential for them; and indeed, that they would have, in part, valued advisers more extensively if they were more involved in actual private-sector activities."

In other words, it's easier when everybody at the table is an oligarch – a reasonable enough argument, though not one that shows up in Shleifer's 1999 book (with Daniel Treisman) on political tactics and economic reform in Russia, *Without a Map*. Indeed, such considerations are ordinarily depicted only in thrillers, when the border-crossing government op flirts with mob ways in order to prove his *bona fides*. He then turns his targets – or is turned himself.

To which Assistant US Attorney Bloom responds in the government brief, "This is not a case where the defendants did not know the rules – it is one where they did not care.... Harvard and its employees, no matter how brilliant, are still subject to the laws of the United States." Every bit as much as Shleifer, Bloom is a central figure in the story, a resourceful and implacable investigator who for five years has withstood enormous pressure to drop the case.

Summers has recused himself from Harvard's decisions about its defense against the government lawsuit – though not before telling outgoing faculty dean Jeremy Knowles how important he thinks it is that Shleifer should remain at Harvard. Who quarterbacks a case as difficult as this one when the university president is involved – and when the issues are not only narrowly legal but moral? The short answer is the Harvard Corporation.

"The Corporation" is the oldest self-perpetuating body in North America. It governs Harvard, quietly and gently, but firmly. The newest of its seven members is Citigroup banker Robert Rubin, who was Summers' boss at the

Treasury Department. Rubin recently replaced Herbert "Pug" Winokur, CEO of Capricorn Holdings and chairman of the finance committee at Enron Corp., who resigned from the Corporation only after some months of backstage maneuvering. Others include Summers himself, ex officio; Harvard treasurer D. Ronald Daniel; Hanna Holborn Gray, president emerita of the University of Chicago; Conrad K. Harper, partner, Simpson Thacher & Bartlett; James R. Houghton, chairman of the board emeritus, Corning Inc.; and Robert G. Stone Jr., chairman emeritus of Kirby Corp.

No less than in the '50s, when in a variety of subtle ways Harvard faced the choice of whether and how to throw its weight against the anti-communist hysteria, the university is once against poised on a razor's edge. This time the dilemma is between financial *realpolitik* and some updated version of semi-insulated disinterestedness. The same choices regularly recur all along a lengthy spectrum extending from the research frontiers of the medical school, to the consideration given major donors, to the seemingly mundane philosophy of undergraduate admissions and athletics. The Shleifer case is only momentarily the leading edge.

As for the economics profession, rivalries among departments surely play a role. Shleifer has no more avid defenders within Harvard than his immediate colleagues, who, as Summers told his interrogators in March, view Shleifer as having been somehow "screwed." The Harvard economists have worked hard over the past 35 years to rebuild their department from the also-ran shambles that it was in the early '60s. They don't want to see one of their strongest drawing cards (remember, the best new students from each year's crop of entrants are the life's blood of any university) defect to MIT – or the University of Chicago.

Meanwhile, the elders of the economics profession have expressed solidarity with the embattled professor by appointing Shleifer editor of the *Journal of Economic Perspectives*. Since the quarterly is intended by the American Economic Association to represent technical economics to the general public, the job is a position of enormous influence. The fact that former World Bank chief economist Joseph Stiglitz doesn't mention the government's case against Harvard in his otherwise incendiary *Globalization and Its Discontents* suggests just how far professional courtesy extends. For that matter, the Shleifer story doesn't come up in *The Oligarchs*, either. Whatever ventilation the issues will receive thus lies ahead. A hearing before the judge is slated for September — September 11, to be precise.

CHAPTER TWO

# Shleifer to Leave Harvard?

*January 12, 2003*

What will happen if one of the brightest and most beguiling economists in the world turns out to be a world-class scoundrel, too?

Andrei Shleifer's stature as an economist is common knowledge. Among the Harvard professor's more striking accomplishments was a 1997 article, "The Limits to Arbitrage," in which he and his friend University of Chicago Business School professor Rob Vishny anticipated in some detail the kind of liquidity crisis that a year later would bring to its knees the giant hedge fund known as Long-Term Capital Management – only to be assured that it couldn't possibly happen, by those to whom it soon did.

In books like *The Grabbing Hand: Government Pathologies and Their Cures* and *Without a Map: Political Tactics and Economic Reform in Russia*, he set a high standard for disentangling the problems of communism and capitalism and bringing them into comparative perspective, thereby illuminating various pathways to transition. And in a series of original papers on corporate governance, he comprehensively surveyed possibilities for managerial misconduct, its remedies (and opportunities) in stock markets, and so influenced the worldwide takeover debate.

In 1999, he won the John Bates Clark Medal, an award presented every two years to the leading economist under 40. Last year he was named editor of the *Journal of Economic Perspectives*, the American Economic Association's flagship organ for general-interest explication of the latest research.

And lest there were any question of resting on his laurels, Shleifer was everywhere at meetings of the AEA earlier this month, presenting or discussing papers on behavioral finance, sovereign debt, law and transition, the regulation of labor, investor protection and the new comparative economics, of which he is a founding father.

A friend says, "He can do Chicago, he can do MIT, he can do the real-world stuff — there are not many others like him." Pretty remarkable for a young man who grew up in the Soviet Union, arrived in Rochester, New York, only in 1976 and was swept off to Harvard College two years later, speaking (he jokes) little more than the English he had learned watching Charlie's Angels.

The trouble is that Shleifer is also a defendant in a high-stakes lawsuit that could cost Harvard University more than $100 million. The US government charges that he misbehaved as leader of the university's US government-sponsored mission to Moscow in the mid-1990s — specifically, that he quietly began buying Russian securities almost immediately after his appointment, despite strict contract prohibitions against such conflicts of interest.

Worse, the government asserts that while he and his deputy, Jonathan Hay, were advising the Russian government on how to set up its markets and create a Securities and Exchange Commission, their significant others (wife and then-girlfriend-now-wife, respectively) illegitimately obtained from the Russian government the first license to operate a mutual fund there.

Harvard recently settled for an undisclosed sum with a Maine financial services firm that had sued the university and its team, claiming it had been improperly elbowed aside in the race for that permission.

All the while, the government says, employees of the Harvard project were raising red flags about their bosses' conduct. They were ignored in Cambridge.

And when one bold consultant flew home to raise the issue with Shleifer directly, the economist ordered her fired.

After whistle-blowers finally succeeded in raising the issue with the government directly in 1997, the US Agency for International Development fired Harvard from its contract. Thereupon the Russian government, angered by the loss of the services of its friends, spurned further US aid.

After a lengthy investigation, the US attorney in Boston filed suit in September 2000 on behalf of the government, seeking treble damages from Harvard for its failure to keep tabs on its employees. The government asserts the whole value of the $34.8 million contract was lost. Harvard contends that its team did a great job.

The case is being argued before Judge Douglas Woodlock in US District Court in Boston. Both sides have asked him to rule in their favor on the basis of the reams of testimony that has been given. He has the option of deciding all the case or some of it, and sending the rest to a jury.

The essence of Shleifer's defense, and that of Harvard, has been to portray the episode as a series of misunderstandings of fine points of law. Never has it risen to the level of the reply that Shleifer gave to a Moscow colleague who raised objections at the time — that in Russia, "above suspicion" was difficult to achieve. And whatever the verdict, the mass of evidence that has been accumulated reflects remarkably poorly on the Harvard mission.

Quite apart from what is decided about the case itself, there is a relatively simple way to address the problem of Shleifer's standing in the economics profession. He should go back to where he came from — return, that is, to the Graduate School of Business at the University of Chicago. Certainly it is hard to imagine that he will continue to teach at Harvard.

*The Chronicle of Higher Education* subscriber-only "Daily Report" reported last week that Shleifer was actively negotiating with New York University's Stern School of Business. Citing "a source familiar with the negotiations," the *Chronicle* said that the Stern school had offered nearly $500,000 in salary.

Shleifer, the report continued, had been "spending time in the business school's finance department over the last several months, giving lectures and talking to faculty members." Shleifer is on leave from Harvard for the academic year.

New York University has made some impressive hires recently, luring theorist Thomas Sargent from Stanford, strategist Adam Brandenburger from Harvard Business School, development economist William Easterly from the World Bank, historian Niall Ferguson from Oxford, among others. Its newly created Center for Experimental Social Science already includes a number of talented researchers and is expected to grow substantially.

Then again, greatly as NYU's economics department and business school have risen in the relative standings in recent years, the atmosphere around Washington Square is still that of a boomtown. NYU's big bang could become a big bust; its fancy new faculty leave for still-greener pastures as quickly as they arrive. Students will have their doubts about the training ethic there.

A better solution, at least for economics, would be for Shleifer to return to the Graduate School of Business at Chicago. That was where he was before he accepted Harvard's offer. He made his name there. It is his spiritual home. At Chicago, he could continue to exercise a significant influence on the profession, train top-notch students, stay in touch with the latest developments – and benefit from the university's reputation for enforcing probity among its faculty.

Why leave Harvard at all? He may be bored. Besides, there's a monitoring problem. The Harvard economics department is so eager for him to stay that it may be only too willing to turn a blind eye to his transgressions, for in combination with professors John Campbell and Jeremy Stein and others, not to mention those at the Harvard Business School, he gives them an unassailable claim to being the best finance section in the world.

Then, too, Shleifer's oldest friend in economics is Lawrence Summers – who, first as undersecretary of treasury for international affairs, then as deputy secretary, was to all intents and purposes his ultimate boss during the period of the alleged transgressions, even though they were separated by several layers of governmental hierarchy.

Maybe Shleifer simply didn't understand what it meant to supply impartial advice with no conflict of interest under American rules. But in that case, what was Larry Summers thinking, then and now? Today he is president of the university. Harvard's continuing contention that its team leaders did nothing wrong requires some explaining far beyond what it has offered in its briefs.

For even if Shleifer's alleged indiscretions arose from a relatively understandable itch to get rich – remember, he was a college junior when Ronald Reagan was elected president – Harvard's dogged defense of its Russia Project has transformed the matter into something completely different — the legal equivalent, perhaps, of George Armstrong Custer's choice of the Little Bighorn as the place to plant his flag. Already Summers' reputation has been damaged by the scandal. What happens if the judge decides against Harvard?

A great deal remains to be seen.

CHAPTER THREE

# A High-Stakes Mediation That Failed

*January 26, 2003*

The stand-off over the Andrei Shleifer case is scheduled to become even more tense next week, when Harvard University lays out the reasons why it believes it shouldn't be prosecuted for the lax supervision of one of its star professors under the provisions of a Civil War statute designed to deter contractors who sold the government tainted meat.

At that point, the question will be up to US District Court Judge Douglas P. Woodlock. He will be in a position to decide the case himself, or to give some part of it to a jury. Looming in the background is the hard bargain, proffered by the government, apparently declined last year by the university.

When Harvard's lawyers asked the judge to decide the case in their favor on the basis of the small mountain of evidence that has been adduced through depositions and discovery, they affected a jaunty stance last summer:

> From December 1992 through May 1997, scores of talented and committed Harvard Institute of International Development advisers, including Andrei Shleifer and Jonathan Hay, gave advice to Russian government reformers regarding, among other things, the privatization of formerly state-owned industries, legal reform, tax reform, and the development of a stock exchange, a Russian Securities and Exchange

Commission, and capital markets. HIID's advisers worked round the clock and, as the government itself has acknowledged, did superb work helping to solidify the political and economic revolution in Russia.

True, the Harvard brief acknowledged, a "handful of nominal personal investments" in Russian securities apparently had been uncovered. Shleifer (or at least his wife) had made them, as had his deputy Hay, while the two were being paid by the US government to serve as advisers to the Russian government. Harvard denied that the investments violated the conflict-of-interest provisions of its contract. And even if it turned out otherwise, its lawyers mocked the US's claim that all the team's work under the contract had been rendered valueless by the behavior of the men at the top. But beneath the bravado there is real concern.

For when it comes to the history of the application of the False Claims Act, the government's argument is strong. When The Boeing Company knowingly delivered helicopters with faulty landing gear, for example, its false claim was judged to be the full price of the aircraft – even though every other component worked fine.

What does Harvard really think about what transpired during the mission to Moscow that it sponsored in the 1990s? It depends, of course, on what you mean by "Harvard." One indicator is the fate of HIID, the university-based consulting service whose ancestry can be traced back to an advisory group founded in 1953 by economics professor Edward Mason to advise the government of Pakistan. Almost immediately after the US government began its investigation of the Russia Project in 1997, the university assembled a task force of blue-ribbon insiders to study the arrangement.

And when HIID's regular biennial report was issued in the spring of 2000, celebrating some 20 country projects abroad and another 20 based in Cambridge, inside the front cover of each report was tucked a printed card. "While the manuscript for this biennial report was at the printer, Harvard University made the decision to dissolve HIID and to distribute its functions and projects to several of the teaching faculties with closely related interests." The vanishing act had been performed by June 30 – even before the report was in the mail. Grand undertakings don't end more unceremoniously than that.

If the decision to disband the institute was intended to forestall further unpleasantness, it didn't work. Three months later, the US attorney in Boston filed suit against Harvard, Shleifer, Hay and their respective wives under the False Claims Act, seeking treble damages. (The judge subsequently dismissed the spouses from the complaint.)

Another measure of Harvard's attitude is to be found in a failed mediation effort. Barely five weeks after the complaint was filed, US District Court Judge David Mazzone had undertaken an alternative dispute resolution on behalf of the court. (It was Mazzone who presided over the highly successful clean-up of Boston Harbor – one of the recent landmarks of court-supervised negotiation.)

According to a source with knowledge of the case, after five months of talking, Harvard offered to settle the charges against it for $24 million, or two-thirds of the total value of the contract. The government insisted on repayment in full, the source said. Negotiations broke down, and Judge Mazzone withdrew from the case last March. A second source confirmed that a settlement was considered to have been near, but was unable to confirm the figure. Harvard declined to comment.

Would it have been better if the government had accepted Harvard's offer to return a startlingly large portion of its fee? Certainly the defendants think so. The government's decision to shoot the moon, Harvard's decision to resist the slam, will be debated in legal and political circles for years to come.

For now Harvard is facing a potentially much more serious embarrassment. The United States wants more than $120 million – a huge sum even for the world's richest university. The government believes that every card in its hand will take a trick. That is some of the background necessary to understand coming events.

CHAPTER FOUR

# Judge Finds Against Shleifer, Hay and Harvard

*July 4, 2004*

The US government's long-running wrangle with economist Andrei Shleifer and Harvard University over Harvard's ill-fated Russia Project in the 1990s was resolved last week, in the government's favor.

A federal judge ruled that, by quietly investing on their own accounts while advising the Russian government, Harvard professor Shleifer and his Moscow-based assistant Jonathan Hay had conspired to defraud the US Agency for International Development (USAID), which had been paying their salary.

Hay was faulted for violating three counts of the False Claims Act, Shleifer for one, with two other counts against him pending a possible jury trial on what it means to have been "assigned" to Russia under the contract's terms. (Shleifer asserts that the conflict-of-interest rules didn't apply to him since, though directing the project, he had continued to reside outside of Russia, in Newton, Massachusetts.)

The decision by US District Court Judge Douglas P. Woodlock, based on motions by all sides that he decide the case as a matter of law on the facts presented, left both Shleifer and Hay liable for treble damages — as much as $120 million apiece, in the worst case.

At the same time, Judge Woodlock cleared Harvard University of the government's most serious accusation, namely that its administrators knew or should have known that their team leaders were investing personally in concert with their wives.

He ruled out treble damages under the False Claims Act, thereby confirming Harvard's view of itself as the victim of a couple of rogue employees.

Harvard couldn't be faulted for failing to investigate "rumor-like allegations" that trickled back to Cambridge, the judge wrote, for the "red flags" identified by the government never quite reached the level of a piercing whistle; they had more to do with gossip about the provision of various goods and services to Russian officials and their families.

The fact that the Project flew the chairman of the Russian SEC and his wife to Idaho for a part-work, part-vacation trip, and that Shleifer paid for training the chairman's wife at his own personal expense "may be ethically dubious," he observed, but they don't demonstrate a clear conflict of interest. Nor could the university be blamed for inadequate supervision.

"A more careful employer might have, for instance, distributed a short memorandum explaining the conflicts provision, and perhaps even required Project staff (whether 'employees' or 'consultants') to fill out a disclosure form," wrote the judge.

"If the applicable legal standard in this case were negligent supervision," he continued, "the government would have a better case against Harvard." Instead, he noted, the fraud law required proof of actual knowledge or reckless disregard.

Paul Ware, the university's outside counsel, said last week, "Harvard is very encouraged that the court has unequivocally ruled that the university neither engaged in nor knew of any fraudulent conduct. Even the breach-of-contract claim, according to the court, is not established as a result of any institutional wrongdoing by the university."

In finding that Harvard had breached its contract to deliver the impartial advice it promised, Judge Woodlock's decision left Harvard liable for damages. Previously Harvard has defended the outcome of its project as, on balance, a great success. The university can be expected to argue that there should be a considerable offset to whatever damages are assessed in recognition of the benefits gained by Russia.

It was in 1992, after Congress passed the Freedom for Russia and the Emerging Eurasian Democracies and Open Market Support Act, that USAID hired Harvard to provide consultants to the Russian government to help design institutions favorable to democratic government and a market economy.

Shleifer in due course became the project director, and Hay his deputy.

Allegations of conflict of interest boiled over among US aid workers in Moscow in 1997, and USAID began an internal investigation. The agency suspended the project in May. An angry Russian government, staffed by friends of Shleifer and Hay, shelved the relationship the same day. Harvard then fired Hay and relieved Shleifer, a tenured professor, of his project duties. USAID then cancelled the contract.

And in September, 2000, the US attorney in Boston filed an 11-count civil claim against Harvard University, Shleifer, Hay, Nancy Zimmerman (Shleifer's wife and a partner in a hedge fund with investments in Russia) and Elizabeth Hebert (Hay's then-girlfriend, now his wife).

US Attorney Donald Stern said at the time that his office had contemplated criminal charges but filed none.

Judge Woodlock quickly dismissed the charges against Zimmerman and Hebert, on grounds that neither worked for Harvard or the government and were not parties to the contract.

As previously reported, Harvard at one point offered to settle its part of the case for as much as $24 million, or two-thirds the value of its contract, in the course of an unsuccessful mediation by Judge David Mazzone, according to attorneys familiar with the case. Now that the government's claim to treble damages has failed, the offer, whatever it was, will have long since disappeared from the table.

Shleifer, who left Russia with his parents when he was 15, only to return as a senior adviser to its government (and a distinguished economist) at the age of 30, remains a Harvard professor.

Until last year, he was a principal of LSV Asset Management, a money management firm for institutional investors that, with fellow economists Robert Vishny and Josef Lakonishok, he co-founded in 1991.

His attorney, Earl Nemser, told Marcella Bombardieri of *The Boston Globe*, "We're pleased now that most of the claims in the case, and against Andrei Shleifer, have been dismissed. We expect the remaining claims will be disposed of favorably to him."

Jonathan Hay, who became a student of Shleifer's while at Harvard Law School, joined the London office of the Cleary Gottlieb law firm as an associate in 2002.

An initial hearing on the damages phase of the trial may be held as early as July 19. Extensive arguments about the ultimate success or failure of Harvard's Russia Project eventually can be expected from all sides.

Judge Woodlock's finding, reported in a clearly written 100-page memorandum and order, came nearly 18 months after both sides asked him to decide the legal issues as a matter of summary judgment.

It was, perhaps, an unusually long deliberation, even for a judge with a reputation for taking his time. On the other hand, his findings were delivered a little in the manner of an O. Henry story, with a sudden twist at the end.

The nub of the case turned out to be the Pallada Asset Management Company. Though evidence was adduced to show that Shleifer had been inviting his former-student-turned-deputy to invest with him in Russian oil stocks as early as the summer of 1994 – and though he and Hay made several other kinds of personal investments in the next couple of years – it was a scheme to win a license from the Russian SEC for Hay's then-girlfriend, Elizabeth Hebert, as the first authorized vendor of Russian mutual funds, that led to Woodlock's decision to find both men guilty of the False Claims conspiracy charge.

The meaning of "assigned to Russia" might be so ambiguous that a jury would be required to decide two counts of the complaint that Shleifer committed fraud by investing in Russia while regularly visiting Moscow from Newton, Massachusetts, Judge Woodlock wrote.

But on the third count, wrote the judge, there could be no such doubt. The available evidence clearly showed that a working understanding existed among Shleifer and Hay to inappropriately finance and assist in the launch of Pallada, in hopes of turning it into a Russian version of market-dominating Fidelity Investments.

Hay's father lent Hebert $200,000 to buy a related business. Shleifer loaned her a similar amount a few months later to advance her plans. The smoking gun here was something called "the Steyer memo," a business plan written by Hebert, reviewed by Hay (and perhaps designed to be signed by him), and addressed to Thomas Steyer, a business associate of Shleifer's wife, in hopes of attracting a further round of investment from him and others.

"We are likely to get a license before anyone else which will give us a significant first mover advantage… Given this project's relationship with the Commission, any other attempts by definition will be in a catchup mode… In the short to medium term, our advantage comes from the fact the regulator wants us to be first…"

Shleifer was adviser to the Securities Commission. Hay was drafting the securities law. At one point, Shleifer consulted a Harvard lawyer to ask if his wife could invest in Pallada. It just wouldn't look right, replied Attorney Michael Butler.

"Tellingly," wrote the judge, "Shleifer did not ask Butler whether *he* could invest in Russia." And so it was, by making the loans and thereby financing the Pallada scheme, that the two men caused the submission of a false claim.

Coming on page 92 of a 100-page opinion, the finding was something of a surprise. It turned out that the meaning of "assigned to Russia" probably doesn't matter in Shleifer's case. One count of fraud is as defeating as three. The decision seemed to render moot any need to resort to a jury trial, and freed the court to move on to the question of who owes what and to whom.

CHAPTER FIVE

# A Walk on the Beach

*September 5, 2004*

It was another summer together on Cape Cod. Two old friends were walking on the beach, deep in conversation, their wives and children momentarily left behind. One was Andrei Shleifer, Harvard professor and chief outside economic adviser to the Russian government in the mid-1990s. The other was Lawrence Summers, former Harvard professor, second in command at the U.S. Treasury Department.

As nearly as one can tell from Summers' testimony, it was the summer of 1996.

Shleifer didn't work for Summers, at least not in the conventional sense. The large team of economists, lawyers and other professionals he led was under contract to the State Department's Agency for International Development. On the other hand, Summers, under Treasury Secretary Robert Rubin, had responsibility for oversight of US economic policy abroad; he had served as undersecretary for international affairs for more than two years.

Thus what the world saw, at least that part of the world that paid attention in Moscow to what passed for the Social Register, was something rather different than the strict reporting lines of an official organization chart. Russia then was in the throes of privatizing its mind-boggling array of state-owned assets, everything from giant factories to mineral rights. It was at once an attempt to destroy the planning system by parceling out ownership to — well, it wasn't yet clear to whom — and a looting spree. Naturally these economic reforms were a matter of great interest to Washington.

Boris Yeltsin had just been reelected president in a run-off election after a campaign of epic scandal and intrigue. His chief adviser, Anatoly Chubais, a bright young enthusiast of the form of all-at-once shock therapy known as "the Big Bang," who had begun his public career selling off half of Moscow's venerable Bolshevik Biscuit Company for $654,000, was jubilant: "Irrevocable," crowed Chubais. "Russian democracy is irrevocable; private ownership is irrevocable; market reforms in the Russian state are irrevocable." Seven men were said to control something like 50 percent of the Russian economy.

Summers and Shleifer were among each other's best friends. The future treasury secretary had been a 28-year-old assistant Harvard professor when he first met the young Russian émigré. He had taught Shleifer as an undergraduate, sent him on to MIT for his PhD, took him along on an advisory mission to Lithuania in 1990, and in 1991, shepherded his return to Harvard as a full professor, where he was regarded, after Martin Feldstein and Summers, as the leader of the next generation. Shleifer, in turn, had hired his own protégé as deputy in the mission to Moscow: Jonathan Hay, a Rhodes Scholar, first in his class at Harvard Law.

The Harvard team in Moscow thus was seen by many to be speaking with unusually high fidelity for the Clinton administration in Washington.

But what could be seen only by insiders in Moscow, Americans and Russians alike, was that the protégés and their wives were apparently loading up on Russian securities for their own portfolios and starting a business seemingly in blatant violation of the conflict-of-interest rules. They were actually running trading operations out of their Harvard offices. No one could possibly tell how extensive were their deals.

About this, however, Summers did not ask and Shleifer did not tell, in the course of their walk on the beach that day. Both men have since testified extensively under oath. Summers' tone in the deposition that he gave at his home in 2002 is by turns hazy and precise, cheerful and combative. At least twice in the four-

and-a-half hours of testimony, he couldn't remember the year that the particular walk in question took place; at another point, moments later, he said, "You know, we're trying to parse what was for me a very casual conversation on a beach six years ago."

Summers acknowledged having known at the time that Mrs. Shleifer — Nancy Zimmerman — was doing well in business in Russia as a hedge fund operator. He knew, too, that Hay's girlfriend (now wife) was involved in Russian capital markets as well.

He advised his friend to make certain that he was operating within the rules; to be careful in his relationship with Harvard. It did not occur to him, he said, that Shleifer might have any obligation under the contract to the United States. They were just two friends enjoying their customary annual summer visit on Cape Cod. "It wasn't my habit to do US government business on beaches," Summers told the assistant US attorney who was prosecuting the case.

Despite his advice, the investment activity of the leaders of the Harvard Russian Project continued in the coming months, as the Yeltsin government prepared for another round of privatization. And the next spring, a series of whistles was blown.

Investigations were mounted. USAID promptly suspended Harvard, mere hours after its first visit to the project offices, and later cancelled the contract. The Russians, angry about losing their advisers and the link to the US government they represented, fired the State Department in turn. Eventually the US government brought suit against Harvard and the leading members of its team.

(For a good glimpse of what was known at the time, you can purchase for $2.95 a copy of an authoritative article which appeared on August 13, 1997, in *The Wall Street Journal* — "Aborted Mission: How an Aid Program Vital to New Economy of Russia Collapsed," by Carla Anne Robbins and Steve Liesman. Robbins is working on an update.)

Last July, Federal District Court Judge Douglas Woodlock in Boston found against Harvard, Shleifer and Hay in a summary judgment. One doesn't say guilty or convicted, for it is not a criminal case (though the US attorney, Donald

Stern, said at the time he had mulled possible criminal charges, presumably for perjury, before dropping them for lack of resources). Nevertheless, the judge held Shleifer and Hay liable for treble damages. Harvard was held liable for simple breach of contract instead of fraud.

Last week, the parties filed a joint memo summarizing where matters stood, preparing for their scheduled September 9 conference before Judge Woodlock. The two-page memo was mainly an agenda of the problems remaining to be discussed.

The memo did contain the news that various settlement talks were underway. Those with Jonathan Hay had made "significant progress," while the likelihood of success of talks with Harvard was still unclear. There had been no settlement discussions with Shleifer, the memo noted. The possibility remained that his case might go to a jury.

The world can only hope that Harvard University's lawyers have the opportunity to fully argue out their case (and that both sides will bring expert testimony to bear on their argument), that no very substantial damage was done, and that the university earned a substantial part of its $34 million contract, because its mission to Moscow did more good than harm.

For the spectacle of Shleifer and Hay and their wives loading up on Russian investment while working out of a Harvard office in one of Moscow's glitziest office buildings, at a time when the company that managed Harvard's then-$11 billion endowment had nearly 2 percent of it actively invested in Russian securities, would be one of the more memorable scenes of the '90s — if only it had been more widely noted at the time.

It is all the more interesting in view of what has happened to the principals since then.

Shleifer has become a leading expert on corruption, on government pathologies and their cures. His 1998 book with University of Chicago professor Robert Vishny, *The Grabbing Hand*, is published by Harvard University Press.

Hay works in London for the law firm of Cleary Gottlieb.

Summers has become president of Harvard University.

No one has accused Summers himself of breaking any law. For example, the Treasury Department never for a moment intervened with State after USAID fired the Harvard team. And while Summers acknowledges having done a certain amount of grumbling about the Justice Department while in office, for having permitted the complaint against Harvard to be brought in the first place, the issue went forward to trial.

Summers' judgment, however, is another matter. He was inarguably present at the creation of the mess.

There is something really haunting about that walk on the beach. It would be a fitting topic for a play by Michael Frayn (*Copenhagen, Democracy*). It is indisputable that the situation in Russia was just short of desperate in those days – the country was tottering on the brink of chaos in the mid-1990s. Nevertheless, surely somebody or something was being betrayed that day.

Was it Shleifer? Did the youthful émigré, who left the former Soviet Union when he was 15, not deserve a better woodshedding from his friend?

Was it Summers? From the standpoint of the Treasury, the brilliant and engaging Shleifer was America's best possible man on the scene, an agent with a feeling for the lot of common folk, yet capable of joining any conversation among oligarchs and government officials. But who could ever tell which side he was on?

Harvard? The university enjoys a reputation for being ethically sensitive. Someday doctoral students will compare and contrast its relationship with the Russian government in the 1990s to the University of Chicago's relationship to Chile in the 1960s.

The United States? The Russia Project was the spearhead of the United States' most ambitious attempt at enhancing order in the world economy through foreign aid since the Marshall Plan, although the situations were very different. Compare the behavior of plenipotentiaries John McCloy and Lucius Clay to that of (elevated) apparatchiks Andrei Shleifer and Jonathan Hay.

Rule-of-law democracy itself? A commonly heard argument in Russia in those days was that "corruption in the service of democracy" was sometimes a necessary tactic. At one point in his deposition, Summers explained the anger of his Russian counterparts at the firing of his friend this way: "I had enough knowledge of Russian mores and Russian practices and Russian views from the conversations that I had with Chubais and [Russian Securities and Exchange chief Dimitry] Vasiliev to be confident that the set of issues contained in the allegations were not issues that were consequential for them; and indeed that they would have, in part, valued advisers more extensively if they were more involved in actual private-sector activities." So was Shleifer exporting US ways to Russia? Or importing Russian ways to the US?

Yet there has been no public falling out among the principals, as might have been expected. Indeed, what has occurred has been just the reverse.

Summers recused himself from the matter of the government suit shortly after taking over at Harvard, though not before conveying to Faculty of Arts and Sciences dean Jeremy Knowles that his friend had "a morale problem" and that he was "concerned to make sure that Professor Shleifer remained at Harvard." Summers was known to have stayed with the Shleifer family while interviewing for the job of Harvard president.

Harvard's lawyers thus have been getting their direction from somewhere else – presumably the seven-member Harvard Corporation (of which Summers and his former boss, Robert Rubin, are members).

Thus that walk on the beach continues to haunt. In it are to be found all manner of hints of why the ruling looms so large for the university; for the economics profession; and for the rest of us as well. For the problem that has so handcuffed Summers to this point is an increasingly acute one in the modern age. It has to do with the individual's capacity to sort through multiple allegiances, to identify the wellsprings of ethical behavior, and perform one's duty. Somebody was betrayed in the course of that walk on the beach; probably several somebodies: but *who*?

These events transpired at the pinnacle of global capitalism. They are still unfolding. It is important that they be understood. There is much about the Harvard matter that remains unknown. There are many lessons of Russia's transition to a market economy that are yet to be drawn. The case continues next Thursday in Boston's Federal District Court.

CHAPTER SIX

# Meet the *Siloviki*

*September 12, 2004*

Half a world away from Moscow and the dreadful sorrows of the North Ossetian city of Beslan, US District Court Judge Douglas P. Woodlock said last Thursday that he wanted a short, tightly focused trial on the failure of Harvard University's mission to Moscow in the 1990s – perhaps a few testimonials by experts for a jury to evaluate, but not "an extended seminar on the role of Russian-American relations in the past century."

A trial on the contract damages that Harvard owes the U.S. State Department ought not to take more than three weeks, he said; it might begin as early as December 6. (Woodlock found in July that the university had breached its promise to furnish disinterested advice.) He told the government's lawyers to prepare a more explicit case for the harm done than the *per se*, speaks-for-itself approach which they had proposed to take. He instructed them to continue to explore the possibilities of settlement.

A dozen years after a Harvard team undertook to Boris Yeltsin's government to introduce economic liberalism and democracy to the former Soviet Union — and in 1996 got fired in the middle of an epic national looting spree, when its team leaders and their wives were discovered to be among those investing on their own behalf — how have things worked out for the Russians?

A particularly good starting point is a survey by Peter Reddaway in the January 2004 issue of *Post-Soviet Affairs*, which just happens to be free. Reddaway, 64, is one of a group of older scholars, generally known as "Sovietologists," who in the 1990s were ridden off the case by young economists enthusiastic about massive and rapid privatization. No critic of the latter's "market Bolshevism" has been more acute.

A political science professor emeritus at George Washington University, Reddaway describes a country in which two great factions are now battling for control, with President Vladimir Putin apparently as chief mediator and balancer in between.

On the one hand are the oligarchs, a handful of clever and daring individuals who, during the improbable gold rush of the 90s, gained ownership of most of the productive assets of the Russian economy – factories, utilities, natural resources, mass media – thanks to head starts given them by Yeltsin and his chief economic adviser, Anatoly Chubais.

On the other are the *siloviki*, a loose, politically motivated faction of former politicians, bureaucrats and military leaders whose power has been quietly but dramatically enhanced in the last few years by Putin. The *chekisty* is a near-synonym, says Reddaway, since so many *siloviks* are former KGB (the Soviet secret police was originally called the *Cheka*). Some 25 percent of the Russian elite are now men and women whose careers were made in the old government ministries, according to one authoritative estimate, up from 11 percent under Yeltsin.

By now, Reddaway adds, both factions have created the well-developed financial, commercial, journalistic and lobbying networks that are characteristic of major political parties. Their interests regularly collide. Institutions are weak. A high degree of corruption is a given. Dealings among the Russian elite remain hyper-personal, promiscuous and unpredictable.

And the liberal market reformers? Their parties received too few votes to have even a single seat in the parliament, Reddaway says. Four parties dominate instead (Unified Russia, the Communist Party, the Liberal-Democratic Party and the Motherland bloc), each of them reflecting in some degree the great-power longing that he describes as the prevalent ideology in Russia today. Meanwhile, ostensibly above party himself, Putin is pressing for reforms that would produce two U.S.-style national parties offering even less real choice.

It was the oligarchs who threw their weight behind Putin and assured his election to the presidency in 2000, after he had been catapulted into power as premier the year before by Boris Yeltsin, says Reddaway. A career KGB officer, Putin had served for several years as assistant to Anatoly Subchak, the first democratically elected mayor of St. Petersburg, before becoming head of the Federal Security Service.

Yeltsin's own oligarchic "family" hoped to control Putin through the use of *kompromat*, politically or legally compromising material, says Reddaway, and so they have, at least to the extent of maintaining their own wealth and freedom. But the tycoons didn't reckon on the extent to which Putin would use his political skills to enhance the power of their natural antagonists, the bureaucrats.

Russians of all sorts were tired of confrontation and change. The oligarchs wanted to consolidate their hold on power; ordinary people wanted their wages and pensions to be paid on time. The oligarchs could continue to modernize the Russian economy: to plow money into new opportunities, to intimidate or co-opt labor unions, to shut down loss-making operations, to move freely between Russia and Western Europe. But, says Reddaway, "An infusion of *siloviki* was required."

That was the situation when maneuvering began last year for the 2004 presidential campaign. The richest oligarch, Mikhail Khodorkovsky, founder and chief owner of the Yukos oil conglomerate, raised a critical challenge. He announced plans to merge Yukos with a fellow oligarch's company to create the fourth-largest oil company in the world – and offered to sell a major piece of it to Exxon-Mobil. He urged the development of a system of parliamentary parties that would weaken Putin's power. He indicated that he planned to retire from business to run for president in 2008. After several months of behind-the-scenes intrigue, he was arrested on various charges in October and remains in jail awaiting trial today. Putin was re-elected by a wide margin in March.

For their part, the *siloviki* are pressing Putin for an explicit program of "de-Yeltsinization," Reddaway says, loosely modeled on the de-Stalinization of the 1950s. He sees the Soviet president as quietly helpful to his fellow former bureaucrats when he can, but not to the point of all-out warfare with the oligarchs. "He is not the strong leader they would prefer, boldly committed to their cause, and unimpeded by *kompromat* or oligarchic constraints," writes Reddaway. "But what other leader do they have?"

What to expect? Reddaway cites three possibilities, none of them very pleasing to those who had hoped that liberal democracy and economic decentralization might take root and flourish in easternmost Europe. A gradual increase in authoritarianism is one possibility, with only small readjustments of ownership. A more pronounced shift towards more government control is the greater likelihood, with Putin retaining power and more oligarchs leaving or facing trial.

The least likely (but not implausible) possibility would find Putin ousted by an alliance of *siloviki* and hard-line nationalists. What could trigger such a seismic shift? A Chernobyl-like ecological disaster or a major epidemic. A military mutiny. A major terrorist attack in Moscow. Or perhaps most dangerous, a decline in the price of oil, with subsequent widespread economic hardship. Only the most optimistic can continue to hope that Putin will successfully play off oligarchs against communists in order to permit genuine market and democratic principles to develop.

Hence the widespread interest in Russia's experience with privatization in the 1990s. It is not just Harvard University that is on trial in Judge Woodlock's courtroom. It is the collective judgment of the economics profession itself.

CHAPTER SEVEN

# The "Assigned To" Trial

*December 5, 2004*

It was in 1974 that Harvard University created the Harvard Institute for International Development. Since 1947, the university's little Development Advisory Service (DAS)(the brainchild of economist Edward Mason) had been providing relatively disinterested macroeconomic advice on development projects to foreign governments, starting with Pakistan soon after its partition from India.

Its small corps of development experts served as links between Harvard professors in the sciences, law and economics and various officials in the countries that they advised. These were latter-day counterparts of the men who built agriculture extension services in the industrial democracies — men and women who could have made livings as college teachers but who preferred life in the borderlands, teaching everything from economic policy and public finance to public health and environmental management to those who otherwise would be bound to traditional methods. They traveled frequently, mastered languages, built their relationships.

And during the long Cold War, they relied on the ideals of academic disinterestedness and universalism to shield themselves from untoward influences.

They cultivated an essential independence from the US government, in order to retain the trust of their governmental hosts.

By the mid-1970s, demand was surging for Harvard's (and many other universities') services as an honest supplier of interdisciplinary knowledge to governments of newly industrializing nations and former command economies. The seven projects HIID inherited from DAS grew to nearly 40 engagements in nations ranging from Indonesia and Vietnam to Ukraine, Bolivia and Mauritius. Some 200 persons worked for HIID all over the world, half of them professionals.

Then in 1992, an economics professor newly recruited to Harvard from the University of Chicago attracted a landmark project – a mission to advise the government of Russia on behalf of the U.S. Agency for International Development on how to quickly build a market economy where there had been none before.

Andrei Shleifer, who had himself emigrated with his family from the Soviet Union as a teenager 15 years before, became the first Harvard faculty member to actually lead an HIID mission himself, rather than defer to a development professional.

He was no stranger to Cambridge, having graduated from Harvard College in 1984 and the Massachusetts Institute of Technology in 1986.

Suddenly, the 31-year-old Shleifer, a theorist and expert on finance, was catapulted into the top-most ranks of the world's "country doctors," traveling frequently to Moscow; vacationing with Russian privatization chief Anatoly Chubais. His oldest friend, economist Larry Summers, was monitoring US economic policy in Russia as assistant treasury secretary for international affairs. His wife became a celebrity manager of a hedge fund with extensive investments in Russia. Within a few years, Harvard University had invested nearly 2 percent of its endowment in Russian securities.

Five years later, his $34 million project collapsed amid charges of corruption. Shleifer, his deputy, former Rhodes Scholar Jonathan Hay, and their wives, were accused of buying several hundred thousand dollars' worth of Russian stocks, bonds and, perhaps most important, jumping to the head of the queue in order to receive, from the Russian Securities and Exchange Commission they advised, the first license to offer mutual funds in Russia – a potential gold mine.

After whistle-blowers in Moscow complained, USAID investigated and fired Harvard. The Russian government, whose senior economic officials had grown close to Shleifer, severed its relationship with USAID in return. Harvard removed Shleifer as project director and fired Hay altogether.

The US attorney in Boston eventually sued Harvard, Shleifer and Hay for civil fraud, seeking treble damages, or something like $120 million from each.

Harvard, meanwhile, had quietly undertaken an extensive internal review. And HIID published its Biennial Report, celebrating 25 years of growing influence and success, just months before the government filed suit in September 2000.

Tucked inside each front cover of the Bienniel Report was a black-bordered card announcing that Harvard had decided to abolish the organization, effective almost immediately.

Many of its people and projects eventually would be moved into various teaching faculties, it said. But the bottom line was that HIID's 200 employees were out of their jobs.

All the while, the government's civil complaint went forward, despite various measures behind the scenes to quash it – including a settlement offer of more than $20 million from Harvard which the government declined.

Last summer, after extensive discovery, deposition, argument and counterargument, U.S. District Court Judge Douglas Woodlock ruled against all three defendants in the civil suit – Harvard for simple breach of contract (reducing its maximum exposure to the $34 million of the contract), Shleifer and Hay for one count of fraud. Shleifer indicated he would appeal.

So why is Judge Woodlock hosting a three-day jury trial this week in his Boston courtroom?

Because, as he prepares for a longer trial next year to assess damages, the judge says there are some preliminary differences of opinion that only a jury can decide – including a second count of fraud.

The three-day trial this week has to do with the meaning of the phrase "assigned to," as it appears in Harvard's contract with USAID.

The government rules seem relatively clear. "No employee of the grantee shall engage directly or indirectly, either in the individual's own name or through an agency of another person, in any business, profession, or occupation in the foreign countries to which the individual is assigned, nor shall the individual make loans or investments to or in any business, profession or occupation in the foreign countries to which the individual is assigned."

Nor is there much ambiguity about why the government insists that advisers not invest in the countries to which they are giving advice. The idea is to prevent actual or apparent conflicts of interest in situations where incentives to curry favor exist in all directions.

What Harvard and Shleifer maintain is that Shleifer wasn't really "assigned" to Russia, despite the fact that he was project director and principal investigator. Therefore, he wasn't covered by the conflict-of-interest rules. After all, he continued to live with his family in Newton, Massachuestts, traveling to Russia only as necessary. (An earlier claim, that he wasn't an employee of HIID, was thrown out by the judge.)

So that's what the "assigned to" trial is all about. Harvard and Shleifer want the discussion to remain as narrow as possible. The three-day proceeding is "neither the time nor the place for an ethics seminar or a debate on the purposes of conflict-of-interest policies or foreign investment restrictions," their lawyers say.

Thus they've sought to bar all witnesses from opining "hither and yon regarding personal morality, moralistic generalities, or about any conflict of interest or investment restriction policy" separate from the government rules — meaning Harvard's own.

The government responds that Harvard is trying to turn the case "into the parsing of a word" apart from its contractual context and real-world setting. In siding with Professor Shleifer, its lawyers wryly note, Harvard is seeking to prevent any discussion of norms that have evolved among other Harvard professors.

The government plans to call five witnesses from USAID to testify about their understanding of the contract, and only one from HIID – former director Jeffrey Sachs, an economist who dismissed Shleifer from the project after the investigation began. Sachs now is director of the Earth Institute at Columbia University in New York.

Harvard and Shleifer, on the other hand, are relying mainly on two former HIID officials to testify to their belief that Shleifer was within his rights to invest in Russian securities: former director and Harvard professor Dwight Perkins and former assistant director Rosanne Kumins. They're calling two experts from USAID as well.

It is not an easy matter to put before a jury. We'll report back next week on how the various parties do.

CHAPTER EIGHT

# "A Narrow and Technical Issue"

*November 12, 2004*

Did the customary conflict-of-interest provisions apply to Harvard economist Andrei Shleifer when, under contract to the U.S. government in the mid-1990s, the young professor led Harvard's mission to Moscow?

After a three-day trial last week, a jury took barely more than two hours to decide that indeed they did.

With the verdict, the government's case against Harvard University and one of its star economists moved to a new level. Harvard's potential liability escalated somewhat, beneath a roughly $40 million ceiling. So did Shleifer's personal exposure, conceivably as much as $120 million, on a charge of submitting false claims.

U.S. District Court Judge Douglas Woodlock entered a summary judgment against both defendants last summer – Shleifer on a previous count of fraud for having attempted to set up a mutual fund business with a colleague, Harvard on breach of its contract to provide disinterested advice – rather than the treble-damages False Claims Act violation for which the government had asked.

What the jury's verdict really changed, according to attorneys for two of the three main parties in the matter, were the incentives to settle the case.

Now that Harvard's bold claim has failed – that it didn't matter if its chief adviser to the government of Russia invested hundreds of thousands of dollars in Russian securities, since he was living in Newton, Massachusetts, at the time and commuting only periodically – attorneys for all sides once again will meet and attempt to come to terms.

If they don't succeed, a second, longer jury trial looms next spring, to determine what Harvard and its errant professor (and Shleifer's assistant, lawyer Jonathan Hay) owe as a result of its team leaders' forbidden investments. They brought the project, which began in 1992, to an abrupt halt in 1997. The potential for embarrassment is huge.

Harvard's reaction Thursday was terse. "Today's verdict related to a narrow and technical issue in the case. Harvard remains confident that as the matter proceeds we will demonstrate that the work on the Russia Project was of great value to both the Russian Federation and the United States government."

\* \* \*

The power entrusted to ordinary people in a jury trial is the more astonishing the higher the stakes. It is, as Judge Woodlock observed, "with the exception of a New England town meeting, the last place in which the individual citizen can make important decisions about government directly."

In the courtroom there are experts on all sides. The lawyers and the judge speak among themselves in low tones throughout the proceedings in a language at once so fluent, terse and hard to follow that it might as well be Navajo. Beforehand, they go over the rules in detail, down to the particulars of where to stand. It is as if they were blocking a play.

At a certain point, 45 prospective jurors troop into the courtroom, sit down and proceed to identify themselves one by one, their towns, their jobs and their spouses' jobs – forklift operator, unemployed, benefits manager, attorney, company president, nurse, attorney, actuary, school teacher and so on. The lawyers among them are immediately excused from duty, as are any others with interests in the matter at hand.

The attorneys trying the case then huddle together — four for the defense, two for the government — comparing notes, darting glances, consulting lists, until, after a seemingly long time, they have assembled lists of those whose presence on the panel they would challenge *peremptorily*, no reasons given, only hunches played, singling out those who might be unsympathetic, occupationally or temperamentally.

Thirty-one citizens are excused on this basis, before twelve are chosen and two remaining candidates returned to the pool. All at once the average age of the panel drops by a decade, to perhaps 35. There are eight women and four men. None knows anything to speak of about Russia, Harvard, or government contracts.

The judge adjures them to pay attention. "Rather than thinking, 'Well, when I get a chance, I'll look at the transcript,'" he says, "You won't get a chance to look at the transcript. It won't be available to you in connection with the trial." No note-taking, either.

The jurors, all of them, remain alert throughout.

And when the government finally rests its case Wednesday afternoon, having invested three days, the jury deliberates for an hour and then goes home. They return Thursday morning. They talk among themselves for a further 90 minutes, enjoy the snack that's provided, and announce that they are ready to return to the courtroom.

They find for the government. The judge polls them one by one, compliments them, thanks them for "a relatively short jury service, but a very significant one," and sends them home with instructions not to talk to the parties to the case without permission.

On the way home, outside the courthouse one of them says, "Are you kidding? Of course he was assigned to Russia. That was clear from the very beginning. How come they had to take three days?"

* * *

Justice Department attorney Sara McLean made the government's opening argument. "This is a case about conflict-of-interest rules and common sense," she began. "Harvard professor Andrei Shleifer was the head of a very important foreign aid project in Russia, and now his lawyers and Harvard's lawyers are going to come in here and tell you that the conflict-of-interest rules for that project didn't apply to him.

"The conflict-of-interest rules in question said that people couldn't invest in the foreign countries to which they were assigned, and as Judge Woodlock has just told you, the question for you is going to be: Was Russia a foreign country to which Professor Shleifer was assigned?" The answer, asserted McLean, would be yes.

The single most compelling piece of evidence the government offered probably was a letter Shleifer wrote in June 1995 to Jim Norris, the Moscow representative of his employer, the US Agency for International Development.

> Dear Mr. Norris,
>
> Thank you for your letter. Indeed I was well aware of your interest in meeting me. It is certainly my intention to keep you informed about the status of the HIID [Harvard Institute for International Development] projects. I very much wanted to meet with you on my last trip, but it was simply impossible. This was a very short trip, made more or less on an emergency basis at [privatization chief] Maxim Boycko's request, and I had no spare time at all.
>
> I arrived in Moscow on Friday evening. Friday night, Saturday and Sunday morning were spent in a meeting with several Russians..., discussing the possibilities of tax reform in Russia. The result of this was a memo prepared for Maxim. Unfortunately, given my understanding with Maxim about the confidentiality of this work, I cannot send you a copy of the memo.
>
> I spent Sunday afternoon at the Legal Reform Project [which was drafting measures for regulatory reform], discussing mostly personnel issues that were absolutely urgent. As you probably know, the reduction by USAID of post-differentials has created huge problems for several

> people, who wanted a compensatory raise and threatened to quit. It appears that these issues have been resolved, but at a great cost of time. I also spent some time on Sunday evening with [Federal Securities Commission chairman] Dimitry Vasiliev and Jonathan Hay discussing the future of the Securities Commission and the GKI.
>
> As you can see, I had a pretty packed trip – even more so than usual. While I realize that it is important for me to see USAID when I come to Moscow, you should recognize the workload that I have since Maxim's and [soon-to-be chief economic adviser Anatoly] Chubais' promotions have been put in place has risen enormously.
>
> You also have permanent access to Maxim, Jonathan and others who reside in Moscow, and who are obviously intimately familiar with all HIID's activities. Thus, while I intended to make every effort to see you, I hope you appreciate the level of activities that I have to monitor and be involved in. And, as I have already mentioned to you..., the efforts to use others to perform many of these tasks simply have not worked. I run an extremely lean operation in the US and most people working for us insist on dealing with me.

Plenty of other evidence was introduced, including various Harvard blandishments of "impartial oversight" in response to the government's help-wanted advertisement that "a completely neutral third party, void of any vested interest in the [privatization] contracting process, is required."

One Harvard proposal promised, "During the first year, Dr. Shleifer will work full time on the project, dividing his time between the US and Russia."

The government also put three top USAID people on the stand to testify to why their understanding that the no-investments proviso applied to Shleifer led them to terminate the contract, as well as former HIID director Jeffrey Sachs, now a Columbia University professor. Sachs testified, "You're assigned to the project, you're assigned to the foreign country because that's your work assignment."

Assistant U.S. Attorney Sara Bloom closed the government's argument. "In this country, no one is above the law," she began. "Today these defendants stand before you literally arguing that the rules, the conflict-of-interest rules of the

United States government, do not apply to the Harvard professor who headed a $57 million US government program in Russia.

"Would it make any sense to read this provision to apply to the American secretaries, to the bookkeepers, to the assistants, and not to the man at the top, the man who was giving advice to the Russian officials on the creation of securities markets in Russia, to the man who directed all the other employees, to the man who had the most information about the financial markets in Russia of everyone on the project?"

\* \* \*

Harvard lawyers, on the other hand, and those for Shleifer, argued that the government was deliberately misinterpreting the meaning of "assigned," in order to hound the leader of a project that had mysteriously fallen into disfavor. And therefore the case was about the government keeping its word.

"Just because it's a famous school, and just because it's a big deal to some people doesn't mean that the government has the right either to back out of or to stretch the language of an agreement with Harvard, and that's what's going on here," Paul Ware of the Boston law firm Goodwin, Procter told the jury.

Early on, Ware spun an elaborate distinction between a homework assignment ("a task or some work") and assignment to a school bus or a homeroom ("as place, a physical location"), hoping to buttress his argument that, since Shleifer didn't have an office, an apartment or a car in Moscow, he wasn't assigned to Russia.

"I was thinking about how we could communicate about the different means of 'assigned,'" he told the jury, "and I think one way in which to do that is to think about the children that you have or you may yet have in your lives. And we often talk, for example, if your child came home and you said to your child, 'Were you given a homework assignment?' You would all know what that meant. That kind of assignment would be familiar to you because it has a particular context. … That's not the assignment that's being talked about in this contract…

"If, on the other hand, in September of the school year, your child came home from first grade or whatever, and you said, 'Have you been assigned to a school bus?' Or, 'What school bus have you been assigned to?' or, 'What homeroom have you been assigned to?' that would have a different meaning to you. That wouldn't be a task. That wouldn't be homework. That would be a place, a physical location."

(To which the government's Sara Bloom later replied, "When you came in here for jury duty, you were assigned to jury duty, right? And not only that, once you got picked for the jury, you got an assigned seat. It's a physical location. But it doesn't mean you have to live there for a year to be your physical location, to be assigned.")

The luckiest man in all of Harvard University last week was surely Dwight Perkins, the Harold Hitchings Burbank Professor of Political Economy, director of the Harvard Institute for International Development for the first two-and-a-half years of the Russia Project, and a man greatly admired for his personal rectitude.

Perkins had been scheduled to testify that Shleifer had brought the Russia Project to Harvard, and therefore it was not one to which he had been "assigned" by HIID; that he himself had been listed as principal investigator on the government grant before Shleifer took over, and that he had not felt that the conflict-of-interest provisions had applied to him, either.

Harvard cancelled Perkins' appearance at the last minute.

In the end, Harvard called only two witnesses – John Owens, a USAID employee who retired in 1994, who had promised to tell the jury that the conflict-of-interest provision was so much "boilerplate"; and Kathleen Mercier, from the Harvard University Office of Sponsored Research, who acknowledged that she was not consulted nor did she volunteer an opinion about the "assignment" issue throughout the process.

But good lawyering often is about taking words out of context. So Harvard's lawyers hammered away at small inconsistencies in the use of the word "assigned" in various e-mails and sworn depositions given by the government's witnesses, including one taken by telephone after lunch the Thursday before the trial began.

"This is not a case in which a bunch of slick guys from Cambridge are trying to put one over on the jury or avoid responsibility," said Goodwin, Procter's Ware at the end of his summation for the defense. Murmured an observer of the local scene, "No, they're from Boston."

* * *

Andrei Shleifer was in the courtroom all three days. Early on, his attorney, Robert Ullmann, of Nutter, McLennen & Fish, introduced him to the jury. Shleifer forced a smile.

At 43, Shleifer no longer exhibits the boyish enthusiasm of the teenager who arrived from Russia in 1976 in Rochester, New York, knowing no more English than what he had learned from episodes of "Charlie's Angels" on television. Within a of couple years, a sharp-eyed recruiter had offered him a scholarship to Harvard College. And there, as a sophomore, he entered into a life-changing friendship when he brashly offered to correct the math errors in a paper by a first-year assistant professor of economics named Larry Summers.

Today, Summers is president of Harvard University. Shleifer, too, has come a very long way. Despite the legal proceedings that have been grinding on against him for most of a decade, Shleifer has continued to rise in the economics profession. He sold his interest in a prosperous money management firm some years ago; he is a moderately wealthy man. Today, he edits the prestigious *Journal of Economic Perspectives* for the American Economic Association. He is considered a leading expert on finance, behavioral economics and, of all things, corruption.

To be sure, there are reminders of the old days. He carries his papers in a canvas bag instead of a briefcase; the middle button dangles by a thread from his suit. He displays the same old seminar-room-bred willingness to engage – behavior his lawyers seek to discourage. Shleifer is, in short, still a man who people want to help.

But also, he is still tough. Still arrogant. By appearances, he is lonely. Mainly, he is a man who does not seem to possess a fundamental understanding of the predicament in which he finds himself – in the dock because of the moral compass of a handful of young government lawyers who considered that even Harvard University with its lofty good intentions must obey the law. He is hoisted on his own petard in the very sort of legal system whose robust checks and balances he was supposed to explain to the government of the Russian Federation.

Attorneys for all sides are to file a joint submission on January 28 on various issues in a prospective damages trial.

\* \* \*

So why did the trial take three days? Why did Harvard spend all that money on a question that took a laughing jury, unanimous from the start of its deliberations (by jurors' own accounts), little more than two hours to decide?

That is the really interesting question. There's something unexplained about Harvard continuing to defend the integrity of its professor, the expert on corruption who began investing in Russian securities with his deputy almost as soon as he got the adviser's job, who argues now that the conflict-of-interest rules didn't apply to him.

That's what makes this such a fascinating case. In putting the meaning of "assigned to" to a jury, Judge Woodlock gave Harvard the benefit of every doubt. The university replied with sophistry and technicalities, and nothing more. The sheer audacity of putting so weak a case before a jury makes you think there must be something more at stake.

At a minimum, when the collective judgment of those who run America's oldest university differs so radically from the common sense of its everyday citizens, as expressed by the jury last week, the institution itself must be alarmed, and enter into a deeper self-examination.

And at a maximum? What if the men and women at the pinnacle of American education simply don't know wrong from right? The "narrow and technical issue" at the heart of Harvard's ill-fated Russia Project may be one of those innumerable pivots on which American history regularly turns.

CHAPTER NINE

# Who Is Minding the Store?

*January 16, 2005*

During the first few days of the new year, the US government's lawsuit against Harvard University and its economics professor Andrei Shleifer had inched forward in the direction of a grinding damages trial.

The case, which has to do with the collapse of Harvard's mission to Moscow amid charges of corruption, is an embarrassing hangover from the corporate and political scandals of the 1990s. The US government was paying the bill for supposedly disinterested advice.

First the government indicated that it wanted to take a year to prepare to argue that Harvard's failure to supervise its team leaders adversely affected everything from the subsequent performance of the Russian economy to US national security.

Harvard promptly responded by asking US District Court Judge Douglas Woodlock to clamp down sharply on the question of damages and to put the case before a jury in the fall. Trench warfare, in other words, same as it's been for more than five years.

Then, last week, three things happened in the space of five days.

- Yale University disclosed it had fired tenured economics professor Florencio

López-de-Silanes, a protégé and frequent collaborator of Andrei Shleifer, for double-billing his expense accounts.

• Jack Meyer announced he was leaving Harvard Management Company with four associates to start his own firm, after 15 years of unparalleled success in running the university's endowment, during which time Harvard's bank account grew from $5 billion to $23 billion.

• Harvard, Shleifer and the government together asked the judge for a 30-day delay in various deadlines. They were working on a settlement, they told the court, and a hiatus might be "productive."

Were the three events in any way connected? And if so, how? It will be years before we can hope to answer with any degree of certainty. We may never really know.

But Harvard Management Company's quiet but extensive program of investing in Russia in the mid-1990s was a part of the government's investigation from the beginning.

And though the investigation produced no charges, the view is common among Russians and those who have worked in Russia that undisclosed behind-the-scenes links are the force that has bound Harvard so tightly to Shleifer.

Consider:

The Yale story by itself was merely interesting; seemingly small potatoes in the scheme of things. Professor López-de-Silanes, 38, had been recruited by Harvard's John F. Kennedy School of Government in 2002 to head Yale's newly created Institute for Corporate Governance in Yale's School of Management.

*The Wall Street Journal* disclosed last Monday that López-de-Silanes had been placed on unpaid leave pending his resignation after an audit found that he had double-billed Yale for around $150,000 in business travel expenses since arriving from Cambridge. A separate World Bank investigation of various contracts he administered is continuing.

Through his lawyer, López-de-Silanes stated: "I deeply regret any unintended harm. I have taken appropriate corrective steps with all affected parties and I can offer no excuse except the intensity of my focus on my work. I am leaving Yale because it is the right thing to do for the institute and all concerned."

So Yale reacted to scandal one way, Harvard quite another. The two universities' differential treatments of its errant economists have raised eyebrows around the world. For while Yale immediately sought their professor's resignation despite his tenure, Harvard has for eight years backed Professor Shleifer to the hilt.

True, the malfeasance which each professor committed is slightly different. López-de-Silanes in effect stole money from his employer. Shleifer, on the other hand, made investments in Russian stocks, bonds and a business while advising the Russian government on behalf of the US Agency for International Development — a flagrant conflict of interest prohibited both by Harvard rules and by his government contract.

But where Yale cashiered its professor, Harvard repeatedly has dug in its heels. Shleifer wasn't covered by the rules, the university argued, because he didn't work really for Harvard (it was the Harvard Institute for International Development, since disbanded, that signed the checks); and besides, he wasn't really "assigned" to Russia anyway, since he only commuted from Cambridge.

Last July, Judge Woodlock threw out the first argument and ruled that Shleifer and his deputy, former Rhodes Scholar Jonathan Hay, had committed fraud by setting up their wives in a mutual fund business which their Russian government counterparts then favored with a licensing head start. And a jury took barely two hours to dismiss the second "assigned to" argument last month.

In other respects, however, the situations were strikingly similar. Both Shleifer and López-de-Silanes grew up abroad — the former in Russia, the latter in Mexico. Both began brilliant academic careers in Cambridge, Massachusetts: Shleifer at Harvard College (where a young assistant professor named Lawrence Summers was his mentor) and the Massachusetts Institute of Technology, López-de-Silanes as a graduate student at Harvard, where Shleifer was his teacher. Both were experts in finance.

Both men consulted to governments around the world. López-de-Silanes was a founding member of the Blue Ribbon Panel on Corporate Governance in Russia and the Committee on Best Corporate Practices in Mexico. Shleifer directed Harvard's Russia Project for several years.

Both were said to behave autocratically. Both were reported to authorities by whistle-blowers among those whom they supervised.

The two also have collaborated extensively. A recent resume lists fourteen recent joint papers (all including permutations of other authors as well), including "The New Comparative Economics," "The Practice of Justice," and "Theft Technologies."

(In the light-of-love, light-of-justice department, it should be said that both men are charismatic, both profess the highest ideals, and nobody has as much money as they'd like. Shleifer, 43, is a senior figure in the profession, a winner of the John Bates Clark Medal, given annually to an American economist under 40, and the editor of the influential *Journal of Economic Perspectives* as well. Most recently, he was honored by the University of Munich.)

Still, López-de-Silanes is out of a job while Harvard has continued to vigorously defend itself, jointly with Shleifer, in court. A difference of opinion of this magnitude between two great universities in their response to professional misconduct would be surprising enough. But there is more.

Meyer and the Harvard endowment are part of the story simply because Harvard Management was an aggressive investor in Russia in the mid-1990s, during the period that Shleifer was advising the Russian government and illicitly investing on his own behalf. For example, *Euromoney* magazine at the time described Harvard as "bolder than most," because it bought stakes in companies themselves, instead of relying on intermediaries such as hedge fund managers.

When government attorneys deposed Meyer in the course of their suit against Harvard, they learned that as much as 1.8 percent of Harvard's endowment had been invested in Russia in the years before the US government fired Shleifer – some $200 million of a portfolio then worth around $11 billion – not the 10 percent that gossip had it at the time.

Though he (and other Harvard Management employees) occasionally had contacts with Shleifer and other members of the Harvard team that was advising the Russian government at the time, Meyer testified that no inside information had been exchanged.

His memory of the trips he had made to Russia proved hazy, though – to the point of forgetting a third trip altogether, until he was shown a record of it.

All the while in those years, Shleifer's old friend and mentor economist Lawrence Summers was serving in the US Treasury Department, first as undersecretary for international affairs, then as deputy to Treasury Secretary Robert Rubin.

While Shleifer didn't report to Summers – the Harvard project's funding came from the State Department – the Treasury Department oversaw US economic policy in Russia. Among insiders, the friendship was widely recognized.

Summers testified that, in the course of a day at the beach during this period (he didn't remember the year), he urged Shleifer to check Harvard's conflict-of-interest provisions – but that the government's interest did not come up.

Far more difficult to explain is that Summers has remained close to Shleifer since the scandal started in 1997, and even after the government filed its lawsuit in Boston in September 2000. While interviewing for the Harvard presidency, he stayed at Shleifer's house. After he got the job, he told Faculty of Arts and Science dean Jeremy Knowles that it was important that Shleifer be retained by Harvard in the face of attractive offers from other schools.

In his testimony, he noted that Shleifer's Russian counterparts may have preferred that he have a stake in the projects on which he was advising. And he repeated the view of some members of the Harvard economics department that their colleague was being "screwed" by zealous government lawyers.

Summers officially recused himself from the matter only at the "insistence" of others among the seven-member Harvard Corporation (of which he is himself a member), according to a report last fall by Carla Anne Robbins of *The Wall Street*

*Journal*. A university spokesperson said the decision was mutual. (Robbins alone in the mainstream press has followed the story that she broke.)

Although Harvard also has a board of overseers elected by alumni, and although certain appointed committees are extremely influential in the governance of the university, the little self-perpetuating Corporation is the ultimate authority. It meets around 15 times a year.

Corporation membership has turned over more than usual in recent years. Summers was named to replace retiring president Neil Rudenstine in March 2001. The next year, long-time Goldman Sachs co-chairman Robert Rubin, Summers' former boss at the Treasury Department, replaced Robert Stone, a veteran of many years of service to Harvard.

At the same time, Robert Reischauer, president of Washington's Urban Institute, replaced Herbert "Pug" Winokur Jr., after the Connecticut financier resigned from the Corporation in the wake of the Enron disaster. (Winokur had been an Enron director and chair of the board's compensation committee.)

In 2004, James Rothenburg replaced D. Ronald Daniel as Harvard's treasurer and became an automatic fellow of the Corporation. And last month Nannerl Keohane, former president of Duke University and Wellesley College, was named to replace Hanna Holborn Gray, when the president emerita of the University of Chicago steps down in June.

Attorney Conrad Harper of New York's Simpson Thacher & Bartlett, a former legal adviser to the State Department, and James Houghton, chairman of the board of Corning, Inc., round out the membership. Harper joined in February 2000. Houghton, a member since 1995, is the senior fellow.

Meanwhile, Harvard general counsel Anne Taylor – a known antagonist of Shleifer – stepped down in June 2002, saying that Summers should be free to assemble a team of his own. A year later, Robert Iuliano, her deputy, was named to succeed her.

In December, Harvard's outside lawyers suffered a humiliating courtroom defeat in a short trial meant to resolve whether Shleifer was "assigned" to Russia.

According to the jury, he was.

Meanwhile, the bill of particulars that the government offered to prove against Shleifer in a damages trial is extensive: that he ran his own business out of government offices; that he elbowed competitors out of the way; that he used USAID funds to buy the votes of Russian officials and legislators favorable to his cause; that he fired, demoted and threatened various Harvard employees who complained.

Shleifer replies that he was passionately advancing the cause of a market economy in the face of old-line communist resistance, and that desperate measures sometimes were required. In *A Normal Country*, scheduled to be published by Harvard University Press in March, he argues that the institutions that he helped shape during the 1990s have ensured that pervasive centralization cannot stage a comeback, and that Russia's escape from communism has been assured.

What are the chances that the Corporation itself has begun to take a more vigorous interest in the Shleifer matter? What are the chances that changes in the mission of the endowment company going forward are one result? It is worth remembering how quietly, in the wake of the scandal, the Harvard Institute for International Development disappeared.

Rubin and Summers are heading the search for Jack Meyer's successor. But with both men apparently recused from the Shleifer matter, it is not at all clear who among the remaining five fellows has active oversight of the case. It is not clear who among the Harvard administration is making day-to-day tactical decisions about its legal conduct.

Nor is it clear what, if anything, has changed in the university's inner councils since Judge Woodlock found last summer that the university had only breached its contract with the government, and not committed the treble-damages fraud with which it had been charged – a reduction of something like $80 million in exposure.

There are many easy-to-understand reasons for Harvard Endowment's Meyer to wish to strike off on his own, after averaging 15 percent a year for 15 brilliant years. (Previously he was chief investment officer for the Rockefeller Foundation and, before that, deputy controller for New York City). His decision, however, came as a surprise.

And students of economics will note that, if there were some sort of guilty secrets between Shleifer and those who in the '90s were investing Harvard's money in Russia, the situation would resemble the standard fable of the prisoners' dilemma, in which two persons accused of wrongdoing find it easy to cooperate in their denial – as long as they can freely communicate. The standard tactic is to split the parties.

What if the people running Harvard are most of all concerned, not with the university's reputation, but with its moral compass? Let's see what happens next.

CHAPTER TEN

# A Theory of the Harvard Mess

*March 27, 2005*

The storm that has erupted at Harvard University turns out to have been building for some time – for three-and-a-half years, or precisely the period that economist Lawrence H. Summers has been president.

Heretofore *Economic Principals* has stuck to covering just one neglected aspect of Summers' presidency, the government lawsuit over Harvard's failed Russia Project in the 1990s. Reporting on a university takes too much time.

But the recent ventilation of extensive discontent, mainly in a series of three faculty meetings bravely and carefully reported by Harvard's alumni magazine, has made it possible to form an opinion about what amounts to a rebellion by a large fraction of the university's core faculty of arts and sciences and senior staff. (Richard Bradley's new book, *Harvard Rules: The Struggle for the Soul of the World's Most Powerful University,* is also useful. It contains a trove of interesting information, but lacks a deep understanding of the institution.) Indeed, it seems safe to say that the circumstances at Harvard have been widely misunderstood around the world – as, for example, by *The Economist* magazine. "Freedom of speech: Harvard's disgrace. Its faculty have censured Larry Summers. They, not he, should be ashamed."

The real problem is a fundamental mismatch between the university and the executive who in 2001 was chosen to head it – "an arranged marriage gone sour," in university professor (of Chinese literature) Stephen Owen's phrase. "This is the first time in my 16 years at Harvard that I have spoken at an FAS Faculty Meeting – and I hope this will be my last," said James L. Watson, professor of Chinese society, at the February 22 session. "I have taught at five universities, some of which were facing serious difficulties. But I have never seen anything like the firestorm currently enveloping us."

It fell to economist Caroline Hoxby to offer the clearest formulation of the problem when, in a powerful statement, she indicted Summers for persistently running against his own team in a bullying manner. Towards the end of her remarks, Hoxby ventured that it sometimes seemed as though the president possessed a view of the faculty, at least some of them, "that is a caricature: self-absorbed people who care a great deal about their privileges and not much about their students and the quest for knowledge."

As a result, Summers seemed to have adopted "a management strategy in which decisions are discussed with only a small inner circle. There are forums for airing views but few mechanisms for incorporating them, and resistance is assumed to stem from obstinacy, not thought and experience.

"I do not know where you got this caricatured view of the faculty, but it is not true to my experience." In her view, she said, the faculty "is passionate about research and passionate about students and struggles every day with the tension between the two."

Where is such a caricature of Harvard to be found? Close to home. It is a cartoon version of a subtle and durable critique that supplied the founding impulse of an institution just down the street at the other end of Cambridge – the Massachusetts Institute of Technology (MIT).

Chances are that Larry Summers acquired it in the early 1970s, when he was an undergraduate at MIT, and at the end of the decade, when he taught there for three years.

To understand, it is necessary to go back more than 150 years, to a time when there was no MIT. Geologist William Barton Rogers, discouraged by the anti-intellectual atmosphere at the University of Virginia, in Charlottesville, moved to Boston in 1845.

He couldn't get a job at Harvard, which was in one of those periods of self-delight that have plagued it periodically since its beginning – in danger, according to historian Samuel Eliot Morison, of becoming "a fashionable finishing school for young gentlemen."

So for 15 years, Rogers sought to form a new-fangled polytechnic institute, based loosely on the model that was revolutionizing science in Germany. He could find no backers. Boston was entering its gilded age.

Then the Civil War broke out. The US Congress passed the Morrill Act, creating the land-grant universities. Massachusetts split its windfall, creating both MIT and an agriculture college in the western part of the state – the present-day University of Massachusetts, in Amherst.

The usefulness of local competition was apparent from the very beginning. When Harvard failed to offer him a professorship, young Charles Eliot quit in disgust and went to Germany to learn more chemistry. In 1866, MIT made him one of its first professors. Three years later, Harvard hired Eliot back — this time to be its president.

Since then, Harvard and MIT have been separately governed, to the great glory of both. Twice when the fund-raising got tough, MIT's administrators attempted to merge their institution into Harvard. The first time, in 1904, Massachusetts' Supreme Judicial Court wouldn't let them sell their headquarters in Boston's Copley Square. The second time, in 1915, MIT's faculty rebelled. On the land it had bought for MIT, Harvard built a business school instead.

The two cultures that have co-evolved over a century and a half could hardly be more different – two campuses of more or less the same university, separated by their motivations. MIT's mascot is the beaver, symbolizing industriousness. Harvard doesn't *have* a mascot. As sociologist David Riesman famously said, "MIT is about merit, Harvard is about grace," – meaning not just the finely turned phrase and the conducive architecture, but the potent doctrine of predestination, on which early Harvard scholars spent so much time, with its implication that some among us are already among the Elect, and that, just possibly, an outward sign of such other-worldly grace was having been "called" to Harvard in the first place.

Any strong school sometimes makes big mistakes. Often MIT has been a safe haven for scholars who didn't fit in at Harvard. Norbert Wiener, Paul Samuelson, Robert Solow, Noam Chomsky and Thomas Kuhn are just the most famous of those who didn't get jobs at Harvard, who subsequently found homes down the river. MIT, in its turn, denied tenure to electrical engineering PhD Robert Noyce, who promptly moved to California and co-invented the silicon chip.

Less attention has been paid to the overlap (or lack thereof) among undergraduate admissions. In *Harvard Rules*, author Bradley reports a fund-raising dinner in 2002 at which Summers was said to have replied, when asked by a student why he had gone to MIT instead of Harvard College, "Because I didn't get in."

In the 1980s, Summers (whose graduate training had been at Harvard) was the first of a substantial number of MIT economics faculty to reverse the trend, leaving what was commonly considered the world's best economics department to take offices in Harvard's Littauer Center. This infusion of MIT's style was said to greatly change the teaching culture of Harvard's graduate school, and at least in economics, probably it did. Before long, Harvard began attracting its share of the best students entering the field for the first time in 30 years.

Whatever possessed Harvard to hire Summers to be its president in the first place? Go back to the beginning of the 1990s, when Harvard missed its chance to hire legal scholar Gerhard Casper, then provost at the University of Chicago, who was widely regarded as the most promising of the next generation of academic leaders. Stanford University acted first.

Harvard then chose Neil Rudenstine, the number-two at Princeton, a scholar of Elizabethan literature, a capable administrator and a thoroughly nice man who, during his 10 years in Massachusetts Hall, was generally perceived as being too eager to please. Non-teaching staff at the university had doubled during his second five years, for example, to 5,100 persons.

Meanwhile, having served as chief economic adviser to the Michael Dukakis campaign in 1988, Larry Summers had gone to Washington in 1991 to be chief economist at the World Bank. During the Clinton administration he rose to prominence with a truly remarkable demonstration of moxie and good sense.

In the out-of-the-spotlight post of undersecretary for international affairs for Treasury Secretary Lloyd Bentsen, he soon became point man for Clinton's top economic adviser, former Goldman Sachs co-chair Robert Rubin – rounding up bond traders to support the Federal Reserve Board's interest rate cuts, crafting strategy in the Mexican peso crisis, practicing shuttle diplomacy in the Asian financial crisis and the Russian default, and helping staunch the panic in their wake.

Along with Alan Greenspan and Rubin, Summers wound up on the cover of *Time* magazine in 1999 as "The Committee to Save the World." Shortly afterwards, he succeeded Rubin in the corner office on 15th Street. It is difficult to overstate the magnitude of the success of the Clinton Treasury. Asset markets boomed and government finances swung from chronic deficit to enormous surplus in eight short years.

It was not surprising, then, when the little corporation that governs Harvard preferred Summers to the two others on their short list, Harvard provost Harvey Fineberg and University of Michigan president Lee Bollinger.

(I'm guilty, too. As a columnist for *The Boston Globe*, I wrote in 2001 that Summers had the potential to be the best president of Harvard since Charles Eliot returned from MIT. I was thinking mainly of his youth, his strategic sense, and the long horizon. About the rest, I could not have been more wrong.)

What no one could have foreseen was that the job offer would precipitate the breakup of Summers' marriage – and that his law professor wife and three children would remain in Washington, D.C. Since then, he has operated with the slightly exaggerated affect of a man no longer modulated by a long and successful partnership. He had more than enough affect to begin with.

It seems unlikely that Summers will choose to remain at Harvard overlong. He is too smart not to recognize that he is not good at it, and too young to give up trying to succeed. His optimal strategy may be to return to Washington and policy-making; to get in shape for another Clinton administration, should there be one, with a different Clinton – to hope, in other words, for a second chance.

And Harvard? How was it that Harvard got to be Harvard in the first place? The tight control, insulated from most outside pressure, of the owner-managers who control the university through its governing corporation surely has had a great deal to do with it. Expect the university to regain its tranquility in a year or two.

\* \* \*

*The following correction was added to this page on April 3, 2005:*

Memory plays funny tricks. *Economic Principals* wrote last week that Harvard University in 1991 missed its chance to hire legal scholar Gerhard Casper, then provost at the University of Chicago, who was widely regarded as the most promising of the next generation of academic leaders. That much is true.

But I had it backwards when I wrote that Stanford acted first. Only after Harvard chose Neil Rudenstine did Stanford successfully recruit Casper to replace Donald Kennedy – to the chagrin of many faculty at Chicago. *EP* regrets the error.

CHAPTER ELEVEN

# A Bigfoot Enters the Harvard Story

*May 15, 2005*

In the dénouement of the US government's successful lawsuit against Harvard University for its failed Russia Project in the 1990s, a scheduled conference again has been postponed, this time until June 2, while the various parties continue their four-month-long attempt to agree on appropriate damages.

A negotiated settlement would avoid an expensive and time-consuming jury trial before US District Court Judge Douglas Woodlock to determine the extent of the harm.

Harvard already has been found to have breached its contract with the US Agency for International Development to provide disinterested advice to the government of Russia; its economics professor Andrei Shleifer and his deputy, Jonathan Hay, to have committed fraud by speculating in Russian securities and trying to start a mutual fund business with their wives.

The really interesting news in the matter, however, came last week when *Boston Globe* columnist Alex Beam surfaced the name of author David McClintick in connection with the case. There was nothing as tangible as a press release or a book contract to report. McClintick spoke to Beam but declined to confirm that he had undertaken the project.

But in calls to others with knowledge of events, the writer had explained he was planning to write a book. There is every reason to expect it will be a good one.

A 65-year-old former reporter for *The Wall Street Journal*, McClintick is the author of three books in 30 years. All three show a remarkable ability to work with a wide variety of sources.

The first was *Stealing From the Rich: The Home-Stake Oil Swindle*, a 1977 cautionary tale of a drilling-rights tax-shelter scam memorable mainly for the energy and precision with which it was told. (A banker's son from Bartlesville, Oklahoma, fleeces well-to-do citizens around the country, including some prominent ones.)

The second, *Indecent Exposure: A True Story of Hollywood and Wall Street*, appeared in 1982 and became a classic, a non-fiction rival to Elmore Leonard's *Get Shorty* as an account of lax morals in the film industry, in this case at its uppermost levels. (Columbia Pictures chief executive David Begelman forges actor Cliff Robertson's name to a $10,000 check and gradually becomes a metaphor for widespread Tinseltown corruption.) McClintick has been dividing his time between New York and Los Angeles ever since.

The third, begun after McClintick had left the paper and entered upon the career of an independent author and published in 1993, was *Swordfish: A True Story of Ambition, Savagery, and Betrayal*. Not to be confused with the computer-scam John Travolta movie of the same name, *Swordfish* also illustrates an essentially timeless tale – a story of espionage and betrayal – with a highly particular tale, the harrowing but successful penetration of a Colombian drug ring by an agent of the Drug Enforcement Agency in Miami.

"I wrote *Swordfish* for a variety of reasons," McClintick explains in a note on sources and methods that itself tells the fascinating tale of how he reported the story (much of the dialogue is painstakingly reconstructed, not just from transcripts of wiretaps, but from complicated conversations with various parties about the contexts in which those conversations took place)."It was an opportunity to tell the story of a group of intriguing people living through a time of crisis. It was an opportunity to study, from the inside, an agency of the United States government under siege from a great international menace. It was an opportunity to write about one of the most intractable social and moral issues of the late 20th century – the drug plague."

As a *Wall Street Journal* reporter for 11 years, McClintick absorbed that newspaper's sense of what constitutes an adequate explanation of a set of facts – the fairest and most sophisticated in the news business. As he wrote in his first book, the *Journal* is "one of the relatively few publications in the world that encourages and enables its writers and editors to practice journalism as a profession rather than as an assembly-line craft."

(Significantly, the *Journal* is the only English-language newspaper to have evinced significant interest in the story of the Harvard Russia Project. It published authoritative front-page stories in 1997 and 2004, both by Carla Anne Robbins.)

Those books, elaborating the canons of fairness and accuracy on projects of steadily increasing complexity, handily qualify McClintick as a 'Bigfoot,' a term journalists reserve for members of their tribe who have won the right to deal with the principals in the stories they cover on more or less equal terms, either by dint of the newspapers for which they work or the importance of books they are expected to publish.

Moscow in the mid-90s was a fabulous story, a gold rush of epic proportions. The Yeltsin government, seeking to render impossible a return to state control of the economy, sold most of the nation's productive assets for a fraction of their value to a handful of savvy insiders who quickly became billionaires. Today they are collectively known as oligarchs.

But what makes Harvard's involvement so interesting is its human dimension. It is essentially the story of a friendship between two of the brightest among the rising generation of economists, Lawrence Summers and Andrei Shleifer. They met and became fast friends in 1979, when Summers was a Harvard teaching fellow and Shleifer was a sophomore student, having emigrated with his parents from the former Soviet Union only three years before.

Seventeen years later, Shleifer was teaching at Harvard and advising Yeltsin on behalf of the United States, while Summers was coordinating US policy towards Russia as deputy secretary of the Treasury. And five years after that, Summers was named president of Harvard University.

All that intervened was a USAID investigation of Shleifer's Russian investments (and those of his wife, his deputy and his deputy's wife and father), which led to the collapse of the project in 1997 and, over Harvard's vehement objections, the lawsuit brought by the US attorney in Boston in 2000.

Shleifer, too, has continued to function at a high level, winning the John Bates Clark Medal in 1999 for having made a substantial contribution to economics before the age of 40, gaining a named chair at Harvard, becoming editor of the *Journal of Economic Perspectives*, a leading journal of the American Economic Association, and last month publishing a book vigorously defending the advice he gave to the government of Boris Yeltsin – *A Normal Country: Russia After Communism*.

Finally, McClintick is well qualified to undertake to tell this complicated story whole in one other dimension. He is a 1962 graduate of Harvard College: close enough to the university to be a member of the largely honorary board of incorporators of Harvard's alumni magazine; sufficiently insulated from its influence by a life-long reputation as an investigative reporter.

Everybody still has to work hard on this case, especially Judge Woodlock. But McClintick's entry onto the scene permits the rest of who have followed the story to relax a little, secure in the conviction that, once justice has been served in the courtroom, the whole episode will be placed in context in a larger sphere.

There are, after all, severe limits to what can be told in a courtroom. As the great physicist Richard Feynman once remarked, "A very great deal more truth can become known than can be proved."

CHAPTER TWELVE

# Adult on Board

*May 29, 2005*

As the US government's case against Harvard University for the collapse of its Russia Project under economist Andrei Shleifer winds towards its suspenseful conclusion, one question more than any other has taken on additional interest. Who has oversight of the legal strategy for the seven-member corporation that rules the university — [for] the President and Fellows of Harvard College, as they are known?

So who is minding the store for Harvard?

According to two sources familiar with aspects of the university's defense, the Corporation's senior adviser in the matter is none other than Derek Bok. The former president has been asked by the Corporation to "look at" not just Russia, said one, but "all kinds of things" within the university.

A standing Joint Committee on Inspections — joint between the seven-member corporation, which has ultimate authority over the university, and the board of overseers, a 30-member advisory panel elected by alumni — presumably also plays a role as the university's audit committee.

Bok is especially well qualified by training, temperament and experience. He is a lawyer, a former professor of law and dean of the Harvard Law School. From 1971 until 1991 he was Harvard's president. Among his salient policies was a thoughtful annual report on significant developments affecting the university.

He has written five books on higher education and two on government: *Beyond the Ivory Tower* (1982), *Higher Learning* (1986), *Universities and the Future of America* (1990), *The State of the Nation* (1997), *The Shape of the River* (1998), *The Trouble with Government* (2001) and *Universities in the Marketplace* (2003).

One case in particular during the Bok years has some bearing on the question of errant behavior among professors. In 1984, tenured government professor Douglas Hibbs Jr. was compelled to resign despite his tenure, after being found to have demanded sexual favors from a graduate student.

Similarly, Yale University earlier this year dismissed tenured economics professor Florencio López-de-Silanes for double-billing his expense accounts to the university and the World Bank. López-de-Silanes, 38, a protégé and frequent collaborator of Andrei Shleifer, had been recruited from Harvard's John F. Kennedy School of Government to head the newly created Institute for Corporate Governance at Yale's School of Management.

Harvard began its Russia Project with great fanfare in 1992, with Shleifer as its 30-year-old team leader. The program came to a dramatic end in May 1997, when the US Agency for International Development cancelled it after a brief investigation, having been tipped off to its team leaders' investments. Angered by the loss of its favorite advisers, Boris Yeltsin's government promptly severed its relationship with USAID.

By then, nearly 2 percent of Harvard's endowment had been directly invested by its managers in Russian assets. They were taking part in the great gold rush that unfolded as the Russian government (which Shleifer had advised) sold off its state-owned assets at bargain prices. As Harvard investigated internally the collapse of its mission to Moscow, the Asian financial crisis spread in early 1998 to Russian securities markets. By August 1998, an abrupt devaluation of the ruble briefly threatened the global financial system with paralysis.

Point man in the US effort to maintain order was Deputy Treasury Secretary Larry Summers. Among his eyes and ears presumably were those of his protégé Shleifer, no longer a US government employee.

The crisis passed. Amid considerable internal uncertainty at Harvard, the decision to aggressively defend the conduct of Harvard's Russia Project was taken in the months immediately before and after the government filed a fraud suit in September 2000, seeking more than $120 million in damages.

By then, Harvard was searching for its next president. Provost Harvey Fineberg, in charge of the Russia matter, was hoping to succeed Neil Rudenstine as president. Summers had become treasury secretary and was an informal adviser to presidential candidate Al Gore. The university has not deviated from the course it set then.

Complicating the oversight process today is the lack of deep experience among members of the Harvard Corporation, the oldest self-perpetuating body in the Western hemisphere. When Robert Stone stepped down in 2002, it was after 27 years of service. Hanna Holborn Gray, president emerita of the University of Chicago, replaced Henry Rosovsky in 1997. She retires next month. At that point, only James Houghton and Conrad Harper will have become members before Summers became president in 2001 — Houghton, recently renamed chairman of Corning, Inc., since 1995; and Harper, a partner in Simpson, Thacher & Bartlett, a prestigious New York law firm, since 2000. [Harper resigned six weeks later, saying, "I have reached the judgment that I can no longer support the president, and therefore I have resigned from the Corporation."]

Citigroup's executive committee chairman Robert Rubin, Urban Institute president Robert Reischauer, university treasurer and McKinsey director James Rothenberg, and Nannerl Overholser Keohane, president emerita of both Duke University and Wellesley College, have joined since. Rubin was Summers' boss through most of the '90s. Also disruptive was the resignation in 2002 of Herbert Winokur Jr., CEO of Capricorn Holdings, who left the Corporation after only two years, when his role as a key director at Enron became a potential source of embarrassment.

All the more reason, therefore, for the President and Fellows of Harvard College to turn to Derek Bok, a man of sound judgment and deep experience in the university, as they prepare to write the end to a most peculiar episode.

CHAPTER THIRTEEN

# Andrei and [the Baseball Star]

*August 7, 2005*

The last great financial scandal of the 1990s wrapped up in court last week when Harvard University agreed to pay the US government $26.5 million to settle charges that its star economics professor Andrei Shleifer had sought to gain a personal fortune while leading Harvard's government-sponsored mission to Moscow.

The settlement put an end to eight years of legal wrangling. US Attorney Michael Sullivan said in a statement, "The defendants were entrusted with the important task of assisting in the creation of a post-Communist Russian open-market economy and instead took the opportunity to enrich themselves."

Shleifer and his wife, hedge fund operator Nancy Zimmerman, will pay $2 million and $1.5 million respectively, according to the settlement (the latter sum having been previously announced). Shleifer's deputy, Jonathan Hay, will pay as much as $2 million over 10 years, if he can earn it as a lawyer in London. Altogether, it adds up to around $31 million, or most of the roughly $40 million that the government paid Harvard to provide disinterested advice to the Russian government.

Adjust for interest cost, on the other hand, which in the worst case accrues at the rate of 1 percent a month on paid-out sums from the moment the contract is first breached (in this case, early 1994) and the actual recovery is less – something less than half the money that Harvard garnered under the contracts.

"An individual can fight the unlimited resources of the government for only so long," said Shleifer in a statement. "After eight long years, I have decided to end this now–without any admission of liability on my part. I strongly believe I would have prevailed in the end, but my lawyers told me my legal fees would exceed the amount that I will be paying the government."

So much for what Judge Woodlock found – that, once installed by the United States as its adviser to Russian president Boris Yeltsin, Shleifer invited his deputy Hay to invest with him in Russian oil stocks despite contract prohibitions against such investments, then gradually upped the ante.

Their illicit activities culminated in an attempt (at a regulatory agency they advised) to vault to the head of the licensing queue a company formed by Shleifer's wife and Hay's girlfriend to offer the first Russian mutual funds. That was the caper which scandalized Harvard's Moscow office. USAID investigated and swiftly shut the project down.

Whatever other undertakings the quartet had contemplated never will be known. Government prosecutors extensively deposed Harvard figures involved in property estate markets – real estate being an asset class that never quite made it to the Yeltsin government "loans for shares" program that created the small band of extremely wealthy Russians known as oligarchs.

The Harvard case is a major story in Russia, where privatization of state-owned assets to the oligarchs is regarded as something less than a complete success. But the *Financial Times* last week ignored the settlement, *The New York Times* and *The Washington Post* ran Associated Press accounts, and *The Boston Globe* buried the story at the bottom of its metro page. Such is the power of money to obscure. Only *The Wall Street Journal* gave the story any ink – the redoubtable Carla Anne Robbins has followed it from the beginning.

Because it was conditioned by conjectures on all sides about the likely findings of a shadow jury, the case ends having provided little illumination of what the defendants are worth. The lawyer Hay, a former Rhodes Scholar and Harvard Law School graduate, is viewed as relatively impecunious. He lives in London with his wife and three children.

His settlement agreement calls for an initial payment of $500,000 over the course of the next year, followed by future payments for 11 years of some fraction of his net after-tax income, unless he can rustle up an exit payment of between $1 and $2 million, depending on the date. Harvard, which fired the unlucky consultant as soon as its contract was cancelled, has refused to pay his legal bills.

Shleifer, however, is another matter. He continues to be employed by the university. His endowed chair in the economics department is intact. Harvard is viewed as being unlikely to pay his legal bills, which are steep. (Apparently the matter is a serious bone of contention.) His house in suburban Newton is mortgaged to the government as part of his promise to pay $2 million over the next three years. But with a long history of successful investing (there is no telling what his gains were while he was advising Russia), a well-to-do wife [who manages a hedge fund], a family house in France (according to fellow economists), a variety of offers from other universities and powerful friends on six continents, he is nothing if not a man with options.

Even so, Shleifer has been the less interesting figure in the case all along. Not that he is not compelling – one of the economics profession's leading experts on corruption now discovered to have been memorably corrupt himself. Raised in the former Soviet Union until he was 15, Shleifer was swept into Harvard and MIT on scholarships, then sent out to the frontiers of policy economics by the time he was 30 years old – hardly long enough to learn the folkways of the university, much less the broader world beyond. Yet [today] he is [considered to be] an academic expert on psychology and economics, on comparative political systems and financial markets, a winner of the John Bates Clark Medal as the best American economist under 40 – in short, probably a bigger factor in luring top graduate students to Harvard economics than all but one or two others in his department.

In fact, Shleifer is more than a little like the famous baseball player Rafael Palmeiro, who last spring raised his voice and jabbed his finger at the members of Congress questioning him as he denied taking steroids ("Period!" "Never!"), who then tested positive weeks later for a drug that may have been the injected steroid stanozolol. Palmeiro is a superb ball player, one of only six to have hit 500 home runs and collected 3,000 hits in the history of the game — a record that would surely have qualified him for baseball's Hall of Fame if it weren't for the steroid scandal. But like Shleifer, Palmeiro is a highly talented refugee from a socialist culture, in his case, Cuba. His contempt for government is built in. It is not surprising that he did not understand his peril when subpoenaed to testify under oath.

The real fault in baseball's steroid scandal is with the people who own the game. In the mid-1990s, they feared baseball was losing its attractiveness to fans — especially after a players' strike shut down the 1994 season in August. It was then that owners [first] turned a blind eye to growing use of steroids by the athletes they employed (and engineered perhaps slight changes to the specifications of the ball as well), in hopes that the subsequent chase for records would lure fans back to the game. About this, at least, they were not mistaken. (Perhaps not surprisingly, President George W. Bush, a former part-owner of the Texas Rangers, for whom Palmeiro played for a time, said he believed the ballplayer's newly qualified denials — "not intentionally or knowingly" — despite the evidence of the drug test.)

A somewhat more intriguing figure than Shleifer in the Russia Project is economist Lawrence Summers, Shleifer's mentor and old friend, who taught him as an undergraduate; sent him to the Massachusetts Institute of Technology to train; took him to Lithuania to practice country-doctoring; brought him back from the University of Chicago to teach at Harvard; helped put him in the Russia job; oversaw, as an increasingly senior Treasury Department official, Shleifer's efforts in Moscow; and, once he returned to Harvard as president, defended his protégé.

Friendship explains much of Summers' role. A combination of patriotism, arrogance, marital hard times and plain bad judgment explains the rest. The Harvard president is in a world of woe. The likelihood that justice will be meted out to him on any separable basis is not great. The Bad-News Train is bearing down on Larry Summers at 40 miles per hour.

So the really interesting figure in the Russia Project case is Harvard itself, meaning the university's headquarters in Massachusetts Hall, the officials then in charge who in 2000 made the decisions to defend their young star: President Neil Rudenstine and Provost Harvey Fineberg; and, of course, the 60-person department of economics itself.

Why not acknowledge obvious wrongdoing? Why prefer intelligence to integrity? In the autumn, the venue of the Shleifer matter will shift to the inner councils of the Harvard faculty and to the economics profession. These are the questions they'll be asking then.

CHAPTER FOURTEEN

# Who Wants to Know? (Or, Why *Economic Principals* Is Not a Blog)

*August 14, 2005*

A lot of ink and pixels have been spilled recently over the relationship between journalism and blogging. As a working journalist who is frequently mistaken for a blogger, I have some ideas. The difference mainly has to do with who the audience is.

A journalist is someone who gets paid to make calls and ask questions on behalf of a set of readers. Usually editors and publishers are involved as well, and very often advertisers who are interested in the readers. Even before the first question is asked, what the person on the other end of the line inevitably wants to know (whether they say it or not) is, "Oh yeah? Who wants to know?"

When I started out as a reporter in Chicago, using dimes to call desk sergeants at police stations around some sector of the city, I sometimes didn't even bother to tell my name. I'd say, "City Press, Sergeant. Anything going on there?" It was a rare cop who didn't have a joke or a beef in return. Kids like me had been covering routine crime and courts in Chicago for the City News Bureau, a wire service cooperatively owned by the city's daily newspapers, since 1890. We reported to a small corps of seasoned editors.

Later, I learned the power that lay behind various brands. What a different reception I got, depending on whether I was asking the question on behalf of the readers of *Pacific Stars and Stripes* or *Newsweek*. If anything, the gap was even greater between *The Wall Street Journal* and *Forbes*. And during the many years I wrote for *The Boston Globe*, to call a source was to risk a substantial discussion of the affairs of the rest of the paper, before we could get down to business. Reporting for a well-established organization invariably meant operating with an extensive and complicated penumbra.

When I started identifying myself as calling on behalf of *Economic Principals*, an awkward silence frequently ensued. If asked, I'd explain that I was working for myself. Professional economists almost without exception returned my e-mails and phone calls. The few who didn't were policy types. Those less acquainted with what I did often had problems. One Russia specialist, for example, slyly described this site as my "hobby." Worse yet, people asked if I had retired. Far from it. This weekly is the regular visible expression of a continuing career in economic journalism. It is, in fact, about to play a more conspicuous part.

*EP*s migrated from a newspaper to the web at a time when blogs were almost unknown. The circumstances were opaque. As a long-time columnist, I had been suddenly forbidden to write about politics by the editor who The New York Times Company hired to head the *Globe*. I tried, but found I couldn't stop altogether. The editor, Martin Baron, killed the column and I quit the newspaper.

Five weeks later I started writing online, keeping the name of the column that had appeared in the paper. Before long, I joined up with Sabre Foundation and went looking other angels to foot the bill for what [at the time] seemed like an unusual enterprise. The only two roughly similar undertakings known to me in those days were those by Mickey Kaus and Andrew Sullivan, both of them well-established journalists.

Today there are an estimated jillion blogs. The community is said to be growing explosively. So powerful a force is the new medium that it acquired a name practically overnight – the blogosphere. What's a blog? Etymologically speaking, it's a contraction of web-log. Editorially, these personal vehicles range from intense explorations of particular angles of vision to a simple daily expression of opinion on everything that comes into the writer's head.

The mechanism that makes blogs work is the ease with which they can call attention to one another through links – a single click and you can be redirected half way around the world; another click and you return, for free. There is no friction on the web. This constitutes a mechanism for what social scientists call collaborative filtering. Blogging and linking to other blogs, becomes an exercise in collective judgment similar to, say, the pop music market, except that no money changes hands. [Rememberr single record sales and payola?] [In the same way]..., [collaborative] linking [identifies] a relative handful of favorites and then amplifyies their influence until they become the favorites of a much larger group. The process also has something in common with the gradual construction of scientific consensus through the etiquette of citation.

But with most blogs, unlike science or, for that matter, newspapering, the prize is much more likely to be novelty than truth. Many of them take the form of intense conversation among a relatively small group of people interested in the same things – the written-down and permanently preserved equivalent of talk radio, rather than a progressive narrowing of disagreement that is the essence of science, or news.

True, if your blog happens to contain material of immediate interest to a large audience – if you are a soldier in Iraq, say, or a particularly witty observer like Wonkette in the middle of an intense political campaign, you can get millions of hits. Just last week *The Washington Post* had a good story on the ups and downs of war blogs from Iraq. And the best-edited websites featuring a portfolio of contributors (I have in mind *Slate* in particular) have managed to create the excitement of a good magazine.

*Economic Principals* has refrained from the practice of [extensive cross-]linking because it is a journalistic enterprise, not a blog. That is, it is directed mainly at readers who are not themselves bloggers, and competes for those readers' attention with other journalists, chiefly newspaper reporters and columnists. [In 2010, *EP* instituted a "j-roll," a list of economic journalists whose work I sought to follow that eventually grew to more than 130 names. In 2015, I installed a short blogroll, and in 2018 sharply pruned the list of journalists.] Which readers does it seek? Economists and intelligent laypersons interested in developments inside economics, of course.

The blogosphere is here to stay. On a truly big story, bloggers have shown that they can interpose themselves briefly [between readers and traditional sources of news] but with great effect, as, for instance, when a tsunami swept the Indian Ocean, or in last year's story of the Swift Boat Veterans for Truth. They are a new and welcome check on entrenched power. But from a global point of view, the blogosphere is a complement to other media, not a substitute.

Newspapers are likely to remain our most powerful engines of discovery for many years to come. For one thing, it is hard to envisage a better device for displaying the news than the familiar paper product – swiftly scanned, easily clipped, a very tangible form of budget constraint. Only so many stories can fit on a front page.

For another, only newspapers will be able to meet the enormous fixed cost of maintaining a staff of expert editors and reporters who work together to perform what they like to call "the daily miracle": the hashing-out of a reasonably coherent answer to the question every morning: What's going on out there? [The significance of the invention of search advertising hadn't yet sunk in!]

You don't have to have a lot of paying customers to represent the public interest, however. A relative handful will do. So after three-and-a-half years, *EP* is switching to a new, a two-tier business model: Early access to the e-mail version for paying subscribers. The regular www.economicprincipals.com site for everyone else.

The first step in this evolution came last year when I gave up foundation support. Now *EP* is looking for around 500 citizens willing to pay $50 a year to support an independent voice in economic journalism. The idea is to put some force behind the questions asked. Something like $25,000 is enough to make the business work.

And what will subscribers get in return? They will continue to receive the e-mail version, which moves Sunday at midnight, Saturday EST, in time for breakfast in Europe, and about a day ahead of the weekly's posting on the web. They'll get regular behind-the-scenes reports as well, and a slightly enhanced level of access. *Economic Principals* welcomes tips, hints, opinions and complaints from all readers. But subscribers get what amounts to a vote.

Mostly, supporters will enjoy the warm and fuzzy feeling that comes from furthering an enterprise that's clearly needed, in a world that seems to be retreating from independent coverage of the economics profession. *Economic Principals'* attention to Harvard University's failed Russia Project (the Andrei Shleifer affair) is an obvious example. But a quick tour of the archives will disclose all kinds of stories that don't get written elsewhere.

The new policy will take effect on October 16. It will be further described in a series of short letters to existing subscribers in coming weeks. And if it doesn't work? The great advantage of having experimented with various alternatives forms of organization is clarity. This time, I *am* prepared to take no for an answer.

CHAPTER FIFTEEN

# The Tick-Tock

*January 22, 2006*

Should Harvard University president Lawrence Summers travel this week to the World Economic Forum in Davos, Switzerland, as he usually does, he'll find that the hottest item in the snowy little Alpine village is the international edition of *Institutional Investor* – the one with the cover story, "How Harvard Lost Russia: The inside story of what happened when the enormous power and resources of the United States government were put in the wrong hands."

Those hands, of course, were those of Summers' close friend and former student, Harvard University economist Andrei Shleifer, whose misbehavior cost Harvard something like $25 million in damages, plus another $10 million or $15 million in legal fees.

Author David McClintick presents in the magazine what reporters sometimes call a tick-tock – a highly detailed narrative account – of what transpired in the 1990s, when the US Agency for International Development hired Harvard to advise the Russian government on how to create a legal and institutional framework for its capital markets – only to see the project collapse in scandal after 4 years, thereby turning "Harvard" into a Russian code word for "hypocritical American greed."

McClintick's article is a *complicated* tick-tock. The one-time *Wall Street Journal* investigative reporter waded through thousands of pages of depositions and courtroom transcripts. He interviewed many participants. The story takes 25,000 words to tell, and even then, McClintick is forced to leave out important parts of the story – its political dimension, for example.

You can read it for yourself online at http://www.institutionalinvestor.com for the price of watching a fifteen-second advertisement – all but the 21 photos, that is, and some of the quote boxes and sidebars. Once an opulent American fanzine for money managers, *Institutional Investor* was purchased a few years ago by London-based *Euromoney*. It is in greatly reduced circumstances now, but the old taste for quality remains, everywhere but the website. The article itself is superb.

Not only is McClintick a best-selling author (*Indecent Exposure, Swordfish*), he is a graduate of Harvard College and a member of the advisory board of the university's alumni magazine.

At last the outlines of the story are clear. (The story a journalist tells is very different from the case a lawyer makes.) Much of what McClintick offers is new, even to close students of the affair. The picture that emerges is not pretty.

"The best and brightest of America's premier university came to Moscow in the 1990s to teach Russians how to be capitalists," writes McClintick. "This is the inside story of how their efforts led to scandal and disgrace."

The Russians in question were two bright economists from St. Petersburg, 36-year-old Anatoly Chubais, and 30-year-old Dimitry Vasiliev, who in 1991 began working on privatization for Yegor Gaidar, minister of economics and finance. Boris Yeltsin recently had elbowed aside Mikhail Gorbachev, and the goldrush was on.

The Americans included Harvard University professor Summers, 36; his arch-rival and fellow professor Jeffrey Sachs, also 36; and Summers' friend and former student, 30-year-old Andrei Shleifer. An émigré from the Soviet Union at 15, Shleifer had gone to college at Harvard, graduate school at MIT, and recently been recalled to Harvard from the University of Chicago and dispatched to Russia by Summers, who by then was chief economist for the World Bank.

Sachs, who had advised the government of Poland on the "shock therapy" by which they had converted their economy to market principles, had been invited to Russia by Gaidar.

Then Bill Clinton was elected and Summers moved to the Treasury Department. In Moscow, Shleifer quickly elbowed aside Sachs, as Chubais and Vasiliev discovered that Shleifer was one of their own. Shleifer soon signed on as director of an ambitious USAID project, and hired a favorite student, Rhodes Scholar and lawyer Jonathan Hay, 30, as his deputy. Shleifer's wife, Nancy Zimmerman, had quit her job at Goldman Sachs and started a hedge fund specializing in Russian investments. At the Treasury Department, Summers was beginning a spectacular rise.

Yet within 18 months of beginning their work for the US government, Shleifer and Zimmerman and Hay began investing in Russia, in direct violation of Shleifer's contracts with USAID and Harvard – some oil stocks, a fund with equity in a group of companies whose privatization they were overseeing, nothing big, just enough to demonstrate a certain canniness in circumventing detection (Channel Island bank accounts, the use of Zimmerman's banker father as a straw).

To be sure, McClintick notes, Moscow in the aftermath of communism resembled the old American West at its wildest. Greed was rampant. Violence was common. Breathtaking corruption was rife. But then that's precisely why the Harvard team was there.

"In running Harvard's Russia project, Andrei Shleifer and Jonathan Hay had an opportunity to preach the importance of integrity, transparency and fairness in shaping a business culture, and to work to enshrine those values in the country's legal and financial infrastructure," McClintick writes.

"Instead, their personal dealings sent a very different message."

The centerpiece of McClintick's article is a painstaking reconstruction of the events of spring and summer of 1996, when Boris Yeltsin was running for re-election against an old-line nationalist named Gennady Zyuganov, campaigning on, among other things, a promise to quickly create a nation of individual investors, the better to soak up the ubiquitous "mattress money" that made fiscal and monetary policy hard to conduct.

Against that backdrop, Shleifer's wife and Hay's new girl friend, Elizabeth Hebert, quietly formed a company they called Pallada (after Pallas Athena, the ancient Greek goddess of wisdom and truth) and began a drive to become the first licensed mutual fund in Russia. To run their back office (known as a "specialized depository"), they contracted with John Keffer, a Portland, Maine, businessman whose firm, Forum Financial, had experience working with mutual funds companies in Poland.

Would-be investors in Pallada, including Farralon Capital Management, the San Francisco hedge fund for which Zimmerman worked at the time, and Boston's Peter Aldrich, a real estate magnate with close connections to the Harvard economics department, were told that Zimmerman and Hebert expected to turn their close relationship with "the regulator" (meaning Shleifer and Hay's advisee Vasiliev) into a powerful "first-mover advantage" – and thereafter into a gold mine. At the World Economic Forum meeting, in Davos, in January 1996, several wealthy Russian oligarchs had recruited Chubais to run Yeltsin's reelection campaign.

McClintick is at his best re-creating the pell-mell scramble that ensued that May, when the Russia regulators tried to install one of Hay's employees, Julia Zagachin, as chief of Pallada's back-office unit, and to limit Keffer to a 49 percent share of the business. Harvard's Hay promptly backed the Russians up, and for a time, the deal went forward, though tensions between Keffer and Zagachin slowly escalated. Yeltsin was re-elected in July; a September 2 deadline was established for the first mutual fund. His regulators were threatened with jail if it wasn't met.

In August, Vasiliev licensed Pallada's specialized depository and registered two of its mutual funds. Seeing several other global securities firms brushed aside, the Western financial establishment in Moscow was agog.

With showtime at hand, Keffer dug in his heels and refused to name Zagachin to the top job. She quit and attempted to shift $400,000 he had deposited for the specialized depository into a bank account to which she had access.

Hebert and Hay, Shleifer and Zimmerman, then began a frantic search for $400,000 with which to take Keffer out of the deal – a quiet solution to which he had agreed at the urging of a Harvard-hired lawyer named Michael Butler. They were ultimately successful when Hebert phoned Hay's father in Idaho (who already had begun investing in Russian securities on his son's behalf) and persuaded him to wire $200,000 of his own money and another $200,000 of his son's to Zagachin, permitting her to become the depository's sole owner.

And all the while, Shleifer and Zimmerman and their son vacationed with Summers and his family in Truro, on Cape Cod, as was their annual custom. The year before, Summers had been named to the number-two post at the Treasury, with oversight responsibility for US economic aid to Russia.

But during a long walk up the beach with his protégé, he could remember under oath years later giving only relatively general advice and eliciting almost no information. "You've got to be careful," Summers recalled telling his friend. "There's a lot of corruption in Russia."

"It wasn't my habit to do US government business on beaches," he told the assistant US attorney who was taking his deposition.

McClintick found the only forthright explanation of what the principals were thinking at the time (or at least saying) in a lengthy quotation that was culled from the sworn testimony of Louis O'Neill, a Harvard Law School graduate who also worked for Hay for a while.

> Julia was Beth's friend. Beth was Jonathan's girlfriend. And Beth Hebert had formed Pallada. Pallada was to be the first share investment fund in the Russian economy. ... What I observed directly was that Pallada received the first license from the Russian SEC, that Dimitry Vasiliev headed. And yet I knew, and the press certainly later screamed, that Credit Suisse First Boston... was way ahead of it in the sort of paper game, get your paperwork in, get your stamps done, get everything approved....
>
> ...I went to Jon [Hay] and said, "This is kind of strange. Why this and not CSFB.... He said something to me that made sense.... He

> said, "Well, this is a very serious pilot project. It will be... basically, the first mutual fund in Russia. We want to have someone as the leader, as the first person, who we are friendly with and who we can monitor very closely for transparency, fairness, proper procedures, proper accounting..." I remember the phrase he used because it made sense. "We'll run water through the pipes on this one, see where the leaks are, fix them, and then we'll open it up to the larger market." That to me was convincing.
>
> ...I then began to notice Beth Hebert in the office using our facilities, our phones, our faxes, our people, our drivers; Julia Zagachin doing the same; their whole staff, both women's staff, doing the same. ... It seems strange to me that Jonathan was running the project, responsible for all the donor money, and his girlfriend was in the office running a private company....
>
> ...I'd gone there sort of out of law school, excited, eager, bright-eyed, maybe to do some good, and it all ended on a kind of a sour note. So I just felt kind of bad about it, kind of wished it would all go away at the time.

Pallada continued to get preferential treatment from the Russian government and Harvard for a time. In December, Hay and Vasiliev recommended to the US Treasury Department that it be included in its official Capital Markets Forum. In February, 1997, Shleifer wired $200,000 from his and Zimmerman's joint bank account, labeling it as a loan but not documenting it.

Shortly after that, the situation in Moscow boiled over. In his article, McClintick carefully traces the channels by which various complaints flowed to Cambridge, where they were ignored, and to Washington, where in April 1997, after a few weeks' behind-the-scenes investigation, USAID abruptly shut down the Harvard project.

The US attorney in Boston began its investigation a few months later. In September 2000, the government sued Harvard, Shleifer, Hay and their wives (Hay and Hebert having married by then), seeking treble damages under the False Claims Act – as much as $120 million in the case of Harvard. The university vigorously defended its team throughout.

The subsequent trial provided much of McClintick's documentation. Harvard paid only $26.5 million for breach of contract in the end, Shleifer $2 million for fraud, and Hay whatever he could afford over the next 10 years. Zimmerman's firm separately had agreed to pay $1.5 million for inappropriate use of taxpayer resources. Keffer sued Harvard in Maine and eventually settled for an undisclosed sum – but not before putting enough material in the record in the Portland courthouse to ensure that the story later could be unraveled blow-by-blow.

When Summers returns to Cambridge from Davos, it will be to a university more determined than ever to understand the history of its failed Russia Project. McClintick's article will circulate hand to hand. The frustration among the faculty that McClintick details will only grow. Some fellow economist may yet come forward to defend Shleifer publicly (instead of grousing anonymously that he has been treated unfairly), but that hasn't happened yet.

It is Harvard's governing corporation which will continue to oversee the matter. The seven-member board perhaps will pay special attention to the collapse of a determined mediation effort by US District Court Judge David Mazzone. It broke down two weeks after Summers was elected president, in March 2001, and before he recused himself in the matter, apparently at the Corporation's request.

This was the point at which the bad outcome in court was sealed. It's not that Harvard's many decisions under President Neil Rudenstine and two of his provosts, Albert Carnesale and Harvey Fineberg, don't deserve scrutiny. Their team leaders had been caught cheating, but Shleifer denied his guilt. So Harvard defended him to the hilt.

By 2001, however, the outlines of the situation were clear. The men and women who hired Larry Summers could have hoped that he would settle the matter as advantageously as possible for the university, on the terms outlined by the judge.

Inexplicably, he did not.

CHAPTER SIXTEEN

# When the Watchdog Doesn't Bark

*January 29, 2006*

A persistent riddle of the Andrei Shleifer case has been the failure of three of the four major English-language papers to report in any detail the story of Harvard's failed Russia Project. *The Wall Street Journal* was quick to grasp its significance in 1997. Carla Anne Robbins' aggressive reporting on page 1 when the investigation was new probably kept it from disappearing beneath the rug. Robbins, who is now a *WSJ* editor, wrote another incisive leader last autumn, after US District Court Judge Douglas Woodlock delivered his verdict of fraud and breach of contract.

But *The New York Times*, *The Washington Post* and the *Financial Times* took a pass, even after Shleifer's close friendship with Harvard University president Lawrence Summers became an issue. Indeed, the *Times* had to run an embarrassing editor's note after a business page columnist quoted Shleifer as an authority on corporate corruption without noting that, only a few days earlier, a federal judge had found the Harvard professor had committed massive fraud himself.

An authoritative account of what actually happened in the seamy affair exists only because an off-shore magazine paid an independent reporter to study the court record and then published his 25,000-word report. "How Harvard Lost Russia:

The inside story of what happened when the enormous power and resources of the United States government were put in the wrong hands," by David McClintick, appears in the January international edition of *Institutional Investor*.

What's a satisfying explanation for the lack of other interest? Simple inattention won't suffice. There were those *WSJ* stories, after all. A more plausible answer in this case can be found in the continual trading of information, appraisal, mentions, column inches, access and other favors that is at the heart of the business of newsgathering everywhere.

What does it take to keep a watchdog quiet? Why did Harvard fail at what would seem to have been the easier task, short-circuiting the government investigation? Some indication of the relative strength of forces at work here can be found in an ingenious study of the checks and balances that underpin democracy by John McMillan and Pablo Zoido, both of Stanford University. It appeared a couple of years ago in the *Journal of Economic Perspectives*. Most political analysts study the institutions of democracy one at a time, they noted, isolating a particular mechanism in order to study it – elections, political parties, the judiciary, the media, and so on.

But the many elements of a democratic system form a *system* of incentives, they stated. Checks and balances work insofar as they interact and reinforce each other. Opposition parties can flourish only where the press is free. The media can't function without judicial independence, which in turn depends on political competition. Which of these mechanisms is the most robust? Which is the most easily suborned? McMillan and Zoido turned to the experience of Peru in the 1990s to make their point. It was tantamount to a laboratory experiment.

Like every other nation in South America, Peru had been jostled by the events of the turbulent 1970s – the oil shocks in particular. A military dictatorship gave way to civilian rule in the 1980s, and by 1990 all the apparatus of democracy was in place – regular elections, opposition parties, presidential term limits, judicial independence (with appropriate safeguards), and a free and competitive press. On the other hand, the economy was a shambles, mired in recession with annual inflation of 7,000 percent, and Shining Path guerillas were gaining strength in the hills.

What happened next was the basis for an opera. University administrator Alberto Fujimori defeated the novelist Mario Varga Llosa for president in 1990. A political neophyte, Fujimori hired as his "security adviser" and intelligence chief Vladimiro Montesinos Torres, an army officer who in the '70s had been cashiered for selling secret documents to the United States, who in the '80s made a living as a lawyer for drug dealers. Montesinos was ideally prepared to play on human weakness on all sides. Together, he and Fujimori – *El Chino* (the Chinaman) to his countrymen – proceeded to take over the state.

There were some striking early successes. Shining Path founder Abimael Guzman was captured in 1992 and his terrorist army collapsed. Meanwhile, "Fujishock" – a series of macroeconomic reforms and privatizations – reduced the inflation rate to around 10 percent by 1995 and stimulated steady economic growth. The CIA liberally financed the regime, despite warnings from the Peruvian military that Montesinos had taken over the government. (Eventually Transparency International would declare Fujimori the world's sixth most successful head-of-state embezzler, after Indonesia's Suharto, the Philippines' Marcos, Zaire's Mobuto, Nigeria's Abacha and Serbia's Milosovic.)

And so through a combination of showmanship, bullying and, mostly, bribery, Fujimori and his secret police chief (or, perhaps more accurately, Montesinos and his puppet president) took over the country. They bribed politicians, judges, bureaucrats, journalists, business executives – more than 1,600 of them were kept on a regular payroll. They killed people, too, but mostly students and peasants. "Remember why Pinochet had his problems," Montesinos told a subordinate in a session that was taped. "We will not be so clumsy."

Instead, they closed Congress, suspended the constitution, reopened the "democracy" long enough to run for re-election in 1995, then persuaded Congress to abolish presidential term limits and won a third term in 2000. Three months later, after an opposition television station broadcast a tape of Montesinos paying a $15,000 bribe to a key congressman to switch sides, the government fell, Fujimori fled to Japan (where he was granted extradition-proof citizenship), and Montesinos sought asylum in Venezuela. (He has since been returned to Peru, and is awaiting trial in a maximum-security prison that he had ordered built.) Then last November, Fujimori surprised everybody by rolling the dice one more time. He flew into Chile and announced plans to run again for president of Peru. He did not make his point. Peru filed extradition papers, and Chile is slowly going through the legal procedures.

McMillan and Zoido's account of Montesinos' activities as a corrupter makes gripping reading. In the videos, he counsels those he is bribing on cooperation: "How do friends help friends?... They do not say, Hey, I give you this so you do this." He gives lessons in the string-pulling arts. He routinely presents himself as a patriot. He is driven, he declares, "to bring peace back to the country" by ending terrorism and the drug trade. "Here we work for the national interest," he tells a television executive on one tape. On another: "I get nothing out of this; on the contrary, only hate, passions, intrigues and resentment. I do it because of my vocation of service to the nation." After Montesinos' arrest, Peruvian police discovered $200 million in his foreign bank accounts. "His patriotism, evidently, did not preclude enrichment," write the authors.

Montesinos' great gift to economic science, however, was that he kept meticulous records. He required recipients of his bribes to sign receipts. He routinely videotaped himself doling out cash and explaining exactly what he expected of those whom he paid (the tapes were quickly dubbed "Vladivideos" when they began to be shown on national television). Stanford's McMillan and Zoido pored over the records, compiling what they described as a price list for bribery, an instrument that could be used to measure the strength of countervailing forces that Montesinos was systematically disabling. They wrote, "The size of the bribes measured what he was willing to pay to buy off those who could check his power."

What they discovered was a well-demarcated hierarchy. A politician was worth slightly more than a judge. But the owner of a television station commanded about a hundred times more than a politician – five times more than the total of all opposition politicians' bribes. "Each channel takes $2 million monthly, but it is the only way," he told a subordinate. "That is why we have won, because we have sacrificed in this way." Newspaper bribes, while higher than those of judges and politicians, were much less than television. The difference had to do with scale. Montesinos explained on tape: "What do I care about *El Comercio*? They have an 80,000 print run. Eighty thousand newspapers is shit. What worries me is Channel 4... It reaches 2 million people."

Thus, McMillan and Zoido concluded, the news media constitute "the chief watchdog" in a democracy. News organizations can provide oversight even where political competition and an independent judiciary have broken down. (It was a small independent television station, one that Montesinos had never bribed, that aired the tape that finally brought the Fujimori regime crashing down.) "Safeguards for the media – ensuring they are protected from political influence and are credible to the public – may be crucial policies for shoring up democracy."

Now the United States is not Peru, and Larry Summers and Andrei Shleifer are not El Chino and Vladi, though aspects of their relationship in the '90s do bear a certain resemblance to the Peruvians' symbiosis – the powerful academician in high office and his worldly agent in the field; the delicate issues of trust and betrayal between them.

And certainly the techniques that Fujimori and Montesinos exploited to subvert the normal functioning of the institutions of democracy are constantly in use with varying degrees of subtlety in nations all around the world. For instance, I thought immediately of Montesinos in connection with the news earlier this month that Richard Scrushy had paid a freelance writer (through a public relations firm) to write several friendly stories about him for a black-owned weekly newspaper, the *Birmingham Times*. He reviewed at least two of the articles before publication, according to the Associated Press, which broke the story.

Scrushy, of course, is the former chief executive officer of HealthSouth who last year was acquitted on 36 counts of fraud, despite the testimony of many of his subordinates that he had been the architect of an accounting scam that caused the insurer's collapse. Audrey Lewis, the author of the articles, told reporters for *The New York Times*, "I sat in that courtroom for six months, and I did everything possible to advocate for his cause." She explained that Scrushy had paid her $10,000, plus $1,000 to buy a computer. He paid another $25,000 to the pastor of a church who was among a group of African-American supporters who frequently attended the trial, according to *The Wall Street Journal*. Scrushy is white. Eleven of 18 jurors were black.

So now to the really interesting question. How did the defendants in the Russia Project – Harvard, Shleifer, Hay and, though he was not charged with wrongdoing in the matter, Summers – convince the *Times*, the *Post* and the *FT* that the collapse of its Russia Project was not a worthy story? What did they say, and how did they say it? To whom, and how often? Let me stress that there is absolutely no question of actual money ever changing hands – of bribery. At the pinnacles of capitalism, the influence exchange is so deep and liquid that cash is almost never required, except, perhaps, within organizations, in the form of golden handshakes and the like.

Instead, the informal economy of capitalism is one of deference and respect, of favors today and the implicit promise of favors later, of jobs and dinner invitations and admissions to exclusive kindergartens. Its texture is extremely uneven: dense around, say, academic medical centers and aerospace contractors; sparse where incentives are weak; and, at least in democracies, full of relatively empty seams in the appropriate places, between countervailing sectors. Anyone who doubts that this informal economy extends to newspapers knows nothing about how newspapers work.

It is here that temptation comes in. Many of the judgments concerning the newsworthiness of the US government's complaints about Harvard's Russia Project were made initially by editors in consultation with correspondents on the ground during the 1990s. All four major papers had series of superb reporters in Moscow in those years. Most of them were partial to the Russians' efforts to bring communism to an abrupt end, and mindful of the allowances that Western experts had to make in order to be useful advisers to their counterparts. John Lloyd of the *Financial Times*, for example, in a lengthy article in *The New York Times Magazine*, spoke for many of those correspondents when he concluded, "Russia suffered from our mistakes and preconceptions, but – barring catastrophe – ultimately will make its own accommodation. It was never ours to lose. Russia lost, not itself but the trust that makes societies civil and functioning."

Matters were seen quite differently in the United States, however, first by investigators for the US Agency for International Development, which paid Harvard to advise the Russian government, then by lawyers in the US attorney's office in Boston to whom they referred their findings. In Boston and Washington, most of the advice that was given to Russian economists who were seeking to create institutions of market economy was completely beside the point. It was the on-the-sly personal enrichment of the Harvard team leaders that was viewed as being wrong. Nor was the case ever seen as mainly a criminal matter: according to government sources, the usual possibilities of criminal charges of perjury having been wisely dismissed in the interests of focusing on the underlying case, a matter of breach of contract and fraud.

Harvard's courtroom defense turned on technicalities: though he was project director, Shleifer somehow wasn't covered by the contract. Its public relations campaign deployed a number of straw men. The prosecutor hated Harvard. Without criminal charges, the government case was of little consequence. The judge had declined to try the charges against the advisers' wives. Janine Wedel, the author of a distinctly left-wing critique of 'shock therapy' in general and the Harvard project in particular, "Collision and Collusion: The Strange Case of Western Aid to Eastern Europe," was from "another planet."

All that's been put to rest now by the McClintick account. It is a straightforward explanation of the case that the government finally proved against Shleifer, Hay and Harvard before a practical and sophisticated judge. It's in the nature of the news business that editors don't ordinarily second-guess themselves and their reporters. They haven't time. But this is one story where the editors of the *Times*, the *Post* and the *FT* may want to "walk back the cat" in order to discover how they got left so far behind on such an interesting story.

For at its heart, the Shleifer matter has always had less to do with the failure to export American values to Russia than with the inadvertent importation of Moscow rules to institutions in the United States. That's why Harvard's cockeyed defense is so alarming, why Shleifer's elevation to positions of ever-greater authority in the economics profession is worrisome. No one doubts that he is an original and productive economic thinker. The good news is that it was Shleifer who, as editor of the *Journal of Economic Perspectives*, published McMillan and Zoido's article on Montesinos. That's the bad news, too, since the editorship confers vast and global favor-trading power.

The worst thing of all is that, starting with his long-time mentor Larry Summers, Shleifer's friends don't seem to understand that they failed the young Russian émigré in the first instance, that they in turn have been betrayed and embarrassed. It is true, as Edward L. Glaeser and Claudia Goldin write in their introduction to the forthcoming *Corruption and Reform: Lessons from America's Economic History* that the United States "changed from a place where political bribery was a routine event infecting politics at all levels to a nation that now ranks among the least corrupt in the world." But it is also true that American aid-giving abroad in the 20th century (Herbert Hoover, George C. Marshall, Creighton Abrams) has been remarkably free of high-level corruption – until now.

CHAPTER SEVENTEEN

# Those Three Weeks in March

*February 26, 2006*

So Larry Summers has resigned the Harvard presidency, pretty much (though not exactly) as predicted here. But the story of Harvard's failed Russia Project and its lengthy aftermath only gets more curious.

In most newspaper accounts, little was made of the scandal and Summers' longtime mentoring and presumed protection of the man at its center, Harvard economist Andrei Shleifer. The two men met in 1979, when Shleifer was a sophomore at Harvard College and Summers an assistant professor visiting Harvard. They have been close allies and fast friends ever since.

Yet at Harvard itself, interest in the matter has intensified, ever since an authoritative account of the affair appeared in a magazine last month, prompting a devastating "no-comment" from Summers at a faculty meeting and a pair of ambiguous denials from the seven-person board, known as the Harvard Corporation, that governs the university.

In a letter to *Institutional Investor* (which published investigative reporter David McClintick's 25,000-word article in January), Harvard general counsel Robert Iuliano asserted (at the Corporation's request) that Summers had removed himself "from any university deliberations or decisions" concerning the US government lawsuit against Shleifer and the university "from the outset of his presidency at Harvard."

In a second letter, James F. Houghton, the senior member of the Harvard Corporation, told Professor Frederick H. Abernathy, a professor in the division of engineering and applied sciences who had raised questions about the matter in a letter and at a faculty meeting, that "President Summers was not present for nor did he participate in any of the Corporation's many discussions about the [Harvard Institute for International Development] matter, including those resulting in the decision to settle the case."

The crucial issue, however, was unaddressed. More than three months passed between the Sunday in March 2001 when Summers was elected by the Corporation and July 1, when he officially took office – presumably the "outset" of his presidency.

And it was in the three weeks immediately after he was elected that a behind-the-scenes court-mandated mediation by a federal judge collapsed in Boston. That was Harvard's last chance to admit its culpability and settle the case, without the additional embarrassment of continuing to maintain its professor's innocence and its own in the face of overwhelming evidence to the contrary.

And there are several reasons why one might wonder if Summers was deeply involved in setting the university's strategy during those three weeks – involved, that is, in "university deliberations or decisions" about the matter. The person who holds the key to the mystery is Anne Taylor, Harvard general counsel at the time, who is not talking. One year later, she was eased out of her job by Summers.

There's nothing difficult to understand about the Shleifer matter. The Harvard professor lined his pockets while under contract to the US government to render untainted leadership and advice to the government of Russia, which was then seeking to turn its bureaucratic nightmare into a decentralized market economy. Not a lot, at first – some oil stocks, some government bonds, shares in a private equity fund. But in flagrant violation of the rules.

But when the Russian SEC chief arranged for Shleifer's deputy, his deputy's girlfriend and Shleifer's wife to receive the first license to start a mutual fund in Russia — a potential gold mine that the trio touted to would-be backers — the Harvard professor's co-workers blew the whistle to USAID. He was quietly investigated and quickly fired.

It is easy enough to speculate about why Shleifer flouted US law. Raised in Russia, he was incompletely socialized in American norms and little supervised on the job. Whether from simple greed, arrogance, idealism or, most likely, some combination of the three, he routinely broke the rules.

Far harder to understand is why Summers failed to distance himself – after Shleifer's misbehavior became known and he was fired by USAID in 1997, after the government filed its suit against Harvard in September 2000, even after the government won its case last year.

As a senior official in the Treasury Department – by 1999 he had become secretary – Summers had oversight of US economic policy towards Russia throughout those years. He stayed at the Shleifers' house in Newton while interviewing for the Harvard job.

Harder still to know is why Harvard defended Shleifer from the moment the scandal broke, on ever more narrow legalistic grounds. He wasn't covered by the conflict-of-interest provisions of the government contract that prohibited investments of any kind in the country he was advising, the university's lawyers argued, because he was a consultant to the advice-giving team that he headed (instead of an employee), or because he didn't actually live in Russia.

Hardest of all to fathom is the stance that Harvard adopted in March 2001, once Judge A. David Mazzone led the parties informally and in private through the arguments of the government's case. US District Court Judge Douglas Woodlock had referred the suit to his senior colleague for mediation less than a week after it was filed, presumably reflecting his sense that the matter could be settled relatively easily.

In late September 2000, when the government filed its treble damages suit, much had been up in the air: George Bush vs. Al Gore in the presidential election,

Harvard beginning its search for a successor to President Neil Rudenstine. If Gore had won the November election, Summers in all likelihood would have continued as treasury secretary.

Instead, the presidential election was a tie, various recounts failed to settle the matter, and the Supreme Court finally decided the result. Summers was out of a job. Two months later, on March 11, he was named president of Harvard, his appointment to take effect on July 1.

We know very little with any certainty about what happened during those next three weeks as concerns the suit against Shleifer and Harvard, except that at the end of them, the negotiated settlement fell through. On Friday, March 30, 2001, the docket notes, "Case no longer referred to ADR (Alternative Dispute Resolution)."

A year later, when Summers was deposed under oath, the government's attorney asked about his conversations with Shleifer about the affair. He replied, "There were various points prior to my removing myself from the case, not long after I took up the position at Harvard, conversations in which he vented a certain amount with respect to his feeling vis-a-vis the way this was being handled."

And, at another point, when exactly did the recusal take place? "Not long after becoming president of Harvard. Just when, I don't recall."

So the three weeks in March remain an enigma. Many lawyers were involved in those settlement negotiations; sources report a deep division of opinion at the time. Harvard is said to have wanted to settle, Shleifer to have refused, unless Harvard promised to pay his legal bills and to indemnify him against a finding of damages. Clearly there was friction between him and General Counsel Ann Taylor. (At one point, Shleifer complained to Summers that she was among the Harvard officials who were "bad-mouthing" him in the press, according to the president's deposition.)

If it wasn't the newly appointed (but not yet inaugurated) Summers who made the argument, directly or indirectly, to defend Shleifer and try the case instead of settling, culminating in the collapse of Judge Mazzone's mediation, then who was it?

Harvard has acknowledged that former president (and former law school dean) Derek Bok entered the case at some point as an adviser to the Corporation. When did he begin? (Bok has been named interim president once Summers leaves, in June.)

*The Wall Street Journal* reported last October that Summers had recused himself "at the Corporation's insistence." When exactly did the formal action take place?

And if Summers was really recused in the matter, what cautionary measures did he take to clarify his judgment when he dismissed Taylor in 2002 as the university's top lawyer and promoted Iuliano into the job a year later? Granted, superintending the Shleifer case was hardly the general counsel's only assignment, but it was probably the most important, with potential exposure to the university of well over $100 million, though the loss turned out to be "only" $26.5 million (plus another $15 million or so in lawyers' fees) in the end.

Harvard's Institute for International Development is dissolved, and soon Summers will be gone from the president's office. But Harvard has not made peace with its disastrous Russia Project. Giving Summers a university professorship, Harvard's top academic rank, is one thing. Absolving him from complicity in the decision taken during those three crucial weeks in March 2001, when he had begun involving himself in management but not yet formally taken office, is something else again. The failed mediation, and the timing of Summers' recusal, are matters that First Fellow Houghton really should explain.

> 15 March 2018: Summers took strong exception to this weekly at the time it was published. He was adamant that he had played no part in Harvard's decision to try the government's case rather than settle it. Though he had been unclear in his deposition about the date of his recusal, and about the timing of his plea to Faculty Dean Knowles that Shleifer be retained, he was presumably certain that he never expressed an opinion about the merits of the government's charges to any Harvard decision-maker, before or after being elected president. Members of the Harvard Corporation have never elaborated on the decisions taken in those three weeks.

* * *

Why did Larry Summers' Harvard presidency fail?

"It would be presumptuous to try to aggregate the opinions of thousands of individual faculty members, or to guess at the private thought processes of Corporation members, and it is far too soon to attempt a history."

So wrote John Rosenberg last week, just before he reminded readers of his own courageous earlier analysis as editor of Harvard's alumni magazine. …[D]istinguished faculty members from a variety of disciplines spoke about their sense that the president, while pursuing change, had claimed 'sole agency' to do so, soliciting and then ignoring informed counsel, and resorting to 'bullying and personal aspersions,' humiliating faculty members and even silencing their opinions."

Two other pieces that appeared last week struck me as especially enlightening.

James Traub, who three years ago profiled Summers in *The New York Times Magazine*, wrote in *Slate*. …[H]e wasn't forced out of Harvard because he stood up to political correctness. If anything, Summers was forced out of Harvard because he behaved so boorishly that he provided a bottomless supply of ammunition to his enemies, both the ideologues and the doctrine-free."

Richard Bradley, author of *Harvard Rules: The Struggle for the Soul of the World's Most Powerful University* (and of a blog that keeps track of subsequent developments as well), wrote in *The Los Angeles Times*, "Summers was ousted not because of a clash of conservative versus liberal ideologies…. The real problem was that Harvard's faculty rejected the encroachment of Washington politics…. Summers spent too much time positioning Harvard to suit prevailing political winds rather than advocating for the university's traditional separation from the corrupting worlds of politics and commerce."

Naturally, I think my own earlier analysis also stands up pretty well – that, having gone to college down the street at the Massachusetts Institute of Technology, Summers was attempting to address a caricature of Harvard that had developed at MIT over the years, and that he possessed no real understanding of the institution of which he had become president, having served eight years as a full professor.

CHAPTER EIGHTEEN

# In Which, At Last, We Meet, Perhaps, Andrei Shleifer's Evil Twin

*April 16, 2006*

Missing in the controversy over Harvard's Russia scandal has been any attempt to explain, much less place a favorable interpretation upon, the actions of its two principals, Andrei Shleifer and Lawrence Summers. It's missing because none of their many friends and allies has come publicly to their defense. They grumble instead among themselves about how the economists have been "screwed."

Let me sketch the outlines of what seems, at least to me, a plausible explanation, if not exactly a defense, of what the two men, individually and severally, thought they were doing at certain points along the way. Why bother to continue to probe the matter? Because it is relevant to understanding what happens next. Summers is 51. Shleifer is 44. Both are among a handful of mid-career professors to have been officially deemed by their peers to be among the world's most influential economists. Each has 20 or 30 more years of productive work ahead – work of some sort. Until both sides of the story are better told and more fully understood, however, neither man can know with any certainty what he can hope to accomplish next.

The story starts back in 1979. What otherwise would be legend, we know with some certainty because Massachusetts Institute of Technology professor Olivier Blanchard wrote it up in 2001 for the *Journal of Economic Perspectives*, after Shleifer won the John Bates Clark Medal of the American Economic Association, awarded every two years to an outstanding economist who is under 40 years old.

(He edged out other contenders, thanks in part, presumably, to the arguments of his Harvard colleague Claudia Goldin, a member of the Honors and Awards Committee. It was Goldin, too, who headed the search committee that a few years later settled on Shleifer to edit the prestigious *Journal of Economic Perspectives*.)

Shleifer arrived with his engineer parents in the United States in 1976, a 15-year-old émigré from the Soviet Union speaking very little English. He quickly enrolled in an inner-city high school in Rochester, New York. Two years later, by a series of fortunate accidents, he entered Harvard College as a scholarship student. As a sophomore there, he went to see his instructor, a young economist named Larry Summers, with a view to correcting certain errors in Summers' math in a recent paper.

"While characteristically unimpressed by the argument that his work contained flaws, Larry was sufficiently impressed to hire Andrei as his research assistant. What followed has been a long period of close friendship and mutual education," Blanchard wrote. He did not speculate on the nature of the bond. Others have felt that Shleifer possessed the gifts of mathematical fluency and penetrating depth that Summers lacked, while Summers brought curiosity, drive and a formidable skill at economic argumentation to the friendship.

Something of the intellectual atmosphere in those early days can be inferred from the toast of J. Bradford DeLong's at the festive party in 1999, after the Clark Medal was voted. To explain Shleifer's success in the years since they were Harvard freshmen together, DeLong (a professor at the University of California at Berkeley who worked for a time under Summers at the Treasury) invoked H. G. Wells' idea of an "open conspiracy," devoted to "the betterment of the human race," and operating in opposition to the "small and secret conspiracies that decided most of history."

Its members would "intensively study the social world, to determine what institutions and practices worked and what didn't – what things contributed to human progress, and what things did not." They would "communicate what they had learned through their studies to others." Most important, "they would be tolerant, listen[ing] to what others had to say, to what others had learned as a result of their studies: for no one has a monopoly on truth or on insight, and good judgments can only be arrived at by close and open-minded scrutiny of evidence and opinions." Others who gave speeches that evening included MIT's Rudiger Dornbusch, Harvard's Oliver Hart, Summers, Blanchard, Shleifer's student Florencio López-de-Silanes (fired last year by Yale University for double-billing his expenses, López-de-Silanes now teaches in Europe), and Andrei's father Mark. But it was probably DeLong who best portrayed the way the members of the group preferred to think of themselves.

Both Summers and Shleifer rose rapidly in the decade after they met. Shleifer got his PhD at MIT, taught at Princeton for a year, then received tenure at the Graduate School of Business of the University of Chicago. Summers went to Washington to work for his thesis adviser, Harvard's Martin Feldstein, at the Council of Economic Advisers during the first Reagan administration, then back to Harvard as one of its youngest full professors.

In 1988, Summers was chief economic adviser to Michael Dukakis's presidential campaign. He returned to Washington in 1990 as chief economist for the World Bank, succeeding Stanley Fischer. In 1991, he took Shleifer along on a Bank mission to advise the government of Lithuania. He also enthusiastically backed Harvard's offer of a professorship, which Shleifer took up in the autumn of that year, with some regret, since his heart in many respects remained in Chicago. Shleifer understood, however, that he could never hope to advise the Russian government as long as he was associated with the famously conservative university.

At that point, things began to get complicated. In August 1991, a coup attempt failed to dislodge Mikhail Gorbachev, who was pursuing a gradualist approach to deregulation in hopes of winning massive aid as part of a "Grand Bargain" with the West. Gorbachev remained in office until December, when Boris Yeltsin and the leaders of Belarus and Ukraine simply withdrew from the Soviet Union. Yeltsin immediately undertook the radical economic transformation of Russia that Gorbachev had long resisted. The US government pledged support, cautiously at first, then with gathering enthusiasm.

In October 1992, President George H. W. Bush signed the Open-Market Support Act, authorizing up to $350 million in aid to Russia, to be managed by the Agency for International Development. A few weeks later, he was defeated by Bill Clinton, and Clinton's advisers, Robert Rubin and Larry Summers among them, took the conn. In December, Harvard was awarded a USAID contract to provide unbiased advice to the Russian government on how to convert its heavily planned economy to one governed by market principles.

In Moscow, there was turmoil. After 75 years during which private property beyond the level of household effects had been all but forbidden, there was no obvious way to place state-owned assets in private hands. Poland had led the way into overnight deregulation in January 1990 with a "big bang" – prices decontrolled, the zloty devalued, private companies permitted open for business and foreign firms to invest in. The economists around Yeltsin were determined to do the same. They were the new *Bolsheviki* (the word means 'majority faction'), *market Bolsheviki*, determined to do everything fast, on the grounds that only an abrupt transfer of state-owned assets to private hands could free the economy of deeply entrenched bureaucratic control.

The best account I know of how this proceeded is *The Oligarchs: Wealth and Power in the New Russia*, by David Hoffman, *Washington Post* bureau chief in Moscow during the second half of the '90s. Embedded in Hoffman's powerful narrative are the views, often transparently self-serving, of many members of the brain trust which presided over the great sell-off, including Yegor Gaidar, Anatoly Chubais and Mikhail Berger, one-time economics editor of *Izvestia*. The tension between what Yeltsin said he wanted – "We need millions of owners, not hundreds of millionaires," he would intone – and what eventuated is painfully apparent in *The Oligarchs*. Consider the following story.

Chubais, the red-haired St. Petersburg economist who played a central role throughout, told Hoffman at one point, "Every enterprise ripped out of the state and transferred to the hands of a private owner was a way of destroying Communism in Russia. This is how we understood the situation, without any exaggeration. And every extra day we worked, we could privatize another ten, twenty, or thirty enterprises. And at that stage it didn't matter at all to whom these enterprises went, who was getting the property. It was absolutely unimportant whether that person was ready for it."

In all this Bruegelesque landscape, one citizen is of particular interest. Meet Boris Jordan, a young American citizen whose grandfather, also Boris, had fought the communists across Europe as colonel in the White Russian army, even making common cause with the Germans for a time, eventually retreating to New York. The younger Jordan, born in 1967, grew up amid tales of the good old days in St. Petersburg before the revolution, went to Russian school on Saturdays and spoke Russian at home. "An incredible hustler," as Hoffman describes him, he yearned to return to Russia. He even took and passed the Foreign Service examination, "but the State Department said he would never be sent to Russia as a diplomat." So the well-connected youth went to work selling airplane leases in Latin America.

It was in 1992 that Hans-Joerg Rudloff, president of Credit Suisse First Boston, hired Jordan and sent him to Moscow – the same year that Shleifer arrived in town for USAID. Rudloff himself had memories, of rebuilding his family's leather factory in Germany after World War II; he had hopes that an economic miracle would unfold in Russia as in Germany. He paired Jordan with Steven Jennings, a veteran of the privatization auctions that had taken place in New Zealand during the 1980s. Their instructions: find ways of making money in the Great Sell-Off of Russian assets.

Jordan and Jennings pursued a time-honored strategy: they hung around the offices of the State Property Committee, furnishing the needy young Russians who worked there with office supplies, coffee, information. They courted Chubais, offering to represent the government for free in the complicated business of its first sale of state property to the public. The enterprise was selected: Bolshevik Biscuit Company was a beloved cookie company that had been doing business in Moscow since 1855. The date was set; the sale took place, in December 1992. Insiders got 51 percent of the company; outsiders, wielding the stylishly engraved "privatization checks" the government earlier had distributed to 148 million Russian citizens, bid for the remaining shares. In the end, Boshevik Biscuit changed hands for $654,000.

Jennings had seen an almost identical company in Eastern Europe sold to Pepsi for $80 million a few months earlier. Jordan later told the *Post*'s Hoffman, "We looked at each other and said, 'We are on the wrong side of this deal. We shouldn't be representing the government. We should be buying the stuff!' We quit!'" And just as quickly, they went to work for the series of bold and energetic insiders who soon would become known to the world as Russian oligarchs.

Here, then, was one of H. G. Wells' ubiquitous "small and secret" conspiracies throughout human history that had been such powerful agents of change – in this case, simply a corporation. In the next few years, Jordan and Jennings built Credit Suisse First Boston's (CSFB) Moscow office into one of the city's most powerful investment banks.

The auction of the cookie company had inaugurated an astonishing fire sale of Russia's assets. Factories, utilities, media, banks, mineral rights, natural resources were sold off to the cleverest bidders over the next few years, with little concern for basic fairness – and CSFB was in the thick of it. Jordan left in 1995 to start his own investment bank, Renaissance Capital, and in 1998 founded Sputnik Group as well. But his relationship with his old employer remained extremely close, and in 1996, as Yeltsin's government rushed to create a mutual fund industry (in the midst of a difficult reelection campaign), it was CSFB that elbowed its way to the head of the queue seeking a license to issue shares.

It was in these circumstances, then, that the mutual fund company with which Shleifer was associated behind the scenes, Pallada, surprised everyone by obtaining the coveted first license from the Russian Securities Commission – one of the many agencies which USAID paid Shleifer to advise. A young investment banker named Elizabeth Hebert had founded Pallada the year before, with the assistance of Shleifer's deputy, Jonathan Hay. Soon she became Hay's girlfriend. A few months later Shleifer and his hedge-fund-manager wife provided crucial investment capital, and before long, Beth Hebert was running Pallada out of the Harvard team's office, using its phones, its faxes, its drivers. Yet it was widely recognized that CSFB had been far ahead in the baroque process of preparing its application.

A young lawyer who worked for Hay on the Harvard project described what happened next when he was deposed years later by government lawyers. Louis O'Neill said, "I went to Jon [Hay] and said, '"This is kind of strange. Why this and not CSFB?'.... He said something to me that made sense.... He said, "'Well, this is a very serious pilot project. It will be... basically, the first mutual fund in Russia. We want to have someone as the leader, as the first person, who we are friendly with and who we can monitor very closely for transparency, fairness, proper procedures, proper accounting..."' I remember the phrase he used because it made sense. "'We'll run water through the pipes on this one, see where the leaks are, fix them, and then we'll open it up to the larger market.'" That to me was convincing.

"... It seems strange to me that Jonathan was running the project, responsible for all the donor money, and his girlfriend was in the office running a private company.... ...I'd gone there sort of out of law school, excited, eager, bright-eyed, maybe to do some good, and it all ended on a kind of a sour note. So I just felt kind of bad about it, kind of wished it would all go away at the time," said O'Neill. A few months later, whistle-blowers attracted the attention of USAID in Washington. After a brief investigation, the government fired Harvard, and the project came crashing down.

A mistrust of CSFB was a current theme in the government's subsequent investigation. For instance, when in 2002 Larry Summers was asked about an attempt to penalize Credit Suisse by excluding it from a Credit Markets Forum sponsored by the US Treasury Department, he answered, "There were certain clouds of impropriety, whose validity I have no ability to judge...."

Fans of "Deadwood," HBO's horse opera set in the Black Hills in 1877 on the eve of South Dakota's statehood, will recognize the moral climate here. An endless series of power struggles unfold among players of widely different backgrounds in an outlaw community in the throes of becoming legitimate. Motives molt, alliances shift and tactics change with each new bit of news. No one's skirts remain completely unsoiled.

But storytelling, however compelling, is not the same as making US government policy. It will require the work of many scholar-years before we can reasonably compare the path not taken in Russia – the gradualism of the Grand Bargain – with the "shock therapy" that produced the oligarchs, the *Siloviki* and the resurgence of the state under Vladimir Putin. But it took a Boston jury almost no time at all last year to decide that, whatever ends Harvard's Andrei Shleifer might have had in mind, he clearly violated his agreement with the US government when he began investing in Russia.

A comparison of the career paths of Boris Jordan and Andrei Shleifer leaves no doubt that the two chose very different paths – a pursuer of commercial interests and a guardian of pursuers of commercial interests. What happened after their careers began to converge in Moscow in 1992 will be a matter of speculation, probably forever. Today Jordan is a man of enormous wealth, though he was fired by the Kremlin in 2003 from his job as head of Russia's third biggest television network. Chubais, who sold Russian assets to the oligarchs in order to break the monopoly of the state, became an extremely wealthy man himself, though with net worth of only around $1 billion, perhaps not quite an oligarch. As head of Russia's electricity system, he has been seeking to break the system into competitive parts, *a la* American Telephone and Telegraph and the Baby Bells.

About Shleifer's innermost ambitions, we'll never know, since his standing as Washington's privatizer-in-chief in Moscow collapsed not long after Yeltsin's second term began, before the scandals of the loans-for-shares program, before Russia's real estate property laws could be reformed. He may not know, himself. Today Shleifer lives modestly with his family in the leafy Boston suburb of Newton, in a house that was mortgaged as part of his settlement with the Justice Department. A villa in France that the family is said to own wasn't in the agreement.

But there remains the matter of the rules, as they have evolved in the United States over the century in which official corruption has become a crime instead of a commonplace. It is instructive to note that whereas the State Department recognized immediately the conflicts and character traits that disqualified Boris Jordan from diplomatic service, Harvard not only cleared their newly hired professor to advise the Russians, but sent the 31-year-old émigré to Moscow as head of its project, without civilian (non-academic) supervision.

But then that's another story.

CHAPTER NINETEEN

# The Light Gray Curse

*November 5, 2006*

So Harvard University has taken away Andrei Shleifer's endowed chair and its privileges – stripped him of his epaulets, in effect. Any day now, the Becker Center on Chicago Price Theory at the University of Chicago, too, will have to do the same, remove the Whipple V. N. Jones Professorship from in front of Shleifer's name on its website. Then the 45-year-old Harvard economics professor will be the only professorial director of that newly formed center without a chair (Ronald Coase, Milton Friedman, George Shultz and Richard O. Ryan, the agribusiness magnate who founded it, are the others). Someday, too, Shleifer may remove himself from Harvard, perhaps to Chicago, where he belonged all along; possibly to the Hoover Institution at Stanford University, where Shultz and Friedman hang their hats; or even to London. Then again, he may remain in Cambridge, Massachusetts. But that's a story for another day.

The question for today has to do with estimating the damage that began accruing – to Harvard University in particular, to the economics profession in general – when, in 1997, while leading a Harvard team advising the government of Russia on behalf of the government of the United States, Shleifer was caught red-handed lining his own pockets with various investments in Russia.

To learn about Harvard's recent attempt to deal with its self-inflicted wounds, read on.

Instead of doing the right thing in 1997, scolding its professor and copping a plea, Harvard then joined him in a bristling defense. The university insisted that in leading its mission to Moscow Shleifer had done nothing wrong by speculating in Russian bonds, investing in a Russian private equity firm, strong-arming a well-established competitor and obtaining for his wife, his sidekick and the sidekick's girlfriend the first license to sell mutual funds in Russia – from the very regulators to whom he was being paid to give disinterested advice.

Elementary ethical common sense, not to mention government contracts and Harvard's own rules, required Shleifer to refrain from investing in the country he was advising.

If, at any point along the way, the university, its department of economics and its errant professor had simply acknowledged that they understood the logic behind this simple ethical precept, expressing appropriate embarrassment and regret, the episode quickly would have faded into the background.

Nine years later, however, after a humiliating trial in US District Court in Boston, Harvard was found to have breached its contract, and was ordered to return $26.5 million, almost all the money it had collected and spent. Shleifer and his protégé/deputy, Jonathan Hay, were found to have committed two kinds of fraud, and Shleifer was fined $2 million, as much as the US attorney could extract from him, having no way to tap whatever offshore wealth he possessed.

And a year after that, Shleifer's friend and mentor Lawrence Summers was gone from the Harvard presidency. Summers' obtuseness on the Shleifer matter is understood within the university to have been a precipitating factor in the Harvard Corporation's decision to compel his resignation. "When the president responded in a manifestly untruthful way to questions that were asked about the Shleifer case, [at a crucial meeting of the faculty], it had a devastating effect on the views of people who were to that point uncommitted, people who, like me, were strong supporters of his agenda," Professor Robert Putnam, a political scientist, later told Sara Ivry of *The New York Times*.

The backstory helps us understand the situation. In 1992, with the Soviet Union disintegrating, Congress authorized aid for the newly elected Russian government of Boris Yeltsin, but not too much of it. The Freedom for Russia and the Emerging Eurasian Democracies and Open-Market Support Act, signed into law by President George H. W. Bush in October, authorized up to $350 million for a mission to advise the newly forming Russian government on how to lay the groundwork for a market economy. The US Agency for International Development selected Harvard, and in 1992 Harvard chose the 31-year-old Shleifer, having hired him from Chicago the year before. Cheering him on at every step was Summers, who had befriended him a dozen years before, when Summers was an assistant professor and Shleifer a brash sophomore.

What had commended him for the job in Russia? The fact that, for one thing, he spoke the language like a native, having grown up in the Soviet Union before immigrating to the United States with his parents when he was 15. That he had learned economics at Harvard College and the Massachusetts Institute of Technology, and taught it at the University of Chicago. That he had turned out to be something of a prodigy, making highly original contributions to the comparative analysis of the legal institutions and financial markets that underpin market economies. That he was an expert on corruption, no less. Above all, that he was an enthusiastic student of applied power. (His wife liked to call him "Boss.") Summers, who at the time was chief economist for the World Bank, first sent him to Russia in 1991.

Shleifer took the helm of Harvard's Moscow office in December 1992 – about the same time that Summers became assistant secretary of the treasury for international affairs in the new Clinton administration. A little more than four years later, USAID shut down the Harvard project, after its inspector general discovered Shleifer to be investing in Russia, with his wife, her father, Shleifer's deputy and the deputy's girlfriend. Just how rich they hoped to become is still not clear – maybe a lot, maybe a little, but definitely some, in contravention of their contract. By that time, Summers had risen to the number-two job at the Treasury, under Robert Rubin. And though, to his credit, he never tried to derail the Justice Department's probe of the matter, it is clear that Summers freely deprecated the government's complaint against his friend from behind the scenes.

The case against Shleifer had nothing to do with inside information. (It is a sure sign of a red herring when someone tells you he was not guilty of a transgression that was never alleged.) It had to do with the self-dealing and the abuse of a position of trust. The only way to understand this is to put yourself in the place of a Russian citizen looking forward to a better deal from the new system. When the American team arrives, it is led by an expatriate crook, flouting the rules of the country he represents, until his subordinates turn him in. (It doesn't help that Summers, his mentor, has oversight of all US economic policy towards Russia.)

In somewhat similar circumstances, the State Department turned down Boris Jordan, another ambitious young Russian hoping to go to Moscow for the US Foreign Service. To Shleifer, however, Harvard said, Go right ahead! The Russian story is like something out of fiction, except that it happened.

(Here, then, is the real scandal: it turns out that Shleifer was boasting of his investments in a Russian private equity fund to his economist friends as early as October 1994, at a party at the home of then department chairman Dale Jorgenson. This is according to David McClintick, who wrote up an authoritative version of the Shleifer story earlier this year for *Institutional Investor* magazine. Martin Feldstein phoned Shleifer afterwards, seeking an introduction. In the end he decided not to invest, McClintick wrote.)

So much, then, for the advice Shleifer was receiving from his colleagues in the economics department. Once USAID blew its whistle, however, there was another opportunity when Harvard's administration could have investigated, discovered for itself the wrongdoing, taken its professor to the woodshed, negotiated an agreement with the US attorney in Boston to make the government whole, and been done with the matter at relatively little cost in cash or reputation. Shleifer was, after all, just a kid who had grown up in the former Soviet Union, hardly a finishing school for good behavior. Even before taking over the Russia Project, he had shown a willingness to bend the rules.

But he was also a likeable guy, bright and quick, intellectually fearless, full of excitement at the possibilities of his new world. It is easy to imagine a time when a stern talking to from someone he trusted – his friend Summers, for example; or chemist Jeremy Knowles, who served as dean of the Faculty of Arts and Sciences from 1991 until 2002; or Harvard provost Harvey Fineberg – would have put the whole matter on a different track.

Why wasn't it done? The mechanics remain a riddle. The cast of characters comprises a veritable Who's Who: Jorgenson, who was chair of the economics department when the scandal broke; FAS Dean Knowles; Albert Carnesale, who was provost when the scandal broke (retired as chancellor of the University of California at Los Angeles, he is back at Harvard's Kennedy School part time); Fineberg, who took over as provost just after the initial flurry of news reports (he is president of the Institute of Medicine of the National Academy of Sciences today); Deputy Treasury Secretary Summers, who may have been consulted through back channels before being elected Harvard president in 2001; Harvard professor and ethicist Dennis Thompson, a friend of Harvard president Neil Rudenstine and the head of a committee that devised the plan to disband the intermediary organization that Shleifer wrecked, the Harvard Institute for International Development; and, of course, Rudenstine himself. The principal faculty whistle-blower was Jeffrey Sachs, who was quickly ridden off the case. (He moved to Columbia in 2002.)

The broad outlines of why Harvard felt it was important to be nice to Shleifer are clear enough. He is a central figure in present-day technical economics; like Summers, Feldstein and Jorgenson, a winner of the John Bates Clark Medal, given every two years to the economist considered to be the profession's best thinker under 40. Sometimes it is said that Shleifer's line of research is potentially of Nobel quality. Maybe so, maybe not. But they give a Nobel every year. Shleifer's real attraction is as chairman of the board of an especially broad line of recent advances, as Larry Summers was chairman of the board of another. (A less flattering term for the role is godfather.) Between them, the pair would command the presence and subsequent loyalty of a steady stream of the very best graduate students for another 15 years – including the brainiest young economists from Russia. Indeed, the parade through Littauer Hall of steller faculty and students from the former Soviet Union during the last few years has been remarkable.

Add to this the fact that the Harvard Management Company was investing aggressively in Russia in the mid-90s – as much as 1.8 percent of the university's endowment in the year before USAID fired Harvard. Did Shleifer possess some bit of *kompromat*, or potentially compromising material, that might have led Massachusetts Hall to prefer to join its defense to his until the very end? The possibility is widely discussed in Eastern Europe, where such stratagems are common. It is, of course, virtually impossible to know.

In any event, in the highly competitive environment of modern economics, the cost of doing the right thing has gone up. As if to illustrate this principle, Yale University last year fired tenured professor Florencio López-de-Silanes, Shleifer's protégé and frequent collaborator, after he was discovered to be double-billing his expenses to the World Bank and the university's Center for Corporate Governance. But, then, López-de-Silanes is a follower in his field, not a leader.

The result today is that Harvard economics' considerable luster is bedimmed by a light gray curse. (There are other problems, too: the department's stewardship of its *Quarterly Journal of Economics* has come under fire in the profession for intellectual self-dealing. Shleifer edited for a decade, and helped choose the current editors, Robert Barro, Lawrence Katz and Edward Glaeser.) On the issue of Shleifer's standing, the department is deeply riven.

Some, including Claudia Goldin, David Laibson, Katz and Glaeser have been outspoken in defense of his academic stature. Others, including Jorgenson (now a high-ranking university professor) and N. Gregory Mankiw (the former George W. Bush adviser who teaches Harvard's introductory economics course), have grumbled over the years about the university's administration, the government and the press, but only behind the scenes. A sizeable faction of the 71-member department, perhaps even a slight majority, deplore the Russia scandal in varying degrees, but prefer not to speak out. In general, the situation seems to have changed only a little from what it was when then-president Summers described it in his deposition in 2002: "…[M]embers of the department, the economics department, expressed and have on repeated occasions expressed the view that Andrei was in some way or other being screwed…."

Undergraduates – a record 965 of them taking Mankiw's introductory course, or nearly 20 percent of the college enrollment – are cowed. For the most part, so is *The Harvard Crimson*. Shleifer's defenders at MIT, where he trained, and the Graduate School of Business of the University of Chicago, where he taught, remain silent. Meanwhile, he remains a powerful dispenser of favors as the editor of the *Journal of Economic Perspectives*, the outreach journal of the American Economic Association.

Thus the light gray curse extends beyond Harvard to the economics profession itself. Friends say that Shleifer will explain himself some day, perhaps in a larger context. Possibly he will take on the very concept of disinterestedness and, perhaps, the principle of transparency as well. Alternatively, he could argue that sometimes agents must do things considered bad in one culture in order to buttress their credibility in another, in order ultimately to do good – a "Mission Impossible" defense whose outlines were sketched here last spring. When, a couple of years ago, Shleifer received a prize at the University of Munich, Tim Besley of the London School of Economics said in his laudation, "There is… a healthy disregard for convention in Andrei's work – a trait that I associate with his mentor Larry Summers. Andrei is willing to challenge accepted wisdom on any topic and many of his contributions take on entrenched views." Whatever the case, a clear and forthright discussion of the issues would seem to be the price of remaining in Cambridge far into the future.

It is in this context that Harvard's decision to take away his named chair is understood. At first glance, it looks fairly deft. Interim dean Knowles (who presumed Shleifer innocent in 1997 and promoted him to the Jones chair in 2002) last month simply took the named professorship away. He may have done more. Who knows? Knowles declined to reveal his actions, to release a report of the faculty Committee on Professional Conduct or the names of its three ad hoc faculty consultants. He left it to *The Boston Globe* to "discover" the rescission by checking the university website. Shleifer shrugged. He told the *Globe*, "I was a professor of economics last week, and I am a professor of economics this week." Yet it seems that no penalty like it has ever been applied. It is enough to place a virtual asterisk wherever his name appears – at the University of Chicago's Becker Center, for example.

Then Harvard quietly applied the same punishment to another faculty miscreant. It took back another chair – the Ernest E. Monrad Professorship, previously belonging to economist Martin Weitzman. (This time it was *The Harvard Crimson* that nailed down the facts.) Weitzman is no less bright a contributor than Shleifer, and, though 64, remains very active in his field. A new book, *Income, Wealth and the Maximum Principle,* is an unusually accessible explication of the mathematical underpinnings of capital theory, hence a guide for serious students of sustainability and "green" accounting. A new working paper – "Risk, Uncertainty and Asset Pricing 'Puzzles'" – is stirring a lively controversy over the deepest assumptions that underlie conventional econometric models of expectations.

It was, however, Weitzman who found his way into the news last year when he drove his truck into a pasture to pick up horseflops – and was promptly penned in by the farmer who owned the land, with whom he had been feuding for years. Trapped, Weitzman offered $20, then $40 for the manure, but the farmer called the sheriff, the sheriff charged Weitzman with theft, and Weitzman eventually agreed in Essex County Court to pay $900 to settle the case ($600 for the farmer, $300 for the town Boy Scouts) – but not before the story spread around the world, providing fodder for many bad puns.

Among the faculty, there were intimations that donor dissatisfaction was at the root of the rescission, but Monrad, a jovial and tolerant Boston money manager, says that he expressed no displeasure, publicly or privately. Nor, apparently, did Dean Knowles consult the faculty's Committee on Professional Conduct before repossessing Weitzman's honorific title. A spokesman for the Faculty of Arts and Sciences said Friday that the dean was under no obligation to explain his decisions.

There is, indeed, a common thread running through both incidents: a rather startling arrogance; in each case a Harvard professor acted as though he were entitled to take whatever he wanted, regardless of the law. Granted, there is not much moral equivalence between a $900 quarrel in a small town, on the one hand, and, on the other, an unrepentant betrayal of an adoptive country, an alma mater, hundreds of employees and a raft of friends (which also cost Harvard well over $30 million and much reputational capital). Applying the same penalty to the perpetrator of a misdemeanor as to a man who smuggled Soviet-style values into the highest levels of government and education in the United States might seem to send no more weighty a message to the Harvard faculty than, "Don't get our name in the newspapers by breaking the law." But perhaps it is too early to say.

Small gestures, cunningly contrived, can have big effects. The price of *not* doing the right thing is going up as well.

CHAPTER TWENTY

# When the Attorney General Was a Mensch

*March 25, 2007*

The resolution of Harvard's Russia scandal last year sheds some light on the recent unpleasantness over the Bush administration's decision to fire eight US attorneys. That successful prosecution of Harvard University, by an attorney appointed by President Bill Clinton, provides a textbook illustration of how the system is supposed to work, to resist political pressure.

Donald K. Stern, the former US attorney in Boston who brought the action, described the institutional arrangement in an op-ed piece in *The Boston Globe* the other day. Stern served from 1993 until 2001; today he is a partner at the Bingham McCutcheon law firm.

> Yes, US attorneys are appointed by the president (and confirmed by the Senate) for a term, can be asked to resign or can be removed. Yet this has rarely happened and certainly never to this extent in the middle of a president's term.
>
> This is because the department generally respected the unique role the US attorneys play in their respective districts, serving as the chief federal law enforcement officer – serving as a representative of the federal government but able to set priorities for the law enforcement

> needs of their local communities.
>
> Moreover, the US attorneys have always enjoyed a special brand of independence, even within the Department of Justice. This unique blend of independence and accountability provides some tension from time to time, but more often affords checks and balances on the enormous power held by federal prosecutors.

Stern should know. He found himself at the center of a tug-of-war that began when investigators for the US Agency for International Development in 1997 shut down a Harvard advisory mission to Moscow after whistle-blowers reported that the team leader, Andrei Shleifer, a professor of economics at the university, was aggressively seeking investment opportunities with his wife, his deputy and the deputy's girlfriend.

Not only did the Harvard administration quickly dispute the charge that any impropriety had occurred, but Shleifer's best friend, mentor and fellow Harvard economist, Lawrence Summers, was deputy secretary of the Treasury, soon to become secretary, replacing Robert Rubin. He had oversight of all US economic policy in Russia.

Clearly Summers was in a difficult position. His man on the inside of Russian policy circles, his trusted friend, had been fired by USAID, a semi-independent agency within the State Department. Shleifer's counterparts in the Russian government retaliated by severing relations with the rest of the American advisory group. Before long, Russian would be embroiled in a currency crisis that would threaten the global financial system; Summers would be lionized on the cover of *Time* magazine, along with Robert Rubin and Alan Greenspan, as "tThe Committee to Save the World."

Summers later testified:

> I came personally to the following judgments during the time when I was in the government: that the project was of enormous value both to supporting the crucial US objective of encouraging privatization, encouraging market-oriented institutions, and to the US objective of establishing relationships of constructive helpfulness to figures within

> the Russian government who the US government had identified as democratic market-oriented reformers whose hand it wished to strengthen.
>
> That the termination of the project, that the termination of Shleifer and [deputy Jonathan] Hay's role had compromised both those objectives by reducing a trusted source of advice supporting policies that were in the broad interest of the US government and rupturing to some limited extent the feelings of harmony between the US government and key officials in Russia.
>
> I had enough knowledge of Russian mores and Russian practices and Russian views from the conversations I had with [Anatoly] Chubais and [Dimitry] Vasiliev to be confident that the set of issues contained in the allegations were not issues that were consequential for them; and that they would have, in part, valued advisers more extensively if they were more involved in actual private-sector activities.

Did Summers do anything to discourage a prosecution he clearly viewed as unwise and unjust? Rumors have circulated for years that he made calls on USAID to abandon its investigation at an early stage. But when asked in his deposition whether he has engaged in conversations with anyone else in the government concerning the case, he recalled none outside the privacy of his office.

Aside from conversations with Treasury attorneys (which were privileged), he replied, "The only other present memory I have is of conversations expressing some irritation about the time commitment and hassle associated with preparation for the discussion we had in my office, expressions of complaint on my part about all of this to members of my personal staff."

What did his staff say in return?

"I think it's probably the case that there's a certain amount of interagency commentary that goes around in which one agency doesn't always think the highest of other agencies, and there was probably a little commentary of that kind vis-à-vis the Justice Department. But there was no effort to engage in contentful conversation about it."

That was pretty much the end of it. For three long years, lawyers for Shleifer and Harvard fenced with the office of the US attorney in Boston, producing documents, giving depositions, even testifying before a grand jury – and seeking to persuade the government to drop the case.

In the end, no criminal charges were filed against Shleifer. Instead, the government sought treble damages from Harvard. Government prosecutor Sara Miron Bloom, an assistant US attorney in Boston, made no attempt to tie Summers to the case. Soon thereafter he was named president of Harvard, and unobtrusively protected Shleifer behind the scenes. US District Court Judge Douglas Woodlock conducted a low-key trial.

Very little is known about whatever representations and back-channel communications took place among Harvard, the Justice Department and the US attorney's office in Boston during those three years, much less what went on in the government itself, among the Treasury, Justice and State departments (beyond simply staring daggers at one another, that is). The US attorney in Boston finally filed his suit near the end of September 2000 – barely a month before the presidential election. Stern and Bloom have maintained principle silence throughout.

What is known is that the attorney general in those days was Janet Reno. Whatever appeals were made to her, she declined to interfere. The suit went forward, resulting in a jury verdict against Harvard and a finding of fraud against Shleifer.

Without that finding, the rise of Vladimir Putin and his high favorability ratings would be harder to comprehend. Commentators routinely note that among ordinary Russians, the sense of having been taken to the cleaners by the Americans is widespread. Then, too, ordinary Americans wouldn't understand that the Russians' grievance was genuine, if Stern and Reno hadn't stood their ground.

Instead, citizens of both nations received a vivid illustration of the meaning of the rule of law – not even Harvard, for all its friends in high places, could break it with impunity. The first female attorney general of the United States set a high standard, by which her successors will be judged.

CHAPTER TWENTY-ONE

# The Un-Marshall Plan

*April 29, 2007*

The death last week of Boris Yeltsin called to mind an important truth – policy never gets made in a vacuum. The United States seriously mishandled its relationship with Russia in the years after the fall of the Berlin Wall, in large measure because of its own internal tax-cut politics. With the benefit of hindsight, three major inflection points stand out.

The first had to do with the failure to extend any sort of helping hand to the Soviet Union during the period of its breakup. Mikhail Gorbachev appealed for aid, privately, then publicly, but was rebuffed. "[W]e need some oxygen," he told Secretary of State James Baker when they met at one point. "We are not asking for a gift. We are asking for a loan. We are asking for specifically targeted loans for specific purposes," perhaps $15 billion or $20 billion "to tide us over." Out of the question, Baker told him. Before long, Gorbachev was outmaneuvered by Boris Yeltsin, who, in effect, declared Russia bankrupt and distributed a large portion of the nation's assets to a handful of insiders.

Had some measure of aid been available, Brent Scowcroft later wrote (he was national security adviser to George H. W. Bush), Gorbachev might have succeeded in shunting the painful process of reform on to some different path. A serious program of assistance to Russia in making the transition to a market economy might not have worked, but it is significant that the Bush administration didn't feel it could try.

The second misstep had to do with the rapid expansion of the North Atlantic Treaty Organization (NATO) during the 1990s. When Gorbachev met Bush in Malta in December 1989, a few weeks after the fall of the Berlin Wall, he handed the American president a map depicting US bases and fleets around the world, in order to argue that while the Soviet Union had adopted a strictly defensive posture, the United States as yet had not stood down.

It turned out that Russia hadn't seen anything yet. Fifteen years later, NATO has admitted to its ranks Hungary, Poland, the Czech Republic, Bulgaria, Estonia, Latvia, Lithuania, Romania, Slovakia and Slovenia. Governments friendly to the United States have been supported in Ukraine and Georgia. American bases have been established in Central Asia to wage war in Afghanistan. And the United States has pressed a "coalition of the willing" – including Polish troops – into its occupation of Iraq.

These were the circumstances behind Vladimir Putin's angry speech in February to the Munich Conference on Security Policy, the one in which he complained of "an almost uncontained hyper-use of force — military force — in international relations, force that is plunging the world into an abyss of permanent conflicts." Not long thereafter *New York Times* columnist Thomas Friedman wrote, "We helped create a mood in Russia hospitable to a conservative cold warrior like Mr. Putin by forcing NATO on a liberal democrat like Mr. Yeltsin."

Finally, there was the advisory role that Americans played in helping the Russians pursue their internal reforms during the 1990s. Specifically, there was Harvard University's tainted Russia Project, the Clinton administration's flagship program to help the Russians build a market economy. When the team leader, a young Harvard professor who had emigrated from Russia at 15, was discovered to be enriching himself, the US Agency for International Development fired him; the Russians then shut down the entire project. Harvard eventually was ordered to pay back most of the sum it had collected.

By then, however, the damage had been done. The old-line Russian intelligentsia was especially unamused. As political commentator William Pfaff wrote the other day in *The International Herald Tribune*, "The naïve and usually self-serving recommendations by the western governments, institutions and consultants heavily contributed to the chaos produced in the 1990s by the collapse of Soviet-era institutions, which is the principal reason for the opinions expressed in Russia today."

It didn't have to be this way. The United States decisively succeeded in its Cold War competition with the Soviet Union and its satellites. It could have well afforded to be magnanimous in victory, at least in some degree. Instead, Washington found itself hobbled by massive deficits and tempted by unexpected opportunities. So it backed a weak and ineffective Russian leader.

No wonder, then, that Yeltsin's obituaries stressed the extent to which ordinary Russians view their first elected president as a man that brought their country to the brink of chaos. He didn't do it all himself, though. He had help, in the form of short-sighted US policies almost guaranteed to return the country's leadership to more authoritarian hands.

CHAPTER TWENTY-TWO

# Climate Change?

*February 24, 2008*

With the Russian presidential election coming up next Sunday, I have been paying more than usual attention to *Johnson's Russia List* (JRL), which arrives nearly every morning at my desk via e-mail, with the complete texts of yet another 30 or 40 news stories about what is happening in Russia, mostly from the English- and Russian-language press, but with plenty of European and Israeli dispatches thrown in. I groan a little each time I call up a new packet.

*JRL* is the one-stop kiosk for anyone interested in what is happening in Russia. It is one of those miracles of the web that more people should know about and more people should support. Let me explain what it is and how it works.

David Johnson, 60-ish, workaholic, resumes the work of the previous evening each morning when his teacher wife leaves for school. A similar service, in a somewhat more edited format, for people interested in the US newspaper, magazine and broadcast news industries, is performed weekdays, by Jim Romenesko, a long-time newspaperman operating out of Chicago. The Poynter Institute, an influential St. Petersburg, Florida, journalism think tank, pays Romenesko to do his work; Johnson subsists on donations from many sources, large and small. There must be many other such prodigies, but these are the two who follow sectors that are of interest to me.

I skim down Johnson's story list, pick out the two or three articles that attract me, and read them. He has access to various sources that translate Russian and other foreign-language media, several US government agencies probably among them. So I read *Pravda* one day, the *Moscow Times* the next, *Interfax* and perhaps *Bloomberg* the day after that; a *Haaretz* dispatch one day, a *Chronicle of Higher Education* dispatch another (its correspondent, Anna Nemtsova, being an especially useful member of the Moscow press corps). In this fashion did I learn last week (from Christian Lowe, of *Reuters*) that Vladimir Putin does not plan to hang Dimitry Medvedev's portrait on his office wall after next Sunday's election, "breaking with the standard etiquette for Russian officials to display portraits of the serving head of state."

A birthright Quaker (his father was for many years an official of the American Friends Service Committee in New England), Johnson studied Russian in high school, traveled there first in 1962. After college at Brandeis University and graduate study at Harvard, Johnson moved to Washington in the 1970s and went to work for the Center for Defense Information (now the World Security Institute) when it opened for business in 1972. He started *JRL* in the spring of 1996, alert to the possibilities of the Internet and "uncomfortable with the policies of [Boris] Yeltsin and the usually uncritical support given to Yeltsin both by the US government and most US media," and has been at it with scarcely an interruption ever since. An interview, from which these quotations and details are taken, appeared in *Moscow News* last year. "While I am not particularly religious," Johnson told Robert Bridge, "I do think that Quakers strive to understand those regarded as enemies… and highly value the need to learn about foreign cultures."

Western economists, you'll remember, split broadly into two camps in the 1980s: gradualists and those who counseled one form or another of "shock therapy." The latter, "market Bolsheviks," in Peter Reddaway's description, quickly gained the upper hand in the feverish atmosphere of the 1990s, as Boris Yeltsin, following a centuries-old pattern of government-led development (Ivan the Terrible, Peter the Great, Nikolai Lenin, Josef Stalin), sought to create a new privileged class of committed supporters – in this case, a relative handful of vastly wealthy robber-barons. Books like *The Oligarchs: Wealth and Power in the New Russia*, by David Hoffman, of *The Washington Post*, and *Sale of the Century: Russia's Wild Ride from Communism to Capitalism*, by Chrystia Freeland, of the *Financial Times*, chronicled the market reformers' stories, but have otherwise failed to keep up with the times.

The original parties to the controversy today are somewhat fatigued, their accounts of their battles inevitably tinged by self-pleading. (An exception is the indefatigable Marshall Goldman, of Wellesley College and Harvard University's Davis Center for Russian Studies, about to publish his sixth book of narrative since 1983, *Petrostate: Putin, Power, and the New Russia*.) We must wait for a new generation of scholars to come of age, steeped in archival sources on all sides, Bush and Clinton, Gorbachev and Yeltsin, in order to form firmer opinions.

Meanwhile, we will make do with what we've had all along: a carefully chosen and well-seasoned press corps, whose veterans advance regularly into the senior editorial ranks of *The New York Times*, *The Washington Post*, *The Wall Street Journal*, the *Financial Times*, *The Economist* and *The New Yorker*, where they continue to refine their opinions of what is happening in Russia. In my view, what comes through from the continual wash of news contained in *Johnson's Russia List* adds up to something very close to Johnson's own appraisal: Putin is receiving perhaps too dark a portrayal; the Yeltsin reforms are still painted in too-cheerful tones. [A recent] *Newsweek* takeout by Owen Matthews sounds about right to me. It is no easier to know what to expect in the next couple decades in Russia than it is in China – or, for that matter, the United States.

Indeed, the expected outcome of the Russian election is useful not just in terms of thinking about Russia, but in thinking about what comes next in Cuba as well. When Fidel Castro announced last week that he would step down, US policy towards Cuba immediately became a bone of contention in party politics.

Here's how *The Economist* framed the issue:

> Look a bit further ahead, and two broad scenarios seem possible in Cuba. The first is one in which the Communist Party oversees the introduction of capitalism while retaining political control – in the mold of China, Vietnam or, closer to home, Mexico in the heyday of the Institutional Revolutionary Party. That seems to be the route favored by senior figures in the regime, few of whom show any signs of

being closet democrats. The other scenario is the one long dreamed of in Miami and in Washington, of the regime's sudden collapse and, it is assumed with a confidence many Iraqis may find worryingly familiar, a swift move to liberal democracy.

Note, however, that in all likelihood, that "dream in Washington" is about to change, decisively (and the dream in Miami is no longer what it was even a decade ago, when Cuban expatriates formed a single, intense generational bloc). Washington had little influence in the 1980s as both China and Vietnam "grew out of the plan." It was mainly on the watches of George H. W. Bush and Bill Clinton that the United States came to feel a responsibility to help manage the transitions of formerly centrally-planned states in Eastern Europe and the former Soviet Union. A president who honed his skills as a community organizer on the South Side of Chicago is apt to view the matter differently.

Cuba came up last week in the debate between Senators Barack Obama and Hillary Clinton. She wants a sequence of behind-the-scenes negotiations; he wants to reverse right away the Bush ban on travel and remittances. Obama capped his remarks this way.

> I do think it is important, precisely because the Bush administration has done so much damage to American foreign relations, that the president take a more active role in diplomacy than might have been true 20 or 30 years ago. Because the problem... is if we think that meeting with the president is a privilege that has to be earned, I think that reinforces the sense that we stand above the rest of the world at this point in time, and I think that it's important for us, in undoing the damage that has been done over the last seven years, for the president to be willing to take that extra step. That's the kind of step that I would like to take as president of the United States.

So many things change when the political rudder is thrown over, as seems likely soon to be the case. Then the van of history itself comes about, and sails off on a different tack. I'll admit to being nervous about Obama. But let's see what he can achieve.

Throw the tiller over! Come about!

CHAPTER TWENTY-THREE

# A Normal Professor

*June 1, 2008*

Perhaps, now that Harvard's Russia scandal is receding into the past, Andrei Shleifer, 47, will take it easy. He has a steady stream of students, presides over a growing literature in comparative economics, and has developed an interesting sideline in the economics of persuasion. His wife, Nancy Zimmerman, runs a hedge fund that has seen explosive growth, today managing more than $3 billion for institutional clients; together the pair, through their start-ups, may have amassed a net worth of $40 million or more. ([Felix Salmon], a columnist for *Portfolio* magazine's website subsequently estimated that the figure may be closer to $1 billion.) Their children are growing, his energetic parents live nearby, he superintends a steady stream of visitors to his villa in the south of France, and he keeps a hand in with developments in Russia.

For example, when Anders Aslund, of Washington's Peterson Institute for International Economics, was in Cambridge, Massachusetts last winter, to celebrate the publication of *How Capitalism Was Built: The Transformation of Central and Eastern Europe, Russia, and Central Asia* and *Russia's Capitalist Revolution: Why Market Reform Succeeded and Democracy Failed*, Shleifer, the author of *A Normal Country: Russia After Communism*, threw a party for him at his spacious home on unpaved Bracebridge Road in suburban Newton.

But if Shleifer has slowed down, he hasn't shown it yet. He just returned from giving three seminars in three days in Chicago. University of Chicago professor and *Freakonomics* co-author Steven Levitt, for one, marveled at the enthusiasm with which Shleifer presented a series of new ideas. Given the uphill battle that publishing requires, the lags, the referees, the harshness of the inevitable criticism: "Usually when people have such rich outside options, they take them. It's refreshing to see the passion with which Andrei pursues academic research."

*EP* readers know Shleifer mainly through this weekly's extensive coverage of the tumult that broke around him in the spring of 1997... [T]hey don't have much of a picture of the man – the sort of thing a proper profile would provide. It's no longer my job to provide that profile. But I can sketch the outlines of what a fuller picture of Shleifer might look like in the aftermath of the scandal, with a view to turning the page.

So what's changed? First of all, Shleifer's defenders, at least those who followed the case, now acknowledge he shouldn't have been investing in Russia while officially advising its government. Moreover, most recognize the negative effect when a Russian expatriate with close links to the US Treasury Department (and, in anti-Semitic Russia, a Jew), is seen to be running a family business out of his USAID-financed Harvard office in Moscow. A little more attention has been paid to the role of his wife may have played in egging him on. Shleifer's long-promised defense of his actions has not materialized.

Meanwhile, healing forces have gone to work within Harvard. The university's endowment, nearly 2 percent of which was invested in special situations in Russia in the mid-1990s, has become less aggressive. Harvard has given up the Investing in Russia conference it sponsored for many years. Other authors, historians and government scholars, including some at Harvard, have joined in the telling of the story of Russia's transition. The economics department, eager to be known as the world's foremost in order to attract the brightest students, remains in bad odor within the university.

Then, too, Shleifer is giving up the editorship of the *Journal of Economic Perspectives*, after serving two three-year terms. (Term limits were adopted after founding editor Joseph Stiglitz served three.) As one of three flagship journals of the American Economic Association, the *JEP* is intended "to fill a gap between the general interest press and most other academic economics journals," according to its marching orders. Its editor thus has great power to reward friends and punish enemies, and the appointment of such an embattled figure in 2003 was viewed with alarm by some senior figures in the profession (though none was willing to do so publicly). David Autor, of the Massachusetts Institute of Technology, takes over in December.

You would have thought that 10 years of backroom battles with Harvard lawyers and the government attorneys would have cost Shleifer dearly in terms of scholarship. But there is little evidence of the disturbance in his CV. Between 1997 and 2005, he published more than 50 papers dealing with finance, behavioral and organizational economics, including "The Limits of Arbitrage," a famous paper in 1997 considered to have anticipated the circumstances in which Long-Term Capital Management foundered the next year. There is, of course, no telling how much greater would have been his influence in such diverse fields had he been able to concentrate single-mindedly on his research, test it more extensively against the evidence, and build bridges to the work of those outside his various networks. But there is no doubt that he has produced a substantial body of work. "Certain people have the inner strength necessary to produce remarkable work in adversity," says his friend and fellow Harvard professor Claudia Goldin.

One arena in which Shleifer works is what is routinely described as the new comparative economics. Traditionally, comparative economics strived to bring capitalist and socialist economies into close comparison, searching out the mechanisms through which markets and central planning achieved their results, gauging the efficiency of each in gaining its ends. Shleifer and several authors (Simeon Djankov, of the World Bank; Glaeser, of Harvard; Rafael LaPorta, of Dartmouth; and Florencio López-de-Silanes, of the University of Amsterdam) wrote in a blueprint for the new field, "By the time socialism collapsed in Eastern Europe and the Soviet Union, this question [the comparison of socialism and capitalism] lost much of its appeal. Socialism produced misery and inefficiency, not to mention mass murder by several communist dictators who practiced it. Capitalism, in contrast, typically produced growth and wealth. If capitalism is triumphant, is comparative economy dead?"

Hardly, the authors say. The entrants to the new field have simply shifted their interests, they explain, to the various public and private institutions that make capitalist economies work in widely differing ways: selecting leaders, securing property rights, redistributing wealth, resolving disputes, governing firms, allocating credit, and so on. Central to the field is an analytic organizing device the authors call the institutional possibility frontier, similar in many ways to the familiar production possibility frontier of present-day macroeconomics. One axis describes the social losses arising from forces of disorder, culminating in a Hobbesian war of each against each; the other, the losses arising from dictatorship. Along the long frontier between them lie the various policies that can reduce disorder without increasing the absolute power of the state: an independent judiciary, regulatory authorities, a competitive press, and so on. How the "new" comparative economics eventually will map into other fields in which somewhat similar work is unfolding, including the "new" political economy and organizational economics, remains to be seen.

Shleifer's friendship with his mentor remains intact. Summers attended the party for Aslund, but in general has gone in the opposite direction from Shleifer, speaking out on higher education, gingerly scrutinizing his own failures and, rather than returning to intensive academic research (from which he had been absent for more than 15 years), serving as a co-editor of *Brookings Papers on Economic Activity*, an influential policy journal, writing a column for the *Financial Times*, and otherwise seeking to re-fashion his role as that of a hard-headed conscience of global capitalism. Summers remains a Harvard economics professor; he joined the D. E. Shaw Group, a global money management firm, as a part-time managing director, as well.

Finally, more attention is being paid to Shleifer as an exponent – and an exemplar – of behavioral finance. It was in 1994 that, along with Josef Lakonishok, of the University of Illinois, and Robert Vishny, of the University of Chicago, he co-founded LSV Asset Management, a Chicago firm making equity investments for large institutional investors, including universities. LSV's proprietary models exploit, among other things, discoveries of judgmental biases (notably the "value-glamour anomaly") that Shleifer and frequent collaborator Vishny had made (and published!) in the course of studying patterns of investor behavior. Earlier this year, the firm was managing $66 billion in equity portfolios; Shleifer sold his share in the firm for a large but undisclosed sum several years ago.

(Nor is Shleifer by any means alone among economists who are both smart and rich. Richard Thaler, of the University of Chicago, co-founded Fuller & Thaler Asset Management some years ago – ("Investors make mental mistakes. Fuller and Thaler's objective is to exploit them.") The Workshop in Behavioral Economics of the National Bureau of Economic Research was founded in 1991 by Thaler and Robert Shiller, of Yale University, with seed money from the Russell Sage Foundation; since 2001, Bracebridge Capital Management, Fuller and Thaler, and LSV have paid the bills.)

So, big house, big furniture, big paintings; a brilliant intellect, a formidable academic position; a hard bargainer: here *EP* seeks to turn the page on the man himself. So close the book on Andrei Shleifer's role at the center of Harvard's Russia scandal. He has become, as he might say, a normal professor, or, perhaps, as another MIT-trained economist put it the other day, a normal *Harvard* professor. You can't help but wonder how different the story might have been if someone in the Harvard administration had taken the matter in hand in 1997 – or even 2001, when the office of the US attorney in Boston made its final proffer.

CHAPTER TWENTY-FOUR

# Is Physiognomy Destiny?

*March 22, 2009*

Bonus-payment fury took center stage in Washington last week. The fever goaded Congress to a terrifying mood, the House and Senate competing to punish *someone*, never mind the Constitution. A classic Washington power struggle unfolded in the background, a reminder of the closing days of the administration of George H. W. Bush, when budget chief Richard Darman and Treasury Secretary Nicholas Brady traded potshots on the front page of *The Washington Post* in the run-up to the '92 election.

Treasury Secretary Timothy Geithner, 47, was under fire again, some of it clearly fratricidal. Meanwhile, a talented and complaisant reporter, Noam Scheiber of *The New Republic*, rolled out a 6,000-word cover story assembled with the full cooperation of National Economic Council chair Lawrence Summers, 54: "Springtime for Summers? Why the White House Needs to Unleash Him."

Unleash him? Presumably he had in mind sending Summers back to the Treasury Department, which he had served for eight years during the Clinton administration, the last 18 months as secretary. There, in theory at least, according to Scheiber, he could bring "far more infrastructure to bear on the economic crisis than NEC."

"Maybe the issue isn't whether Summers plays well with others, but whether Obama's economics effort should be led by an ensemble cast or a single virtuoso performer," Scheiber concluded.

An unfortunate coincidence? Perhaps.

It's as good a time as any, though, to review why Geithner is at the Treasury and Summers is not.

Exhibit A is the Harvard Russia scandal – a chain of events that played a key role in Summers' dismissal from the Harvard presidency. It is a black mark that, for some reason, rarely is taken into account when relating the key events of his career. It hasn't become part of the record. It's not mentioned in Scheiber's *New Republic* piece, for example. But then neither did it come up in the *Newsweek* or *Time* accounts of Summers' return to Washington, either. Not even David Leonhardt, economics columnist of *The New York Times*, brought it up when he explained "The Return of Larry Summers" last fall, though he had to ignore his newspaper's own clips. (Registration required.)

And yet it *did* happen – a story straight out of a Tom Clancy novel. *EP* readers don't need to be reminded of how Summers' protégé, Andrei Shleifer, was hired by the US Agency for International Development to head a Harvard mission to provide advice to the Russian government of Boris Yeltsin, but quietly went into business for himself in violation of his contract, got caught and fired, but retained the sympathy and protection of his mentor, even as Summers served as treasury secretary and president of Harvard. A US District Court judge ultimately found Shleifer and Harvard to have committed fraud. The episode has become a standard item in Russia's anti-American lore.

Exhibit B is what happened at Harvard during and after Summers' five years as president there – not so much the well-publicized friction over his blunt manners as the outcome of his business plan for the university. Many of the details have just begun to emerge: the big-bang expansion of the university's campus into the Allston neighborhood of Boston; the heavy hiring of administrative staff; the recruitment of his former boss, Robert Rubin, to Harvard's governing corporation; the running-off of legendary Harvard endowment manager Jack Meyer and much of his senior staff, and his short-lived replacement by Mohamed

El-Erian; and some costly endowment bets made on Summers' watch. Summers probably feels he could have handled the downturn if he had been permitted to stay. But a substantial reinterpretation of the overall story is underway.

Exhibit C is Summers' role in overseeing the Clinton-era deregulation of the banking industry. He was secretary when the Glass-Steagall Act separating banking from commerce was repealed by a Republican Congress in 2000, and his 1998 dressing-down of Commodity Futures Trading Commission chairman Brooksley Born when she sought regulatory authority over derivatives trading has become a focal point in reconstructions of the period. Nor is it clear what Summers did or how much he earned as a part-time managing director of a leading hedge fund/venture capital firm, D. E. Shaw, after leaving the Harvard presidency.

Which, at least in the conventional wisdom of Washington, is why Obama chose to nominate the younger and less-experienced Geithner to the post of treasury secretary – he feared Summers' nomination could bring about a lengthy confirmation hearing. (He also is said to have simply liked the younger man, whose youth and background overseas are similar to his own; in fact, Geithner's father apparently oversaw the Ford Foundation program that took Obama's mother and her young son to Indonesia.)

Then Geithner himself ran into confirmation problems – those $40,000 in underpaid taxes in the years when he was moving from Washington to New York – and barely squeaked through on a 60-34 vote. His first tentative plans to restore banking stability underwhelmed markets; his role in the initial AIG bailout (when he was president of the Federal Reserve Bank of New York) came under fire; Democrats criticized his communication skills; and last week he was caught in a wicked crossfire over those bonuses. Both the president and Senator John McCain went out of their way to defend him. That set the stage for this week, when Geithner will unveil a more detailed version of a $1 trillion plan to cleanse bank balance sheets of their questionable assets. It may work, but there is blood in the water. He will not survive another prolonged bout of market despair.

After the election, Summers made no secret of preferring an appointment as treasury secretary. When that didn't materialize, he bruited it about that he would be available to replace Ben Bernanke at the Federal Reserve Bank when his term as chairman expires in January. The job as chair of the National Economic Council made sense not just because he briefed the president every day, but because it was from that position that Summers' mentor, former Goldman Sachs co-chair Robert Rubin, ascended to the Treasury under Bill Clinton.

No doubt that Summers possesses the skills to be a highly effective finance chief, beginning with the fact that he grew up as an economist in an intensely competitive arena, the quasi-official non-governmental policy institute that is the National Bureau of Economic Research (NBER). Since moving to Cambridge, Massachusetts, from Manhattan, in 1973 – and especially after Harvard professor Martin Feldstein (Summers' thesis adviser) became its president in 1978 – the NBER has become policy economists' West Point, a highly selective academy in which future leaders of the profession from all over the world meet, match wits, and learn to assess each other's strengths and weaknesses.

Indeed, much of the aura of unquestioned deference that Summers enjoys among his policy-circle peers derives from having successfully persuaded others of his credentials as an alpha male in innumerable late-night bull sessions in the early 1980s in the NBER offices, located midway between Harvard and the Massachusetts Institute of Technology. He has been remarkably good at forging alliances as well. Since entering the political world full time in 1990, as chief economist for the World Bank, he has honed a second array of skills, including a deliberate manner of speech that conveys gravitas, disarming humor, a comfortable girth, and a baleful glare.

Geithner, on the other hand, has no such base among an academic discipline. Nor do his boyish face, runner's frame, or matter-of-fact delivery convey authority through a microphone (he has plenty of power in a conference room). A Dartmouth College graduate with a degree in international studies from Johns Hopkins University, he has made his career in civil service, as a regulator rather than an economist. One of his principle recommendations all along, from Rubin and others, has been that he is one of the few persons in Treasury circles to have been able to say "no" to Larry – precisely because he is not a member of the guild. If Geithner goes, it is crucial to find him a position of relative independence, in the likelihood that future government service will be required. (Each time Paul

Volcker left government service, he sheltered at the then-thoroughly-respectable Chase Manhattan Bank.)

Would the country be better off in the current emergency if Summers were somehow or other "unleashed"? Would the Senate go for it? As a long-time enthusiast of Summers, I have to say: it beats me. (I wince when I remember the newspaper column I wrote touting his candidacy for the Harvard job: "By temperament and training, he is uniquely suited to this momentous task.")

Certainly he is a man who knows the plays and wants the ball. And I'm pretty certain that Noam Scheiber is dead right about one thing: an ensemble cast of economic advisers simply won't work in the current circumstances. Tim Geithner? Larry Summers? My bet is that one or the other will be gone by the first of June. [March 15, 2018: Summers remained in the White House for another 21 months.]

CHAPTER TWENTY-FIVE

# The Asterisk

*February 27, 2011*

I'm always interested to see a new book on the transition of the Russian economy from central planning to the oil-based, *siloviki*-dominated oligarchy of today. *No Precedent, No Plan*, by Martin Gilman, stakes a claim to being the definitive word on some of those events. The impact of the crash of August 1998 needs to be appreciated in order to understand contemporary Russia, he says. The English edition is a slimmed-down version of a longer Russian book.

Gilman should know. He was named a senior member of the International Monetary Fund's (IMF) Russia team in 1993, just after the Clinton administration took office. He moved to Moscow in November 1996 and remained until 2002. Along the way he married a prominent Russian political columnist, Tatiana Malkina, gaining thereby unusual access to the Russian government at its highest levels, and, as well, "a special insight into the way that Russians really see their world."

Today he is a professor at Russia's new State University Higher School of Economics in Moscow. And it is from this vantage point that Gilman seeks to set straight various "dangerous stereotypes" and to put to rest a lingering "suspicion of corruption that accompanied the discussion of Russian financial matters" in the second half of the 1990s.

*No Precedent, No Plan* ascribes the various scandals of 1999 to fabrications designed to discredit opponents, a familiar enough tactic in Russian political campaigns, and expresses indignation about an especially prominent story, a series of allegations in *The New York Times* concerning money laundering by the Bank of New York. "The remarkable media feeding frenzy probably deserves a serious study in its own right," he says, "including what in my view was unwarranted self-righteousness on the part of much of the foreign press."

So it is strange that *No Precedent, No Plan* contains no mention of the well-documented [Harvard mission to] Moscow scandal [in 1997] that set the scene for various perceptions of U.S. intentions that followed the IMF-supervised restructuring of Russia's external debt in August 1998…. [It is all the more so since] when [Lawrence] Summers returned to Washington in 2009 as chief economic adviser to President Barack Obama, Shleifer's wife, hedge fund operator Nancy Zimmerman, was noted by the *Times* to be among his inner circle of informal advisers, along with Laurence Fink, chief executive of BlackRock, the large money management firm, and H. Rodgin Cohen, chairman of the Sullivan and Cromwell law firm, and several others.

Yet not even Shleifer's name makes the cut in *No Precedent, No Plan* when Gilman writes, "The World Bank staff members and those of other international agencies, some western think tanks and academic advisers such as [Anders] Aslund, [Richard] Layard and [Jeffrey] Sachs, and the G-7 financial attaches based in Moscow also had privileged access, but none were able to have such a comprehensive overview of the macroeconomic situation on a continuing basis as [had] the IMF."

So when Gilman last week spoke at Harvard's Russian Research Center about his book, I stopped by to hear him. Towards the end of his talk, I asked about the Harvard project, and he gave what seemed to me a genuinely forthcoming answer.

> I'm going to say something very politically incorrect. I think it was a tempest in a teapot, a teacup. I thought the whole thing was overblown and exploited. I'm not saying that there weren't elements of poor judgment involved. I think that in terms of foreign technical assistance

> to the Russians, I think they actually made a valuable contribution, compared to some other institutions that were involved there. I think it was a sad outcome, sloppy, as I say, poor judgment, but I just don't think it should have been exaggerated the way it was. There were a lot of enemies out there.... I don't really know enough about the details and I don't like to get involved in that kind of stuff.

The collapse of the Harvard mission, amid widespread publicity in Russia, caused no discomfiture to the IMF?

> No. No. Because if every time there was some impropriety, or accusation – we're not judges – if every time there was an impropriety, we could have never done anything. You raise a good point, because later, we were not able to overlook improprieties, not in 1997 or '98, but when scandals that I mention [in the book] started… then minor charges of these kinds… the IMF could [no longer] ignore.

But, in fact, I noted, the Harvard charges were not minor. They had been brought, not by Russian disinformation specialists, but by American whistle-blowers. Harvard's Institute for International Development itself had fired its team leaders, and the US Agency for International Development in turn had fired HIID, for inadequate supervision. The case had been investigated extensively and tried in US District Court in Boston. Harvard and Shleifer's defense had been curtly rejected by both a judge and a jury. Both were found to have committed fraud. The dismal end of "the so-called Harvard Boys," as Gilman described them in passing in his book, was, in other words, a *proven* case. So why wasn't the episode worth mentioning in the book?

In conversation after the talk, Gilman at first thought he must have included it. Then, he speculated, perhaps it had been left on the cutting-room floor when the longer Russian version was translated into English. But when he returned to Moscow, it turned out the original didn't include a reference either. In an e-mail, he wrote:

> I would still maintain that at least from what I know of the scandal, in the scheme of things, it seems marginal to what was happening in Russia. I stress "in the scheme of things" because there were so many purported improprieties that this rather Americo-centric one just

> did not rise much above the radar. Maybe it should have had more visibility and perhaps there is something fundamental that I'm missing, but in the big, chaotic mess that was Russia in the 1990s, I just don't get it. All the other "scandals" that I discuss in my book concerned accusations that Russians broke Russian laws. In this case, where the perpetrators were Americans who were accused of breaking US laws, few eyebrows were raised in Moscow where the Russian authorities and the IMF, quite frankly, had more immediate concerns. Perhaps it reflects my Moscow perspective at the time, but I thought that the accusations were exaggerated and mainly just another stick used to beat on Chubais' reputation.

Even granting that IMF had big macroeconomic worries in Russia, that seems obtuse. A kid who grew up in Russia, returns to Moscow as a 30-year-old Harvard professor ast the head of a US mission, with big plans to privatize the place. He, his wife and his deputy get caught with their hands in the till. The most prominent economic collaboration between the two superpowers collapses. But in America, the Kissinger-like figure appears to be shielded from the ill consequences of his acts by his good friend, the soon-to-be treasury secretary. Harvard defends him to the hilt.

Is it really plausible that Russians, from Yeltsin and Putin to everyday newspaper readers, didn't pick up on that as a clear signal of US intentions? Professor Timothy Colton, of Harvard University, didn't mention the episode either, in *Yeltsin, A Life*. "I didn't think to include it," replied Colton, when I asked him about it last year. "It would not have reached the level of Yeltsin."

Alas, *No Precedent, No Plan* is another book about Russia in the '90s to enter the world with an asterisk firmly affixed – the typographical device that in sports history indicates a record tainted by circumstances. It could be, I suppose, that Gilman has accurately reflected what a broad swathe of Russian public opinion thinks about US-led interventions in those years, but I doubt it. Certainly he doesn't know much about the deeper currents of American opinion.

… Yes, it was in a foreign country, and, [yes], the wench is dead. But the subtle suborning of the scholarship of the community of students of the American involvement in the Russian transition, and of the journalists who cover them, by the little foursome that was chosen to represent the government of the United States to the government and the citizens of Russia, was, to my mind, a more serious matter than any single thing that has yet surfaced on Wall Street. Martin Gilman deserves his asterisk – and so do all the [others], including, especially, Harvard University.

CHAPTER TWENTY-SIX

# Larry Swings for the Fences Again

*July 28, 2013*

For the sixth time in five years, Lawrence Summers has mounted a campaign for a top job in Washington. He has won one of these and lost four so far. He's not likely to get this one, either. But even if he fails, the 58-year-old Harvard professor won't be going away.

Summers and his mentor, former treasury secretary Robert Rubin, joined the Obama campaign in September 2008, three days after Lehman Brothers declared bankruptcy, just as the financial crisis entered its most serious phase (*EP*: A Fan's Notes).

After the election, Summers hoped to be named treasury secretary, a job he had held for the final 18 months of the Clinton administration. Instead, Timothy Geithner, his former subordinate, got the nod. Summers became director of the National Economic Council, with an office in the West Wing of the White House – a job that required no Senate confirmation (*EP*: More Rivals).

Eighteen months later, Summers unsuccessfully sought to jostle Geithner out (*EP*: Is Physiognomy Destiny?). When that didn't work, he campaigned in 2010 to replace Ben Bernanke at the Fed (*EP*: Is Summers Headed Home?).

Bernanke was reappointed and Summers returned to Harvard and to a variety of consulting engagements, including the advisory board of a competing online for-profit university.

In early 2012, he actively campaigned in Davos to be appointed president of the World Bank. President Obama chose Dartmouth University president Jim Yong Kim instead (*EP*: One Thing Obama Could Have Done Differently).

This time Summers is trying to shoulder aside Vice Chair Janet Yellen to become chairman of the Federal Reserve Board when Bernanke's second four-year term as chief ends in January. Summers seems unlikely to get the nod. Damian Paletta and Jon Hilsenrath, of *The Wall Street Journal*, surfaced previously undisclosed consulting ties to Citigroup Inc. and the Nasdaq stock exchange.

Summers is qualified for the Fed job mainly by ambition. He's a macroeconomist, with little background in monetary policy. He possesses few of the consensus-building skills the job requires. And while he has proved to be an excellent leader in harness with others, as when assembling the framework in 1992 that became Rubinomics, or serving as the Clinton administration's ramrod in various international financial crises in the 1990s, he has displayed a remarkable lack of judgment when in charge himself.

He was forced out as president of Harvard University after running off the university's star endowment manager and replacing the well-loved dean of the college, both with many ill effects; alienating a substantial swathe of faculty; and digging himself in deeper with Harvard's Russia scandal, a matter which would presumably receive renewed scrutiny if his nomination came before the Senate (*EP*: The Asterisk).

Summers' gifts include an agile mind, a passion for debate, a lust for power, a knack for friendship, and, of course, by now, a wealth of experience. (He entered politics in 1988 as an adviser to Michael S. Dukakis's presidential campaign.) He is able to remain in competitive play thanks equally to the backing of his one-time boss, Robert Rubin (formerly of Goldman Sachs and, more recently, Citigroup), as well as to a legion of his own former staffers still working in the White House and elsewhere. The current round of speculation commenced, for example, with an enthusiastic endorsement by Edward Luce, Summers' former Treasury Department speechwriter, now the Washington Bureau chief of the *Financial Times*. Every policymaker hopes for favorable coverage from friendly journalists, but Larry's admirers sometimes overdo it (*EP*: A Rice Bowl Should Not Be Carelessly Threatened).

You can't blame Summers for trying. Yellen, 67, a former chairman of the Council of Economic Advisers, has plenty of experience of Fed team play (three years as governor, then president of the Federal Reserve Bank of San Francisco, 2004-2011, before Obama re-appointed her governor and vice chair). She is a highly regarded macroeconomist and has a bevy of friends in Congress and is married to Nobel laureate George Akerlof, but seems to lack enthusiastic backing, at least for the top job, among monetary economists, who include students of financial markets and of the central bank. Thus Summers might win and can't lose for being so furiously mentioned.

If neither Summers nor Yellen is chosen, who might serve? Before the financial crisis Rubin might well have been chosen – certainly economic policy was successful under his management during the Clinton years. Today the best candidate, bar none, is Stanley Fischer, 69, formerly of the Massachusetts Institute of Technology (where he was Bernanke's teacher), a US citizen who enjoyed great success for eight years as governor of the Bank of Israel, now living in Manhattan and looking for a job (*EP*: The Head of the Table).

There is the usual list of dark horses, as well, which presumably includes Kevin Warsh (no relation!), 43, who went through the crisis with Bernanke, and Roger Ferguson Jr., 61, Fed vice chair from 1999 to 2006, now chief executive of the enormous TIAA-CREF retirement fund. It is always possible that in an emergency, Bernanke could be persuaded to stay on but he has made it clear that he has no wish to do so (*EP*: Bush's Best Pick).

CHAPTER TWENTY-SEVEN

# Summers: A (Mildly) Exculpatory Note

*August 25, 2013*

Larry Summers is leaning in – he badly wants that job as chairman of the Fed. Many find his candidacy hard to fathom. To understand Summers' motivation, it helps to know something about the career of E. Gerald Corrigan. Just as Corrigan, now 72, was the greatest US crisis manager of his generation, so Summers, 58, was the greatest crisis manager of his own – that is, until Ben Bernanke came along. No wonder then that Summers wants a second chance. Arrogant and ambitious he may be. But as a veteran player, he knows the game.

To this point, very little attention has been paid to what is required of a central banker. Gillian Tett, of the *Financial Times*, citing Binghamton University anthropologist Douglas Holmes, thinks they need to be storytellers. But that's more her job and mine, and, before us, that of the community of economists on whom all journalists depend. Central bankers really have just two jobs: the conduct of monetary policy and crisis management.

Monetary policy – the management of money, credit and interest rates – is a collegial, cerebral business. Managers of the US Federal Reserve System mostly think about whether the economy is overheating or not, or assuming a distended shape and, if so, what can be done about it, chiefly by manipulating the banking system via the market for the US Treasury debt, but sometimes, as in the present case, by entering broader financial markets, [a practice they call] "quantitative easing."

Crisis management is something else again. Here are Milton Friedman and Anna Schwartz on the topic, from *A Monetary History of the United States: 1867-1960*:

> The detailed history of every banking crisis in our history shows how much depends on the presence of one or more outstanding individuals willing to assume responsibility and leadership.... Economic collapse often has the characteristics of a cumulative process. Let it go beyond a certain point, and it will tend for a time to gain strength from its own development. Because no great strength would be required to hold back the rock that starts a landslide, it does not follow that the landslide will not be of major proportions.

(There are those who think banking is like any other industry, and that if some simple measure were adopted, crises would disappear. This is wishful thinking. The latest example is *The Bankers' New Clothes: What's Wrong with Banking and What to Do about It*, by Anat Admati, of Stanford's Graduate School of Business, and Martin Hellwig, of the Max Planck Institute for Research on Collective Goods.) It's not that banking regulation doesn't need to be carefully thought out; rather, it's that bank-like innovators can be expected to devise ways to wire around it. In *Shadowy Banking*, Edward Kane, of Boston College describes the latest maneuvering. "Shadowy banking is the inevitable *yin* to regulation's *yang*...," he writes. "Financial crises are a fact of life."

The inevitability of crises puts a premium on experience. Bernanke and Alan Greenspan showed that there are other ways to lead the Fed. But the path that Summers traveled, like that of Gerry Corrigan, is a more traditional one, namely by working for a time as understudy to a master craftsman.

Corrigan, a career Federal Reserve employee, apprenticed to Paul Volcker. The two met in 1975 when Volcker was president of the Federal Reserve Bank of New York and Corrigan a vice president. After Volcker became Fed chairman, in 1979, Corrigan served briefly as his special assistant, overseeing the aftermath of the Hunt brothers' [unsuccessful 1980 attempt to corner the market for silver], before becoming president of the Federal Reserve Bank of Minneapolis. From there he oversaw the rescue of Drysdale Securities and Lombard-Wall, Inc.in 1982, and Continental Illinois National Bank and Trust, the nation's seventh largest bank, in 1984, before returning to head the New York Fed in 1985. He staunched potential panic in October 1987, when the Dow Jones Industrial Average lost nearly 23 percent in a single day.

Summers, a Harvard University economist, [also apprenticed] as an assistant [a bold leader] to former Goldman Sachs co-chair Robert Rubin, devising details of the budget agreement of 1993 in the days before the Clinton administration took office. [Summers] then signed on as undersecretary for international economic affairs in Secretary Lloyd Bentsen's Treasury Department. [He] advanced to deputy secretary when National Economic Council director Rubin replaced Bentsen. [Thereafter, Summers] was deeply involved in the serial financial crises of the 1990s: Mexico in 1994, the Asia economies in 1997, and Russia, in 1998. Between 1998 and 2001, he, Rubin and Alan Greenspan presided over the climactic phase of the vast deregulation of the US financial industry that had begun 25 years before, under Richard Nixon. When Summers returned to Washington in 2009 as director of the National Economic Council for President Obama, he played a key role in the decision to keep the US auto industry afloat.

Both men are the product of strong value systems: Corrigan in the Jesuit traditions of Fordham University, where he was an undergraduate and earned his PhD; Summers in the commitment to open give-and-take of big-league technical economics. Both men have become supremely well connected over the years. And both understood from the start of their careers that force of will, and even physical mien, have much to do with successful crisis management. Thus each learned to wear the command manner as if it were a power suit. Corrigan, lumberjack large, shaggy, gravel-voiced, physically intimidating; Summers intellectually nimble, scowling, speaking hyper-deliberately, as if he were delivering blank verse. In each case the manner is calculated to elicit obedience. These are men who repeatedly have been in battle and who each time have held the line.

(There is no tradition of heroic fiction set in the world of central banking as there is of, say, naval leadership. Even so, financial crises have their fans. The late Charles P. Kindleberger made something of a hobby of them, at one point compiling an annotated 50-book list of *Retirement Reading for Bankers*; at another, boiling it all down in his classic *Manias, Panics, and Crashes: A History of Financial Crises*. And David Landes, of Harvard University, who died earlier this month, at 89, in *Bankers and Pashas: International Finance and Economic Imperialism in Egypt*, made something of a thriller out of the story of the building of the Suez Canal.)

There are some important differences between the men as well.

Corrigan was a favorite to succeed Alan Greenspan in 1995 when, in January 1993, he unexpectedly [and without explanation] resigned from the New York Fed. A year later, he joined Goldman, Sachs. What happened? Signs now point to a personal crisis of sorts. Several bad habits, chain-smoking among them, he put behind him. A few years later, he married the woman who had been first vice president of the New York Fed, Cathy Minehan, by then president of the Federal Reserve Bank of Boston. The prior marriages of both had dissolved. Corrigan told *The New York Times* that the romance began in 1995. Minehan served until 2007. Today she is dean of the School of Management of Simmons College.

Summers, whose meteoric rise commenced just as Corrigan's ended, also separated, and later divorced, as he was leaving Washington, D.C., for the presidency of Harvard University in 2001. Several years later, he, too, remarried to good effect. But where Corrigan enjoyed 20 years of quiet life since leaving government, Summers walked into a buzz saw. A series of missteps led to his being forced out of office after five years by Harvard's governing corporation. None was more costly than his handling of Harvard's Russia scandal, in which Summers' close friend and collaborator Andrei Shleifer was found to have attempted to muscle into the mutual fund business for himself while advising his Russian enablers on behalf of the US State Department.

The closer you look at Summers's not-so-tacit approval of the affair, the more appalling it becomes. That fact that no one in economics has mounted a defense of Shleifer's and Summers' conduct – not Andrei, not Larry, not any of their numerous seconds – should tell you all you need to know: their actions were indefensible. All the more alarming has been Summers' ability to suppress criticism. Taken altogether, my hunch is that the story is more than enough to put the kibosh on his appointment. He can make money, give advice, mentor students, but no more running for high office.

So who should be chair? If the otherwise highly regarded Fed vice chair Janet Yellen is considered by insiders to lack this rally-to-me taste for crisis action, it should come as no surprise. It is not the part of the job for which she has prepared. Yellen has a splendid record as a forecaster, analyst, and colleague, both as president of the San Francisco Fed and of the seven governors of the system. But that constellation of gifts for monetary policy is almost the opposite of the visceral instinct required to take charge when circumstances suddenly darken. Among her colleagues, Eric Rosengren of the Boston bank, James Bullard of the St. Louis Fed, and governor Jeremy Stein, are better suited to the master-and-commander role. It is time for President Obama to end his indecision.

CHAPTER TWENTY-EIGHT

# Toward a Climax

*September 15, 2013*

Gene Sperling, 55, President Obama's top economic counselor, will be leaving his job as director of the National Economic Council at the end of the year, the White House announced last Friday. Named to replace him was Jeffrey Zients, 46, who until April served as acting director of the Office of Management and Budget.

Did Sperling jump, or was he pushed? We can leave the question to the well-sourced Ezra Klein, of *The Washington Post*. A Yale Law School graduate, Sperling entered national politics in 1993 as deputy to National Economic Council director Robert Rubin. He met his wife, Allison Abner, while she was writing episodes for the TV series *The West Wing*. They have a five-year-old daughter and a bi-coastal marriage, according to Wikipedia. To my mind that's more than enough reason for Sperling to want to quit his high-pressure job after three years (and two before that at the Treasury Department).

But it is also the case that, as NEC director, Sperling orchestrated the highly public run-off between Lawrence Summers, his long-time mentor, and Federal Reserve Board vice chair Janet Yellen, over the nomination to the head the Fed. With the appointment of Zients, Obama gets a neutral manager and a source of disinterested advice. A graduate of Duke University, who rose rapidly through the ranks of Mercer Management Consulting, Bain & Company, and David W. Bradley's highly successful Washington consulting firms, Zients has no ties to Summers.

The competition to succeed Fed chairman Ben Bernanke when his term expires in January has become a major headache to the White House. Zients, who left his White House post as acting budget director only in April, may already have begun to reframe the choice. *The Wall Street Journal* reported Saturday that mounting opposition among Senate Democrats signifies that Summers' prospects have dimmed.

Meanwhile, Alan Blinder, of Princeton University, a former vice chairman of the Fed himself, circulated a letter signed by some 300 economists urging the president to nominate Yellen. Her candidacy is widely viewed by students of the Fed as a more reasonable proposition than that of Summers. She may not be a force of nature, like Paul Volcker; a magician, like Alan Greenspan; or a student of history, like Bernanke. Or so the argument goes. But she is a superior intellect who has met every challenge she has faced in order to rise to the top of the profession, in an era when opportunity customarily was denied to women.

If there's a criticism of Yellen, other than looking like a kindly grandmother, it has to do with her identity as a product of the somewhat amorphous "Yale school" of macroeconomics. (See David Colander's interviews in *Inside the Economist's Mind* for background.) A proud tradition associated with influential figures of the 1960s such as Arthur Okun, Henry Wallich and James Tobin (the Nobel laureate whose student and collaborator Yellen was), Yale macro today also includes Robert Shiller, William Nordhaus, Ray Fair and William Brainard. (CORRECTION: Lael Brainard, currently treasury undersecretary for international affairs, mentioned recently as a possible Fed governor, is not Brainard's daughter, as earlier asserted here. They are not related.)

The problem with present-day Yale dogma is thought to be, at least by many financial macroeconomists, that having defined itself long ago in contradistinction to Irving Fisher – the legendary Yale economist who went broke in the Great Depression – [Yale macroeconomists] may have [overlooked] or misunderstood key aspects of the recent crisis. (Robert Dimand's presidential address to the History of Economics Society last summer dealt with some of these issues.) In other words, there is plenty of discussion among experts about how to lead the Fed forward, based on what we know now. Both Yellen and Summers have their partisans; so do others who loom just out of the spotlight. Former Fed vice chairman Donald Kohn has been mentioned by the president himself.

In the background is Jon Hilsenrath, chief economics correspondent for *The Wall Street Journal*. Last week he was in Durham, North Carolina, leafing through the trove of letters the late Paul Samuelson deposited in the Duke University library. In "A Close Bond and a Shared Love for 'Dismal Science'", in the *WSJ* Saturday, Hilsenrath ranged widely over Summers' relationship with his two famous uncles, Samuelson and Kenneth Arrow, both Nobel laureates. At one point he described a letter from Samuelson to his former colleague Stanley Fischer. Hilsenrath wrote:

> Mr. Samuelson expressed mixed feelings about the relationship between Mr. Summers and Robert Rubin, a former US treasury secretary who would become a Summers mentor in the Clinton administration.
>
> "Rubin taught Larry some tact – but nobody could keep his shirt tails firmly tucked in," Mr. Samuelson said of his famously argumentative, sloppily dressed nephew....
>
> But Mr. Samuelson believed Mr. Rubin, who was a member of Harvard's governing board, had failed to properly advise Mr. Summers when he was Harvard president. In particular, his uncle was upset about the handling of economics professor Andrei Shleifer, one of the issues that contributed to faculty unhappiness with Mr. Summers....
>
> "Rubin should have compelled Larry to stay out of the Andrei Shleifer Moscow business," Mr. Samuelson confided to Mr. Fischer.
>
> Mr. Summers and Mr. Shleifer didn't comment on the Samuelson letter.

As a journalist, part of my job has been to keep alive the memory of Summers' role in Harvard University's Russia scandal. In that strange affair, Shleifer and his wife were caught trying to go into the Russian mutual fund business for themselves in 1996, while leading a Harvard team advising the Russian government on market design on behalf of the US Agency for International Development. Summers, their close friend, was deputy secretary of the Treasury at the time and, soon thereafter, secretary. Harvard defended Shleifer to the hilt, both before and after Summers returned to the university as president. (At a certain point, Summers recused himself from the matter.) In 2004 a federal judge ruled that both Harvard and Shleifer had breached their contract to provide disinterested advice. He ordered the university to return its fees.

By now, even the most casual reader of newspapers will have noticed that Harvard's Russia scandal doesn't come up in most discussions of Summers's fitness to lead the Fed. Only the *WSJ*, which originally reported the story, has kept up with it. *The New York Times* and *The Washington Post* didn't cover the fracas, so they have no fistful of clips from which to reason now. *The Financial Times*, which hired Summers as a columnist after he was forced out of Harvard, has likewise given the story a good leaving-alone. So have the authors of many books on the privatization of the economy of the former Soviet Union during the 1990s, none more conspicuously than Strobe Talbott, onetime *Time* magazine Moscow correspondent, in *The Russia Hand: A Memoir of Presidential Diplomacy*, his account of his years as deputy secretary of state from 1994 to 2001. Today Talbott is president of the Brookings Institution. It's this very invisibility that, to my mind, is the best argument against letting Larry Summers anywhere near the Fed.

CHAPTER TWENTY-NINE

# The End of the Saga

*September 22, 2013*

A few last words about Lawrence Summers and the Federal Reserve Board:

Although the White House was already moving to reframe the choice, it may have been a magazine story that precipitated the end of Summers' candidacy. Felix Salmon, the finance blogger at *Reuters*, wrote:

> Michael Hirsh's anti-Summers *National Journal* cover story landed on the desks of everybody who matters in Washington at the end of the week, and it had its intended effect: no matter how much the White House wanted Summers to get the job, those pesky Constitutional checks and balances would conspire to ensure that it would never be his.

Hirsh's aptly-titled "The Comprehensive Case against Larry Summers" touched all the bases, including the Harvard Russia scandal. ("Of course he's brilliant. But he also displays all the attributes – arrogance, bullying, stubbornness – that you don't want at the head of the Fed.")

By the end of the day, Senator Jeff Merkley (D-Oregon) phoned the White House to say that as many as five Democrats were prepared to vote against

Summers on the 22-member Senate Banking Committee, according to Annie Lowrey of *The New York Times*. Last Sunday the candidate withdrew from consideration.

The episode is damaging to Obama's presidency. It is too soon to judge how much harm has been done. Now that Congress has been told to expect Janet Yellen to be the nominee, the debate can turn back to more important matters.

Summers will remain at Harvard, and his opinion will continue to be sought, like that of his mentor, Martin S. Feldstein, another one time aspirant to the Fed's top job.

LOOKING BACK

CHAPTER THIRTY

# Meet John Keffer

1.

In April 2011, three months after Larry Summers left the White House, I drove up to Bretton Woods, New Hampshire, to hear him talk about the recent financial crisis. The Harvard-Russia story seemed to be over. I was putting away my files. There was, however, one loose end that I wanted to tie up – a second complaint against Harvard, Hay, and Shleifer, filed just 30 days after the government's case, by a little-known Maine mutual fund administrator.

Forum Financial hadn't been mentioned in the government lawsuit. It wasn't clear what the firm had been doing in Russia in the first place, competing among internationally known firms such as Credit Suisse First Boston, Pioneer, and Franklin Templeton. Whatever Forum's complaint had been about, the matter was quietly settled by the defendants in 2002, 18 months before the first verdict was reached in the government's case, and reported in a few paragraphs in the local papers. On the way home, I drove to Portland, Maine, and stopped at the courthouse to examine the records of Forum Financial v. the President and Fellows of Harvard, Jonathan Hay, and Andrei Shleifer.

From the docket, I discovered that the case had been settled on the eve of trial, presumably on Harvard's, Shleifer's, and Hay's initiative, just before jury selection was to begin. But the terms of the agreement had been sealed. Some of the depositions taken and the documents discovered had been purged. Even the paper filings that remained public had been shipped to Denver for storage. I called the president of the company, John Keffer. I had talked with him before, in the course of seeking to understand the government's suit. Always I was pressed for time; each time the conversation reached a dead end.

This time I went around to Keffer's office for lunch. It became obvious that there was much he couldn't talk about; he had signed a non-disclosure agreement. Keffer told me, "I made sure there was enough in the public record that anyone who was interested could see what happened." After lunch, I went through a large box of publicly available documents from his storage room. By the end of the afternoon, I understood that Keffer was someone I wanted to get to know.

The significance of the Harvard Russia scandal had been hard to explain to readers over the course of a decade because it was an apparently victimless crime. Harvard had broken its promise to deliver disinterested advice. Besides the reputations of USAID, the United States, and, of course, Harvard, had anyone been hurt? Whistle-blowers had caught the leaders of the Harvard team lining their pockets. But that was the 1990s. Didn't everyone want to get rich? The Russians in charge had expected as much of their counterparts. Harvard president and former treasury secretary Summers said as much in his testimony.

From the documents I learned that Keffer had been an outright victim of the leaders of the Harvard team. He had been invited to Russia by Dimitry Vasiliev on the advice of Jonathan Hay and Elizabeth Hebert, Hay's girlfriend, to open a Russian government-endorsed-and-supported, back-office record-keeping facility (a "depository") for a mutual fund that Hebert hoped to start. Hay and Hebert, abetted by Shleifer and his wife, had then sought to inveigle him out of the Russian firm he had started. All of this had been well established in the government's case, but in a manner incidental to its complaint. Separately, Keffer had sued Harvard for permitting its employees to pursue their plot, and Shleifer and Hay as well. Apparently he had won.

But what had he received? Keffer couldn't say; he was prevented from discussing details of the case that were not already in the public record. As a result, the underlying nature of what happened with the Harvard Russia Project had been widely misunderstood. I went home and beefed up my deposit with the online system of federal court records. Over the next five years, I periodically revisited the matter. Keffer and his company turned out to have been at the center of the Harvard-Russia story.

2.

Born in Washington Crossing, New Jersey, in 1942, Keffer would have been unlikely to find himself in Moscow in 1996, except for one thing – his father had been persuaded of the value of higher education. Paul Keffer had been taken out of school midway through eighth grade, in 1924, to go to work. He turned out to have a knack for it: a few years later, he was part-owner of a Lambertville, New Jersey, hosiery mill. When the mill wiped out its shareholders during the Great Depression, the young man retooled as a part-time salesman for its products. This much, in the family telling of it, was typical Pennsylvania Dutch: entrepreneurial, hard-working, persistent. What was new, by virtue of experience, was dedication to higher education.

The elder Keffer had two sons, David (b. 1938) and John (b. 1942). He played bridge every week at the local YMCA – in Princeton, 10 miles away. There he learned about the Hun School, a small private high school offering 50 percent scholarships to highly motivated and athletic day students. A Princeton University mathematician, John Gale Hun, had founded it, in 1914, to prepare prospective college students (athletes in particular) in math. He acquired a small campus on the edge of town in 1925. By the 1950s, the Hun School was a well regarded little boarding school able to top off its enrollment with day students, all of them expected to play three sports. David Keffer enrolled in 1953; his brother John followed in 1956.

Four years later, Keffer went off to Amherst College, having graduated salutatorian of his Hun School class; his best friend and constant competitor, valedictorian Paul Steiger, attended Yale. Keffer thrived for a time in the western Massachusetts institution, then dropped out his junior year and moved with his motorcycle to San Francisco in search of adventure. He worked, took courses at San Francisco State and UC Berkeley, returned to Amherst 18 months later, graduated in 1966, married, honeymooned on his motorcycle in Europe for the summer, worked a year with Chubb in New York City, and then joined the Peace Corps.

Keffer spent most of the next three years in a small town in the mountains of central Panama. Local subsistence farmers in Coclé Province fed themselves, but seldom earned more than $100 a year, growing oranges, grapefruit, pineapples, and rice. With the support of the minister of agriculture, Keffer commandeered a truck, organized a marketing cooperative to deliver produce to towns around the province, and partnered with a canning factory owned by Swiss transnational Nestlé to build a demonstration and training farm – then saw it all come apart when he was not replaced for several years after he left. This was not an uncommon outcome in those early Peace Corps days, he says.

Back home in 1969, Keffer enrolled in the management school of Carnegie Institute of Technology, today Carnegie Mellon University (CMU). The Graduate School of Industrial Administration (GSIA) was, at the time, an outlier then among American business schools, emphasizing various know-how that had emerged from World War II, including operations research, financial economics, and computer science. Eventually CMU faculty, past and present, would be recognized with half a dozen Nobel Prizes; Keffer took courses from both Robert Lucas and Herbert Simon, thrived among its international student body, and graduated with distinction. He joined Citibank, then just beginning to develop yet more expansive global ambitions. Walter Wriston had taken over as chief executive in 1967, emphasizing computers and automation as a key to profitability.

Keffer spent the next 10 years mastering the new technologies, learning to navigate the shifting boundaries of the firm: controller in the bank's real estate division, manager in its dividend re-investment group, head planner for its leasing subsidiary, then head of financial reporting for the Manhattan consumer bank. In 1976 he transferred to Detroit on an especially tricky mission: CFO of the second-largest mortgage-lending firm in the United States, newly acquired by Citi. It was his introduction to the growing permeability of the 40-year-old Glass Steagall Act, designed to keep banking separate from commerce.

In 1980, Keffer left Citibank for the money management company Reich and Tang, sponsor of what had become the nation's fourth-largest money market mutual fund. Money funds were a recent innovation: they enabled banks to offer higher interest rates than those permitted under Glass-Steagall regulatory ceilings. Keffer found a further loophole in the law: if banks could offer money market mutual funds to their Trust Department customers, why not to all customers who simply requested a "sweep account," never mind that its assets were short-term debt. Keffer was hired to find a way. He did, and so did many others. Before long, trust and bond departments of major banks all over the country were merging and re-opening with "capital markets" painted on their doors.

Successful mutual funds require that accurate records be kept of both the assets owned by the fund (the depository function) and how claims on shares of the fund itself are distributed among its legitimate shareholders (the transfer agency function). Keffer had become something of an expert on systems of back-office record-keeping and custodial arrangements before moving to Reich and Tang. In 1985, with R&T's blessing, he hived off to open a business of his own. His Forum Financial would do money fund record-keeping, first for Citibank, and then would offer other banks the same. In 1987, he moved the business to Portland, Maine. As his father had, he traveled relentlessly for work. Within a few years, he had become the largest privately owned provider of back-office services to money market funds in the country. He competed with giants such as State Street Bank, DST Systems and Bank of New York.

It was a small corner of a very large, complex, and rapidly changing industry. Financial deregulation, first proposed in the Nixon administration, had gone forward under President Gerald Ford. By the '80s, the consequences of "Mayday," as the first, seemingly inconsequential deregulatory step in 1975 was known to denizens of Wall Street, were ramifying all around the world. Investment banks, having been forced to compete with one another, soon moved into banking, underwriting high-yield, or "junk," bonds. Commercial bankers pushed back, inventing the newfangled technology known as securitization. China entered world markets. In Britain, firms prepared for the radical reform of the London Stock Exchange in 1986 known as "the Big Bang."

3.

Starting in the late '70s, Poland led the way to Eastern Europe independence: Solidarity, by Lech Walesa; its Roman Catholic Church, by Karol Wojtyla, who became Pope John Paul II in 1978. The reasons for the breakup of the Soviet empire in the 1980s were complex. The pace of technological change had quickened in the 1970s; world trade had expanded dramatically as well. Japan led the way. China had entered world markets after 1978. Disproportionate and uncontrolled defense expenditures sapped the strength of the Soviet economy. The USSR found itself unable to keep up with either China or the United States.

Reluctantly, the Soviet authorities began loosening up, proclaiming *perestroika* and *glasnost*, restructuring and openness. The changes loosened their grip on the satellite countries of Eastern Europe. At every step, but especially after the Berlin Wall came down in 1989, Poland was in the vanguard.

Until the Soviet occupation began after World War II, Poland had been a well-evolved market economy. People remembered market ways; farms were still family-owned. Moreover, an independent labor union, Solidarity, had developed during the late '70s to negotiate with the government. Its managers prepared a plan to privatize state-owned companies and create competitive markets. Macroeconomic conditions would have to be stabilized; infrastructure aid sought from multinational lenders including the World Bank, the International Monetary Fund, and the UN's International Bank of Reconstruction and Development. Advocacy would be required.

Enter Jeffrey Sachs, an audacious young Harvard professor. Only a few years before, Sachs had been Larry Summers's rival, competing for leadership in the economics department. In 1985, Sachs had become adviser to the government of Bolivia as it attempted to stabilize its economy's stratospheric inflation rate. Solidarity and the Polish government hired him in 1989. "If Hollywood were casting it, Sachs might be the Indiana Jones of economics," wrote Leslie Wayne of *The New York Times*. Summers, meanwhile, prepared to become chief economist of the World Bank.

Polish economists devised a plan for privatization of government-owned portions of the economy – a deregulation far more extensive than the "Big Bang" that had rocked London's financial industry in 1986 and slowly turned it into a global powerhouse. The Polish government would distribute shares representing ownership of its enterprise – to workers, banks, and government ministries. A stock market would be established, and the biggest institutions would sell their blocks of shares to core investors. A rapid reshuffle of ownership would occur through mergers, acquisitions and buyouts. If all went according to plan, a relatively well-functioning market economy would emerge practically overnight. At first citizens' shares would be held in a handful of diversified mutual funds. Gradually, broad and deep asset markets would emerge.

If Poland was to have mutual funds, arm's-length back-office systems to keep their records would be required. Adam Jakubski, a Polish expatriate, living in Portland, read a newspaper story in the *Portland Press Herald* about Keffer's business. Jakubski understood the structure of Polish banking better than most: three or four large government banks in Warsaw, a smaller government bank in every province. He was also adept at talking his way through the door – any door. He persuaded Keffer to finance a prospecting trip to Warsaw.

Soon Jakubski and Keffer were traveling together around the country, the Polish consultant arranging their meetings, the American businessman explaining how well-kept transaction records would lead to access to more capital. At Bank Handlowy, the most important among Warsaw's banks, their meeting included a former member of an international Philadelphia firm, a Polish citizen thoroughly familiar with American securities law, who had returned to Warsaw several years before. After he pronounced Forum "just what was needed," Forum created a joint venture to do back-office processing for Handlowy. By 1995, Keffer had established a solid business in Poland. He had begun thinking about Russia.

4.

Russia had developed very differently in the 70 years since the 1917 October Revolution. Its root-and-branch communism had thoroughly erased collective memory of market culture. By the second half of the '80s, however, it was clear that Moscow, too, would need to enter the increasingly high-tech world economy, and would require help in doing so. When Mikhail Gorbachev took over the leadership of the Politburo, in 1986, he seemed, at least to many, to be the right man to tackle economic reform.

But Gorbachev vacillated, proposing and abandoning one plan after another. He invested in heavy industry instead of encouraging family farming and the production of consumer goods. The Soviet president was clearly sincere about his desire to end military competition with the United States; arms control talks demonstrated as much. But as "Gorby" became a hero abroad, the Soviet economy continued to stagnate. In June 1991, Boris Yeltsin was elected president of the Russian Soviet Socialist Republic.

Yeltsin was a very different sort of Russian leader. Born in 1931, he grew up to become the party boss of Sverdlovsk, the largest city in the Urals (today once again called Yekaterinburg). Lured to Moscow in 1985 as a construction administrator, he quickly assumed responsibility for supervising the urban affairs of the entire sprawling Soviet capital. There he regularly butted heads with Gorbachev over the pace of reform – as an outsider, Yeltsin felt little attachment to the ossified communist order. The Central Committee of the Communist Party fired him ("forever") in February 1988. At a time when Gorbachev was promoting *glasnost* (openness and candor), Yeltsin couldn't be silenced in the usual ways, and he quickly became the spokesman for rapid change, with Gorbachev arguing for a middle way.

Russia was invited to join the G-7 in June 1991, but when Gorbachev returned home from London with no financial aid in hand, old-line Communist Party leaders attempted to displace him with a coup. The plotters arrested him in his dacha near Sochi, but Yeltsin climbed atop a tank threatening the White House, the seat of government in Moscow, and the plotters decided not to attack the crowds surrounding him. Their troops returned to the barracks. Gorbachev returned to Moscow and was recognized with a Nobel Prize for Peace in the autumn, but henceforth Yeltsin was in charge.

The Communist Party's failure to regain control exposed the scrawny character of rival institutions. Suddenly the nation had very little government. Russia had first-rate educational institutions, strong diplomatic and intelligence services, the enormous administrative class known as *nomenklatura*, but its civil society was otherwise underdeveloped: no contending political parties, no free press, few centers of independent professional authority. Ninety-nine percent of the citizenry had possessed no real political power under the Soviet system.

Yeltsin had been catapulted into power in a profoundly dangerous situation. Did he have any alternative to immediately adopting market reforms? He thought not. There were Russian economists who had worked under Gorbachev who still advocated gradualist plans, Grigori Yavlinsky in particular. But Yeltsin chose economist Yegor Gaidar, 35 in 1991, to finally put into effect the 500-day plan that Gorbachev's economists had talked about for years. Gaidar had a certain standing – his grandfather had written *Timur and His Gang*, a beloved 1940 children's book about a squad of neighborhood teenagers doing patriotic good deeds around town – and Gaidar himself founded an Institute for Market Reform in St. Petersburg in 1990. Many of its members came with him to Moscow, chief among them Anatoly Chubais and Dmitry Vasiliev – well-educated young reformers steeped in Hayek and the literature of deregulation. Inevitably they were dubbed "Gaidar's Gang."

In a speech to the nation on October 28, 1991, Yeltsin announced that Russia would undertake "shock therapy," based on the Polish experience. A one-time change-over to market prices would make things worse for everyone for six months, he explained, but after an initial surge, prices would fall, consumer goods would fill the shops, and stability would return "by the autumn of 1992." Yeltsin participated in one last half-hearted attempt to save the political union that was the USSR, but in December, Mikhail Gorbachev, eighth and last leader of the Soviet Union, announced its dissolution in favor of the emergence of 15 newly independent states. Yeltsin was elected president of a newly independent Russia the next spring.

5.

George H. W. Bush had succeeded Ronald Reagan in 1989, and for the next three years it seemed as though the United States was succeeding on every front around the world. Germans tore down the Berlin Wall. Poland, Czechoslovakia and Hungary cut their ties to the Soviet Union. Estonia, Latvia and Lithuania declared their independence. The USSR itself dissolved. A Statue of Liberty was erected in Beijing's Tiananmen Square. When Iraqi dictator Saddam Hussein invaded and occupied Kuwait, the United States deployed an enormous coalition force to drive him out. The United States paid Ukraine, Belarus, and Kazakhstan to surrender their nuclear weapons to Russia, greatly diminishing the threat of pell-mell nuclear proliferation. In an essay in 1989, "The End of History?," political theorist Francis Fukuyama argued that mankind's ideological evolution was complete, and the norms of Western liberal democracy would become "the final form of human government."

The euphoria waned quickly enough. The government of China cracked down decisively on its student demonstrators. Bush faced a conservative revolt on the eve of the Gulf War, when he sought to raise taxes on gas and alcohol. In the end he acquiesced to Democrats' demands to create a new tax bracket instead: 31 percent on high incomes, up from 28 percent. When the ground war in Kuwait began in February 1991, it was over in 96 hours. True to their war aims, the Americans stopped short of invading Iraq (Baghdad) to remove Saddam Hussein.

America was uniquely powerful, but US Secretary of State James Baker warned Gorbachev in June at the G-7 Summit in London, that, on the eve of an election year in the United States, Russia could expect no financial help with its looming transition. There would be no currency stabilization fund, no loans to finance budget deficits, no rescheduling of the debts run up in the last days of the Soviet Union to buy American grain. Gorbachev complained that if the United States could come up with $100 billion to fight a war, surely it could spare something for its old competitor. He then returned empty-handed to face the attempted August coup. The Bush administration warily greeted the Yeltsin ascendancy and, a few weeks before the election, signed the Freedom Support Act, authorizing a range of programs to support market and democratic reforms in Russia, Ukraine, and the other states of the former Soviet Union – $410 million in bilateral assistance.

There might not be much money in the scheme of things, but in early 1992 Moscow was teeming with consultants eager to help spend it. Harvard held the inside track among American university teams in Russia, with no fewer than four competing experts on the ground. There was Graham Allison, dean of Harvard's Kennedy School of Government, an expert of the Cuban missile crisis, author of *Window of Opportunity: The Grand Bargain for Democracy in the Soviet Union*. Jeffrey Sachs was there, too, on the strength of his successes advising the governments of Poland and Bolivia. So was Marshall Goldman, of Wellesley College and Harvard's Russian Research Center, an old-style "Sovietologist" whom Russians knew the best. Finally, there was Andrei Shleifer, a leader among the young economists who were elbowing the "Sovietologists" aside.

Shleifer stood out. He had grown up in the Soviet Union, but left at 16 with his engineer parents, and had found his way to Harvard College two years later. Befriended there by Summers, he had raced through graduate studies at MIT and by 1989 was a rising star as an affiliate of the National Bureau of Economic Research. Founded in 1920 as a quasi-governmental organization at the intersection of business, labor and government, the NBER had become the arbiter of policy-related research among academic economists. Harvard professor Martin Feldstein, who had been among Ronald Reagan's economic advisers, led the organization in a joint conference in Moscow with the Soviet Academy in the summer of 1989. It was there that the close connection between Russian reformers and American economists began.

Feldstein's translator, a young mathematical economist named Maxim Boycko, was invited to spend six months in Cambridge. There Boycko met Shleifer. By then, Summers was chief economist of the World Bank; Shleifer was teaching at the University of Chicago's business school. Summers involved him in World Bank visit to Lithuania and Moscow in the summer of 1990. On that trip Shleifer first met Chubais, Vasiliev and other members of the Gaidar team. Harvard Law School graduate Jonathan Hay had already gone to work on a pilot program in Moscow under a USAID grant. "And so," wrote reporter Fred Kaplan in *The Boston Globe* in September 1992, "on the fourth floor of an old Soviet ministry building, just east of Red Square, some recent Harvard graduates are helping three Russians in their thirties [Chubais, Vasiliev and Boycko] manage the next stage of the post-Communist revolution."

The smooth transition promised by Yeltsin in his Shock Therapy speech the year before had failed to materialize. Consumer prices had tripled in January alone – inflation was 2,520 percent for the year 1992, destroying the savings of millions of people who had no place to put their rubles except mattresses, which were viewed permitting spontaneous actions by factory directors and local officials; managers and workers were sometimes permitted to lease factories during their off-peak hours. Chubais was desperate to privatize the rest.

Chubais had learned about the details of privatization in other lands – Poland, Hungary, Czechoslovakia, and, especially Great Britain, where Margaret Thatcher's government had been selling off nationalized industries and government utilities for years. He calculated the value of Russia's commercial and industrial assets and divided by the number of citizens, 148 million. Parliament dug in its heels, insisting that those operating going concerns deserved most of the swag. Only in June did Chubais get a deal. Two-thirds of the whole would be set aside for inside managers and workers; citizens would get the rest. The value of each voucher was set at 10,000 rubles in August, and by the end of the year, more than 146 million Russians had picked up one of their own. They were perhaps $50 at then-current exchange rates, but there was no telling what they would be worth in the coming auctions. Chubais boasted he was creating a bourgeoisie.

It was more easily said than done. Eager to demonstrate, Chubais hired Credit Suisse First Boston to conduct an auction for vouchers. Managers of a much-loved Moscow bakery, founded by the Swiss in 1855, agreed to be the first to privatize itself. Vasiliev, Hay and Boycko worked night and day with the investment bankers to get ready. And in December, the Bolshevik Biscuit Company sold for $654,000, unbelievably little. With prices like that, those 10,000 ruble vouchers had real value – at least to those who possessed a lot of them. Nevertheless, the demonstration was considered a success. Parliament backed off its opposition to privatization.

George Bush may have presided over the end of the Cold War, but in the late stages of the 1992 election campaign, he received very little credit for it. Republicans remained furious at him for raising taxes to pay for the war in Kuwait. Democrats argued that recovery from the post-war recession lagged behind. Populist billionaire H. Ross Perot complained about deficits and the proposed North American Free Trade Agreement. There were scandals on Wall Street. Bush, 68, seemed somewhat weary himself.

In November 1992, 46-year-old Bill Clinton won the election with 43 percent of the popular vote, compared to 38 percent for Bush and 19 percent (but no electoral ballots) for Perot. In Washington, as in Moscow, a new generation was in charge.

6.

Clinton had been elected on the strength of his promise to foster job growth. "It's the economy, stupid," had been written on his campaign's war room wall. He asked adviser Robert Rubin, co-chairman of Goldman Sachs, who would become his chief economic aide, to work out a budget package that might induce Federal Reserve Chairman Greenspan to ease interest rates. Rubin employed Summers, whom he had known since the Dukakis presidential campaign four years before, to assist him, sampling opinion and forecasting various policy effects.

Little noticed was the degree to which Clinton considered himself especially well equipped to manage relations with Russia. Though known mainly as a four-term governor of Arkansas, Clinton and friends had been aspiring to the presidency since 1963, when, as a high school student attending a jamboree, he shook hands with President John F. Kennedy in the Rose Garden of the White House. He had spent the first week of 1970 in Moscow, on the advice of his fellow Rhodes Scholar and Oxford classmate Strobe Talbott, a Russophile who had traveled there the year before. Talbott would go on to translate Khrushchev's diaries; write a well-received book about arms control negotiator Paul Nitze; and spend the '80s writing about Russia for *Time* magazine. Talbott would flatter the incoming president for having been "his own best Russia hand," but it was Talbott who became the architect of the Clinton administration's Russia policy.

One lever immediately available to the incoming administration was that Freedom Support Act, passed by Congress in the summer of 1992. The bipartisan Nunn-Lugar Threat Reduction Act the year before had appropriated substantial sums to pay the former USSR to consolidate in Russia its widely dispersed nuclear arsenal. By keeping Belarus, Ukraine, and Kazakhstan out of the nuclear club, that legislation had made the world far safer. The Freedom Support Act had a different goal: assist Russia and the other newly independent states to make their transition to market economies, mainly by making available expert advice. Bush presumably had expected to choose the experts. Clinton did instead.

A month after the election, the US Agency for International Development (USAID), the office responsible for administering civilian foreign aid, chose the Harvard Institute for International Development (HIID), the consulting arm of the university, to advise to the Russian government. The swift award of the no-bid contract brought objections from bidders who had been shut out. USAID replied that Harvard, with its young economists, was the institution the Russian reformers preferred.

Sachs was to become the marquee name, on the strength of his Polish experience. Shleifer, 30, would become second in command, living in Cambridge. Hay, fresh out of law school and already living in Moscow, would head the project there. In an incident that would later seem telling, Shleifer's bid on a house close to campus was thrown out when a bankruptcy judge ruled he had cut corners in describing his offer, omitting the fee he had paid an agent. His wife, Nancy Zimmerman, commuted to New York, where she worked as a fixed-income derivatives trader for Goldman Sachs.

The young reformers of the Yeltsin government had other advisers, notably

Richard Layard, of the London School of Economics, and Anders Aslund, of the Stockholm School of Economics. But the HIID program was its largest and most important source of technical assistance and prestige in Russia. It became the crucial channel of communication between economic reformers in Russia and the government in Washington. In 1997, after news broke of an investigation of the Harvard project, I described the enterprise as it had been described to me:

> HIID might never have had the contract in the first place but for the rump State Department that was the USAID mission in Moscow – with something like 300 hard-to-control employees. In fast-moving events after the attempted coup against Mikhail Gorbachev in 1991 – and especially after Bill Clinton moved into the White House – the Harvard Institute came to be used as the principal, if unofficial, instrument of US macroeconomic policy in Moscow, responsive to instructions from the White House in ways that the well-entrenched USAID mission in Russia never was.

When Rubin became director of the National Economic Council, Summers joined the Treasury Department, working for Secretary Lloyd Bentsen as undersecretary for international affairs. In early 1994 Talbott became deputy secretary of state, under Warren Christopher. As economic growth resumed in the United States, Rubin replaced Bentsen as treasury secretary in January 1995, and Summers became deputy secretary, with responsibility for economic policy towards Russia.

7.

The US economy was slowly expanding in 1993, but Russia continued hemorrhaging jobs. Not until 1997 would employment there begin growing again. At least the terrible year of 1992 was over. Gaidar, leader of the market reformers, had been dismissed at the end of "shock therapy's" first turbulent year, replaced by the more cautious Viktor Chernomyrdin. The overall commitment to market reforms had survived; a referendum in April 1993 endorsed Yeltsin's economic program.

Privatization was no longer the main issue. A contest for control of the government itself had developed. The Russian Parliament – the old Supreme Soviet, full of old-timers, democratically elected amid the enthusiasm of 1989 – was on one side, Yeltsin, the president, on the other. The central issue was the budget: slash more jobs and balance it? Or continue borrowing and feed inflation? By now the Harvard team was advising Russian counterparts on all manner of issues, including a new commercial code, and new real estate law. Sachs would work with Gaidar on central banking, currency stability, and the elimination of price controls; Shleifer, with Chubais and Vasiliev, focused on privatization.

Tensions escalated through the spring of 1993. Parliament sought to impeach Yeltsin and fell only a few votes short. There were street battles between factions on May 1. John Lloyd, of the *Financial Times*, later described the situation this way:

> The corruption was fabulous, shameless, and at the highest levels; it was the confirmation of the suspicions which hard-pressed men and women harbored as they saw the Mercedes swish by, the boss in the back, attended by crewcut thugs.... By midyear [1993] little else counted except the struggle for power.

In September, Yeltsin reappointed Gaidar; in October, he took absolute control. In a television speech, the most important of his career, Yeltsin announced he was dissolving the old Supreme Soviet, permanently. New elections would be held in December, he declared, under a new constitution, to elect a parliament with more limited powers – the Duma, it would eventually be named.

Supreme Soviet deputies flocked to the White House; Yeltsin turned off the lights, then the water. Most of the legislators left, but 200 or so remained, and a few days later some of those marched out to join an angry mob of supporters in another attempted coup – seeking to occupy City Hall and then Broadcast House. They were repelled, after no little violence, and the next day Yeltsin ordered tanks to fire on the upper floors of the White House – a spectacle witnessed by thousands of Muscovites and millions on national television. Gaidar broadcast a dramatic appeal to Muscovites to back the president or see their country "turned into an enormous concentration camp for decades." The parliamentary leaders were led out under guard and taken to prison. Sachs resigned his advisory role in late 1993, complaining that, in the impasse between president and legislature, his advice hadn't been followed. Yeltsin's advisers were furious. Shleifer was now fully in charge.

Two-thirds of the vouchers hadn't been used. Chubais procured an extension to June 30, 1994. The auction of Russian industry was about to become "a new Klondike," as David Hoffman, of *The Washington Post* described it later in *The Oligarchs: Wealth and Power in the New Russia*. In May, *The Economist's* cover proclaimed "The Sale of the Century." The opportunities were comparable to those seized by British investors who made fortunes in the surging US economy in the century, the magazine said. Promoters convinced holders to swap vouchers for shares in what they called "voucher funds." By February 1994, more than 600 of these were in operation. A few months later, half of them had collapsed, their money squandered or, in some cases, simply stolen.

It turned out later that Shleifer and Hay had begun investing on their own account that summer, in violation of the rules – Shleifer, $200,000 in a fund run by Russian expatriate Leonard Blavatnik, a 1989 graduate of Harvard Business School, already an oligarch; another $165,000 in a Russian oil company, Purneftgas, via an elaborate ruse (they used a Channel Islands account and ascribed ownership to Zimmerman's father). At Shleifer's urging, Hay added $66,000 of his own. The deal had been arranged by a partner of the San Francisco investment firm that put Shleifer's wife in business, Farallon Capital Management. David Cohen, of Farallon, later explained: "We wanted to get as much protection as we could… and we thought Andrei provided some of those things. People might have been more hesitant to hurt Andrei than to hurt Farallon."

Among his Harvard colleagues, Shleifer made no secret of his investing in Russia. If asked, he explained he was exempt from the usual conflict-of-interest provisions because he hadn't moved to Moscow. At a cocktail party that autumn, at the Cambridge home of Harvard professor Dale Jorgenson, attended by several of the economics department's most worldly members, including David Landes, Zvi Griliches and Martin Feldstein, Shleifer boasted of the opportunities. Before long, almost 2 percent of Harvard's $11 billion endowment was invested in Russia.

By early 1995, a severe budget crisis and accelerating inflation put the fledgling government to its most serious test – too many promises, too much debt, too little cash. Publicly, Yeltsin promised those who had seen the value of their vouchers vanish that he would create a proper mutual fund industry, in order that the gains that were becoming apparent might be legitimately shared; and to generate much-needed tax revenue in the process. There was still plenty of cash on the sidelines in Russia – "mattress cash" – to be invested.

Behind the scenes, Chubais worked on a plan to raise some real money with which the government could pay its claims – by selling the biggest enterprises remaining in the government's portfolio, including the dozen largest in Russia: six in the energy business, three in minerals, and three in shipping. This was the loans-for-shares program, an artful deception – up-front cash in the form of loans from a consortium of Russian banks in exchange for a pledge to auction firms, including should the government fail to repay what it owed. The banks had been formed by enterprising *nomenklatura* a few years before; when auctions followed two years later, the great enterprises were awarded by the bankers to insiders, in every case, at scandalously low-ball prices.

The loans-for-shares was presented by reformers as a measure to get big industry out of the hands of conservative "red directors," even if its effect was simply to place management in the hands of young Russian entrepreneurs soon to be dubbed oligarchs – Vladimir Potanin, Mikhail Khodorkovsky, Boris Berezovsky et al. All had excelled in the famous specialist schools of the old Soviet Union; they had been quick to embrace the opportunities of *perestroika* to start banks. Privatization had become "the fantastic gamble of throwing the state sector into the hands of whoever would prove resourceful and ruthless enough to grasp it," as *Financial Times* correspondent John Lloyd later described the process. And indeed, once privatized, the big companies were well run.

By autumn 1995, however, the deception of the loans-for-shares ploy was clear. The Communists gained 23 percent of the Duma in the December elections. In January, Yeltsin fired Chubais. "He sold off industry for next to nothing," said the president. "We cannot forgive this." Bad news for the reformers, and their Harvard advisers. The nation was turning back towards old-style communism.

Yeltsin had suffered a heart attack in October 1995. He was often drunk in public. His prospects for a second term couldn't have seemed dimmer; he was running dead last in polls. Communist party head Gennady Zyuganov was the front-runner. In early February 1996, Zyuganov delivered a commanding performance at the annual Davos Conference in the Swiss Alps. A Communist return to power seemed all but certain.

Whereupon a group of seven newly minted oligarchs met to consider their options: either plan to leave Russia, or rally to the Yeltsin banner and attempt to govern the country themselves. After Chubais boldly countered Zyuganov with an equally commanding press conference of his own at the glitzy meeting, members of the "Davos Pact" agreed to support Yeltsin. They hired Chubais to manage their campaign. The Clinton government decided to back Yeltsin energetically.

On February 15, 1996, Yeltsin announced that he would indeed stand for a second term. Among the first of his campaign promises was a new mutual fund industry. There would be no more of the chicanery that characterized the "voucher funds." The big financial companies doing business in Russia – Pioneer Investments, First Boston, Chase, Franklin Templeton – prepared to get in line.

8.

These were the circumstances in which John Keffer met Elizabeth Hebert. He had been visiting Forum's Warsaw office, preparing to travel to Moscow, to call on Russian banks to explore the depository business there. A friend from Flemings, a well-known British investment bank, had told him that the manager of the firm's Moscow office was thinking about starting a mutual fund of her own. He called on her as well.

Hebert explained that she managed a $30 million Russian investment fund for the International Bank for Reconstruction and Development, an agency of the United Nations. She and her associate, Julia Zagachin, had ambitions of their own to join the queue of those seeking licenses to operate in Russia. Following the Polish example, the Russian Securities and Exchange Commission planned to require that funds companies sign contracts with a regulated specialized depository, an independent record-keeping business operating at arm's-length from the fund companies. The government didn't want a replay of the embarrassing voucher funds/Ponzi schemes and other frauds of the sort that had flourished in the first privatization drive.

Pioneer and First Boston already possessed up-and-running specialized depositories of their own. Hebert and Zagachin peppered Keffer with questions about how such back-office operations worked. The big international companies wouldn't permit her to buy into their services. A company like Forum, with its proprietary technology and its entrepreneurial tendencies might be just the sort of well-established firm whose services she – and Russia – needed.

She had an inside track, Hebert told Keffer, with Dimitry Vasiliev, head of the Russian Securities and Exchange Commission, via his American adviser, Jonathan Hay, whom she knew. She phoned Hay, who then met with Keffer for an hour, handing Keffer his HIID business card, interrogating him about his business, stressing the importance of the nascent mutual fund business to the Russian president's reelection campaign. Chubais apparently had promised Yeltsin that the first funds would open by the election. The date was later moved back to September 2.

Sure enough, a few days later, a letter arrived by fax from Vasiliev inviting Keffer to start a company to "supply fund administration services to the large number of mutual funds that are being launched in Russia," holding out the possibility of financial assistance from the Russian government to get it up and running quickly. The Russian asked if Jonathan Hay, "one of my advisers," could visit the Warsaw facility on March 7 and 8. Mysteriously, Hebert and Zagachin, showed up instead. Hebert assured Keffer that Hay had drafted the letter. Intrigued, Keffer replied to Vasiliev that he would be willing to try. He returned to Moscow on March 18.

In his landmark *Institutional Investor* article (chapters 11, 15), David McClintick presented myriad new details as he described the close-knit group of associates whom Keffer encountered in February 1996. They were not yet quite plotters, not yet quite friends. Each had many different and sometimes conflicting ambitions. At the center of the affair that brought the Harvard project down, it turned out, had been the love affair between Hebert and Hay – catalyzed by that other potent stimulant, greed.

Hay, then 32, a graduate of Williams College and Harvard Law School, Rhodes Scholar in between, was the idealistic young lawyer from Idaho whom Shleifer had hired to run the Moscow office of the HIID project, a "brain-on-overdrive academic with a piercing stare, limited business experience, and no time for haircuts," in McClintick's description. He "dazzled everyone he encountered." Hay had grown close to Vasiliev, his Russian counterpart, in the years since they shared an office with a handful of others in 1991. Vasiliev and his wife had visited Hay at his parents' home near Boise as Hay's mother lay dying. Vasiliev had arranged for Hay's widowed father, a physician, to be invited to work on a project in Moscow. Jonathan Hay, an associate told McClintick, "wanted to be buried in the Kremlin wall."

Hebert, an Ohio native, then 33, had earned a master's degree from Columbia in business and international affairs, learned Russian, and had been sent to Russia by Flemings. Now she wanted to start a mutual fund company of her own in Russia. For this she needed a back office, hence the invitation to Keffer. Keffer himself was impressed. In McClintick's description, she was "the kind of person who would arrive at a meeting promptly, wearing a trim suit, carrying a leather portfolio of meticulous notes. "Hay would blow in late, hair flying, clothes askew, without a pen." He was "brilliant, but with no sense for business."

Zagachin, then 28, had been born in Russia, but moved to the United States with her family when she was 11. After graduating from George Washington University, she had gone to work in Moscow for the international accounting and consulting firm Deloitte & Touche. Hay hired her in 1994 to run an AID-funded start-up intended to become a clearing house settling trades for securities transactions, the Depository Clearing Company Forced out of DCC in favor of a Russian citizen, she agreed to work with Hebert in November 1995. "High-strung and intense," wrote McClintick.

Hebert had first met Hay in the summer of 1992. Over the next three years, they talked at times over meals about his business and hers. Hay described the plan to bring mutual funds to Russia on which he was advising Vasiliev and the Russian SEC. By early 1995, Hebert decided to try to enter the business herself. In due course, she named her firm Pallada Asset Management Company – Pallada being both a sobriquet for Athena, ancient Greek goddess of wisdom, and the name of a famous Russian frigate that voyaged around the world in 1852-55. As plans for the industry advanced, Hay and Hebert became closer.

In November 1995, Hay and Hebert separately attended a dinner at the Shleifer family home in Newton, in honor of Alexander Livshits, a Yeltsin adviser who would go on to serve as minister of finance. There they each met Peter Aldrich, a Harvard college alumnus, former Peace Corps volunteer, and Harvard Business School graduate who remained close to the university's economics department. Aldrich had founded Aldrich, Eastman & Waltch Capital Management (AEW), an international investor in real estate trusts. He had begun investing in Russia, and was eager to get to know Shleifer. At the urging of Shleifer, Zimmerman and Hay, Aldrich received Hebert the next day in his downtown office to hear about her business plan. (He wasn't impressed.)

In December, Hay made a prohibited investment in Hebert's mutual fund; since the vehicle was available only to those residing in Britain, she had his papers sent to her home in London. After Christmas, Hebert left her family in Ohio to fly to Idaho to join Vasiliev and his wife, and Hay, for a day at Hay's father's home. She then flew to Boston for a cozy New Year's Eve dinner at the Shleifer home in Newton – "our first real date," Hay later testified. (Zimmerman's business partner, Gabriel Sunshine, and his wife were the other couple.) The next day, Hebert and Shleifer walked around Harvard Yard discussing plans for Russia's asset management industry.

Soon they were a couple. In January, the Hebert-Hay romance gradually became an open secret in their Moscow circles. They flew to London together in February, and by April, Hay was helping her raise her fund, with Aldrich, the Boston real estate fund proprietor whom she had met at the Shleifer's home six months before. Like Farallon's Steyer, Aldrich was eager to be close to Shleifer, and seen to be close.

By February, Shleifer's wife, Nancy Zimmerman, began to take an interest in Hebert's business. Daughter of a Chicago real estate investor and race horse owner who also happened to be a director of a local bank, Zimmerman was herself a promising investor from an early age. After graduating from Brown University, in 1985, she joined Chicago's secretive O'Connor and Associates, a derivatives trading firm then expanding all over the world on the strength of a billowing wave of financial innovation pioneered by Chicago commodities markets. Three years later, she joined the legendary risk arbitrage department of Goldman, Sachs that Robert Rubin had built. She and Shleifer married in May 1991. By December 1992, she was head of worldwide trading of fixed-income derivatives.

After her maternity leave, in 1994, Zimmerman left Goldman to open a hedge fund of her own. She obtained seed money from two important Yale alumni: Thomas Steyer, founder of Farallon Capital Management, of San Francisco, who in the 1980s had worked for Robert Rubin as an arbitrageur at Goldman, Sachs; and Steyer's friend, David Swenson, manager of Yale's then $4 billion endowment. Zimmerman had been introduced to Steyer by Farallon partner David Cohen, with whom she had worked at Goldman; as it happened, Cohen, a former Rhodes Scholar, had known Hay at Oxford as well. Steyer and Swensen each invested $25 million in Zimmerman's Farallon Fixed Income Associates; Farallon would clear her trades. "Though she called her husband 'Boss', wrote McClintick, Zimmerman, 31, "was a charging financial wizard in her own right.... [She] earned far more trading bonds than Shleifer did teaching economics: $1.06 million to his $191,000 in 1994."

Hebert and Zagachin pitched their plans for Pallada to Hay and Vasiliev in February 1996 – various prominent Russians were prepared to back her, Hebert said. Zimmerman sat in on the briefing. Afterwards, she promised to invest $200,000 of her own in the business and to help Hebert raise the rest of what she needed. (Many years later, Jeremy Knowles, dean of Harvard's Faculty of Arts and Sciences, would tell a grand jury in Boston, "[O]bviously, it is common sense, surely to us all, that if one's spouse were doing something, that is awfully close to doing it one's self.")

9.

None of this was known to Keffer when he returned to Moscow, in March. Hay grilled him about the business. How long would it take to be ready to create a Russian depository? Keffer told him 60 days. What about Vasiliev's insistence that Russian investors own 51 percent of the business? No problem, said Keffer, as long as he retained the rest and had management control. After an hour, Keffer and Hay travelled to see Vasiliev, who on the spot offered Keffer $2.5 million to help him start his Russian firm, in the form of a lump-sum contract, with a $450,000 advance. The Russian SEC would borrow the money from the World Bank. Vasiliev emphasized the importance of a timely start to the privatization campaign, and its significance to the election campaign.

Behind the scenes, HIID employees in Moscow began questioning the use of

World Bank funds to finance a private start-up when big Western banks were already beating down the door. Keffer didn't view the money as a gift. If the Russians truly wanted a depository unaffiliated with the leading money managers then operating in Russia – Pioneer and CSFB – then Forum was the obvious candidate, based on its experience in Poland.

Once his staff had drafted the World Bank contract, Keffer chartered a new Russian subsidiary and returned to Moscow with his team to begin work and search for a Russian partner for its initial venture – First Russian Specialized Depository (FRSD), it would be called. Not long after, it turned out later, Hebert and Zimmerman began seeking to sell some or all of FRSD to two big-league investors – Farallon's Steyer and AEW's Peter Aldrich – behind Keffer's back. Their plan was described in a document that came to be known as "the Steyer memo." The presidential campaign gathered steam; there were delays. After a month, Hay told Keffer he must renegotiate the contract on a different basis – time-and-material as opposed to lump-sum. A second contract was drafted, only to be turned back to be rewritten in July. Forum finally began work in June, at Hay's insistence, still without a contract. Only in late July was a third contract finally agreed upon.

A second tug-of-war emerged over the summer between Hay and Keffer. Hay insisted Zagachin, Hebert's assistant, be named president of Forum's Russian subsidiary. Keffer wanted no part of her, judging her undependable and inept. Zagachin had told Keffer's assistant that she viewed Forum as a technology vendor and that she expected to be in charge of FRSD in the end. She found a large suite in an expensive office building and asked him to lease it for her and Hebert. Proposals flew back and forth between Forum and Hay's office. Oral agreements were reached but never signed.

Meanwhile, behind the scenes, there were various domestic arrangements to attend. Hebert finally quit her job at Flemings at the end of June and began working on Pallada out of Hay's office. Hay and his father invested $150,000 in Russian Treasury bills, $50,000 of it the son's own money. They employed a firm owned by Zimmerman, designed to shield profits from Russian taxes, via a conduit to her father's bank. (Real returns that summer were running around 75 percent.) Shleifer sought Aldrich's help with the admission of his son to Cambridge's exclusive Shady

Hill School. The Shleifer-Zimmerman family prepared for their annual August vacation week on Cape Cod with the Summers family.

The pressure on Keffer grew. By August, the carrot of the World Bank contract became a stick. Keffer's team was far along to finishing the work they promised, converting and translating Forum's record-keeping software to Russian specifications; their back office was almost ready to go. The contract was finally signed. But Hay refused to approve payment unless Zagachin, his girlfriend's associate, was designated general director of Keffer's firm. By now Keffer had deposited $400,000 in FRSD "founding capital" in a Moscow bank; Vasiliev in return had awarded him the promised business license. Keffer named various prospective Russian partners. Hay vetoed each one, insisting that, one way or another, Zagachin be put in charge. Keffer flew to Moscow in August and complained to Vasiliev. The Russian SEC chairman again promised that Keffer would control the depository, but stressed he needed a working system by September 2. He declined to sign the memorandum of understanding that Keffer had drafted.

The tension came to a head when Keffer decided to explain the squeeze he was experiencing to Michael Butler, an attorney who, according to Keffer, had implied he was an intermediary between Harvard and its Moscow team when he requested the meeting. Gradually Keffer came to understand that the lawyer actually worked for Shleifer, and was paid via HIID. When Zagachin tried unsuccessfully to transfer Forum's $400,000 to her own account the next day, and a friend warned him he might be in physical danger, Keffer decided that risks outweighed any plausible reward. He sent his wife home to Maine the next day.

Keffer dug in. He now possessed everything that Hebert needed to open her Pallada Fund – a depository license, system software, employees to operate it – but neither Hay nor the Russian SEC could force him to contract with Hebert to keep records for Pallada, which itself was about to be licensed. Instead, Keffer offered to sell the FRSD, its license, and the "founding capital" he had deposited, to Zagachin, for $400,000, that being the sum of the money he had in the bank (plus another $8,000 to cover the cost of the transaction). The Russian government's tight deadline remained in force.

In his *Institutional Investor* article, McClintick described the scene that evening:

Shleifer and Zimmerman flew into Moscow that Monday afternoon and found themselves in the midst of a crisis. Over dinner at the ornate National Hotel, Hebert and Hay, flanked by Zagachin and Sokin [Vasiliev's political adviser], briefed the Shleifers on Keffer's "blackmail."

Panic gripped the group. Sokin implored Shleifer to devote himself personally to resolving the problem before the September deadline. Then all heads turned to Zimmerman. Was she still hesitant to invest with Hebert? If not Pallada, would she consider helping with the FRSD? Conflicted Zimmerman asked a lot of questions. Could it be a loan instead of an equity investment? What would secure the loan? By the end of the dinner, Zimmerman was weighing the notion that she might become a lead investor in the FRSD.

After returning to vacation with the Summers family in Truro the next week, Zimmerman eventually agreed, in an e-mail, to loan Zagachin $200,000 she had promised months before and to invest another $200,000 in the depository she was about to acquire. But, she said, she couldn't send the money in time to prevent the license from expiring if the transaction weren't completed by September 2. So over the Labor Day weekend, a desperate Hebert asked Hay's father to lend Zagachin the necessary sum. Dr. Hay wired $400,000, half his own funds, half from his son's account, to Zagachin's Delaware bank. Later, Zimmerman and, ultimately, Shleifer himself, engaged in a series of transactions designed to unwind that transaction, creating another prohibited investment for the Harvard professor.

Thus at the last possible moment, the deal went through. Keffer gave the demonstration he had promised (known as a "light show" in the trade). Zagachin had a depository license but no software. Keffer returned to Portland with laptops, his $400,000, and the hope the World Bank would eventually pay at least some of the money it owed. His Russian adventure had lasted six months.

By now Hebert's Pallada fund and Zimmerman's Farallon fixed income fund were being run out of Hay's HIID office. Later that year, Hay would move in with Hebert in her apartment. Zagachin now owned a depository that didn't work. Moscow newspapers were raising questions about the depository deal. When Louis O'Neill, a USAID project staffer returning to Moscow from law school, asked Hay why Vasiliev had licensed Hay's girlfriend's fund and a depository that by now belonged to Zagachin, rather than the far-better-established Credit Suisse First Boston, Hay explained,

> "Well this is a very serious pilot project. It will be the first, basically the first mutual fund in Russia. We want to have someone as the leader, as the first person, who we are friendly with, and who we can monitor very closely for transparency, fairness, proper procedures, proper accounting.... We'll run water through the pipes on this one, see where the leaks are, fix them, and then we'll open it up to the larger market.

Whistle-blowers within USAID went to work. Attorney Holly Nielsen sought to warn Shleifer. He first disregarded her, then sought to fire her. Veteran administrator Janet Ballantyne, newly arrived in Moscow as head of the entire USAID mission, notified the agency's inspector general in Washington and an investigation began. After two months, the project came to a screeching halt when USAID called a press conference to announce it had fired the Harvard Institute. *The Wall Street Journal* ran the story on its front page on May 21, 1997; *The New York Times* followed a day later.

There is no record of whatever message traffic passed between the Moscow embassy and Deputy Treasury Secretary Summers and Deputy Secretary of State Talbott in Washington during the 10 weeks before USAID announced its decision, much less what Summers said to his boss Robert Rubin and vice versa. Shleifer and Zimmerman were considered valuable observers of the Russian scene and their discomfiture cannot have gone unnoticed among Treasury officers who worked regularly on Russia. Project director Shleifer's May 9 letter to Harvard provost Albert Carnesale, seeking to short-circuit the investigation, was produced as evidence in the government lawsuit. It is included it here as an appendix for the vivid picture it paints of a decisive actor who has suddenly lost his bearings.

The Russian reformers stuck with their friends. Soon after USAID fired Harvard, an indignant Chubais, by now first deputy premier for macroeconomics, fired USAID, describing the work of the Harvard advisers as "fantastically important and supportive for the Russian reform process." The Russian government,

Chubais said, would continue working with Shleifer and Hay. A second *Wall Street Journal* story appeared in August – the one that featured woodcuts of Hebert and Zimmerman, and spelled out the story in considerable detail.

In September, Moscow celebrated the 850th anniversary of its founding. Harvard's (and the NBER's) Martin Feldstein was among the dignitaries who visited and, in "Russia's Rebirth," on the editorial page of the *WSJ*, declared that "Russia's privatization of virtually all businesses and housing has been one of the late 20th century's most remarkable achievements anywhere in the world." Despite some policy mistakes – he singled out the amassing of enormous wealth by a few individuals – and much turmoil, the progress had been impressive. "Although more problems and setbacks will inevitably arise, the future of the Russian economy now looks very bright indeed." The Russian stock market peaked a month later; the financial crisis came 10 months after that. Hebert and Hay married in December 1998.

10.

USAID had already referred its case against Harvard to the Justice Department in June 1997. The US attorney in Boston went to work; by the autumn of 1998, a grand jury had been empaneled. For a year the investigators pursued a criminal case. For one thing, Harvard's endowment had invested extensively in the Russian economy – by the end of 1997, around $195 million, or nearly 2 percent, of its then $11 billion fund – and questions had arisen about links between the management company and the HIID team. Issues of back-dating and perjury were explored as well. In the end, no criminal charges were brought.

In September 2000, the Justice Department filed a civil case, accusing Harvard of fraud and would charge Shleifer and Hay with making a series of investments in Russia, in violation of their contracts. Three weeks later, in US District Court in Portland, Keffer sued Harvard, Shleifer and Hay.

The government suit in Boston took over the headlines. US District Court Judge Douglas Woodlock was assigned the case. Hoping to save the court time and money, he referred the case to senior District Court Judge David Mazzone for mediation. The effort failed in March 2001, three weeks after Summers was named Harvard president. (See chapter 17, "Those Three Weeks in March.") A year later, Robert Rubin joined the seven-member corporation that governed Harvard. (Like Summers, he recused himself from the Russia matter.) Depositions in the dual lawsuits commenced after Labor Day, complicated by the events of 9/11. They were pretty much completed by the end of 2002.

After both sides moved for summary judgment, Judge Woodlock ruled that the Harvard team leaders had indeed broken the law, investing in Russia and breaching their contracts: Hay four times, Shleifer three. Moreover, Harvard itself had failed to deliver the disinterested advice that it had promised. As for the False Claims Act, with its treble damages, it didn't apply, Judge Woodlock wrote, because there was insufficient evidence that university employees in Cambridge knew about the illegality in Moscow. "Warning signals," including "rumor-like allegations of impropriety and favoritism," were not enough to warrant the heavy penalty under existing case law; had the relevant standard been "negligent supervision," he wrote, the government would have had a better case.

There remained to be tested Harvard's main line of defense. The university argued that Shleifer was free to invest in Russia because he was technically a consultant to HIID, not an employee, like Hay; therefore the government's rules (and its own) didn't apply. Shleifer hadn't moved to Russia; he lived in Newton. He worked in his economics department office, not in HIID headquarters, a few blocks away. On the other hand, he traveled to Moscow frequently, and he was known there, as in Cambridge, as the project director. Judge Woodlock referred that argument to a jury. What did "assigned to" Russia mean, in terms of the project?

After a trial lasting three days, it took the 12-person panel just two hours to decide (chapter 8, "A Narrow and Technical Issue"). Jurors walked away from the courthouse chuckling. Of course Shleifer was an employee, one said, not a consultant, they had concluded; of course he had been assigned to Russia under the contract. Harvard didn't appeal. The case entered its remedy phase and, in the end, Harvard agreed to give back $26.5 million. Shleifer paid $2 million; Zimmerman, $1.5 million on a related claim; and Hay, between $1 million and $2 million, depending on his earnings in the years ahead.

And there the matter rested* until McClintick's article appeared, in January 2006. Six weeks later, after a third raucous faculty meeting, Summers resigned. A few days after that, *New York Times* reporter Sara Ivry investigated whether

McClintick's exposé had contributed to Summers' decision. Absolutely not, said Summers' spokesman, John Longbrake. Rifts with "certain factions" of the faculty "made it infeasible to advance the agenda of renewal that he saw as crucial to Harvard's future."

*Wellesley College economist Marshall Goldman, the kind of expert on the Soviet economy known as a Sovietologist, was highly critical of the "shock therapy" approach in Russia, of the Harvard Institute for International Development in particular, especially after Shleifer and Hay became embroiled in scandal. Goldman told me that, in the years during which Summers was president, he was warned – by whom he did not say, on whose authority he did not know – that his crucial association with Harvard's Russian Research Center would be imperiled if he were publicly critical of the Harvard mess. Notwithstanding the threat, Goldman wrote a good terse account of the scandal in *The Piratization of Russia: Russian Reform Goes Awry* (2003), and defended Sachs against assertians that he had similarly misbehaved. There is some reason to think the warning was general. The Harvard scandal was not mentioned in Harvard professor Timothy Colton's 2008 biography, *Yeltsin: A Life*.

Certainly Summers had been embroiled in plenty of other controversy over the previous two years. Robert Putnam, a former dean of Harvard's John F. Kennedy School of Government, saw the matter differently. "When the president responded in a manifestly untruthful way to questions that were asked about the Shleifer case, it had a devastating effect on the views of people who were to that point uncommitted, people who, like me, were strong supporters of his agenda."

11.

A year later I met Keffer, in Boston, when he was passing through town. He had sold Forum to Citigroup for a hefty sum. He was looking for someone to collaborate on his life story – not as a story about Russia, but about how a kid with attention-deficit disorder had managed to build the business he did, having various adventures along the way, starting in Panama, wending through New York, Warsaw, Moscow, and back to Panama. My interest lay elsewhere. His story didn't seem to be a vanity project: I immediately thought of books about recondite accomplishments of colorful characters by accomplished writers such as John McPhee and Tracy Kidder. I sought to fix him up with a ghost writer, and turned back to my chores. Summers had resumed teaching and was continuing his education by consulting to D. E. Shaw, a large hedge fund. I had little to say about that.

Then came the financial crisis of 2008. Summers joined the Obama campaign the week that Lehman Brothers failed, and proved indispensable thereafter – especially since Rubin, having earned $115 million over nine years as a high-level strategist at Citigroup, had been rendered a toxic asset himself by the giant bank's precarious position. By January, Summers was back in the government, as national economic adviser to Barack Obama, a position requiring no Senate confirmation. His immediate task was devising the president's stimulus bill, but Summers hungered for a line job. He sought to displace, first, Treasury Secretary Timothy Geithner, then, a year later, Federal Reserve Board chairman Ben Bernanke, when Bernanke's reappointment came up.

In *Economic Principals*, I periodically reminded readers of the salience of the Harvard story. Nancy Zimmerman, Summers had told the *Times* not long after taking office, was among his inner circle of advisers, along with Lawrence Fink, founder of BlackRock, the asset management firm; Kenneth Brody and Frank Brosens, of Taconic Capital Advisers, a hedge fund; and bank industry expert H. Rodgin Cohen, of the Sullivan and Cromwell law firm. For the next two years, he jousted occasionally with Christina Romer, chair of the Council of Economic Advisers, whom he had recruited, only to disagree over the design and effect of the stimulus bill. With no further government job in immediate prospect, a disappointed Summers returned to Harvard in 2010.

After I called on Keffer in Portland, in March 2011, I began to think of his story differently. The more I read through the various depositions, the better I understood what had happened in Moscow. Harvard's lawyers had succeeded in concealing the fire, leaving only the smoke. As I thought through the implications of the non-disclosure agreement that Harvard must have demanded, I was infuriated not to know the details of the settlement. What else had Harvard hushed up?

12.

The lawsuit Keffer filed in Maine had been very different from the government charges. Hay, Hebert, Shleifer and Zimmerman had conspired to "misappropriate" the firm that Hay and Vasiliev had encouraged him to found, he charged, "misappropriate" being an appropriately cautious word for "steal," and Harvard, through lax management, had enabled them to succeed.

Forum was not mentioned in the government's complaint. From the various motions, depositions and exhibits I had collected and put away, it was possible to piece together Keffer's side of the story. Unfortunately, his initial deposition appeared to have been purged as part of the settlement, making his experiences that much harder to understand. Especially useful were a pair of timelines prepared by corporate counsel Dana Lukens, who had been Keffer's principal lieutenant on the ground in Moscow. He compiled the first in the heat of battle, in August '97; the other, eight months later, in preparation for the legal fight. And, of course, former employees are not covered by the agreement.

Easy to miss – certainly I missed it – was the glancing reference near the end of Judge Woodlock's 2004 opinion to Keffer's now-settled claim. "Fraud that either [Shleifer and Hay] may have engaged in towards third parties under Harvard's apparent authority is not an issue in the present litigation (Forum Fin. Group vs President and Fellow.)" At the time, Woodlock's short discussion of the Steyer memo seemed to lead nowhere. Viewed through the prism of Forum's case, it was penetrating.

The Steyer memo is a spirited eight-page document in which the plotters outline their plans for Keffer's company – what they hoped would be a sure-fire recipe for success. It is something of a smoking gun, since all four schemers – Hay, Hebert, Zimmerman and Shleifer – were clearly involved in its preparation. The Keffer team didn't see the memo until the government, having obtained it by subpoena, turned it over to them. The document was, in effect, a bold plan to sell a company that Hebert and Hay didn't own.

Significantly, the Steyer memo lacks a "from" line. "As you know," it begins, "we are seeking $1.2 million to create a fund management company and a fund administrator/custodian ('specialized depository') in Russia. I understand from Nancy that you wish to have some more information on the specialized depository." The Russian SEC plans to issue only a few licenses to back-office operators, the memo confidently explains; FRSD will be the first. Strong "first mover" advantages will ensue, for the Russian SEC intends to keep Credit Suisse First Boston, their most formidable competitor, out of the market, at least for a time. Hebert, who has operated the best-performing public fund in Russia for the last two years, is to receive the first license to offer a registered mutual fund. Zagachin, said by the author to be a woman of stellar accomplishments, will be president of FRSD.

A "strategic partner," Forum Financial, is to be "involved in the set-up," the memo says, serving to "shadow" the local management team, preventing mistakes in the choice of systems. Forum may even flow down to FRSD some revenues from the World Bank contract it had won to design systems to be used by the depository. The depository was projected to earn pre-tax profits of several million dollars, growing to 238,000 accounts in its first five years. "[I]f we were to assume that this Specialized Depository has a large market share and if it were to process millions of accounts, it would be an extremely profitable operation!"

But time was of the essence. Farallon must decide quickly whether it wanted to invest. FRSD "already has financing in place," thanks to the presence of Forum Financial. "If worse comes to worst... we would still get 51 percent" of the company. For the moment, there was room for more, but if Steyer wanted in on the specialized depository, he would have to invest, at least on a modest scale, in Hebert's Pallada fund as well. "We... are tying our futures to this strategy. We would like our backers to do the same...." Only in the last line of the memo does its author re-assert himself: "I look forward to talking to you about the proposal."

So who was the author of the memo? Judge Woodlock dug through the testimony and concluded that Hebert had drafted the memo, in such a way as to make it appear to have been written by Hay. Hay reviewed a heavily annotated copy, with the understanding that both Zimmerman and Steyer were seeking an expression of "his opinion and his support"; Hay suggested that Hebert make this clearer, and that she also mention the Russian SEC's favorable views. Hay's office then sent the draft to both Zimmerman and Shleifer, and made sure that Zimmerman had received it. The "we" is Hebert and Hay.

As for the *how* – how the authors planned to either obtain Keffer's assent to a massive dilution, or wrest the company away from him altogether – recipients were left to read between the lines. Judge Woodlock concluded that the document in evidence hadn't been faxed to Steyer or received by him; Hebert faxed a version of it to Zimmerman and Zimmerman thence to AEW's Aldrich (though the latter parties said they had no memory of receiving it). Both Aldrich and Steyer were still talking about possible investments in August. It is inconceivable that each executive wouldn't ask who actually owned FRSD. In short, it is hard to imagine that Keffer eventually wouldn't have won his case.

Harvard battled to quash the Forum case, or at least transfer it to Boston. The judge ruled it could go forward in Maine. The university, Shleifer and Hay settled just as jury selection was set to begin. Might Keffer have won his case? We'll never know. What did he gain in the deal? The terms were not disclosed; all the parties signed a non-disclosure agreement. The news occasioned only a short wire story. Harvard had swept it under the rug.

Why did Keffer settle? Dana Lukens, his lieutenant, explained that even if Keffer had persuaded a jury in Maine, Harvard was in a position to appeal the verdict, expensively and indefinitely, perhaps all the way to the Supreme Court. The case could have dragged on for years, costing Keffer far more proportionately than Harvard, never insulating him from the possibility that he might lose at the next stage. By settling, he succeeded in his basic goal: making Harvard pay a price for its toplofty disregard of principle.

By muzzling Keffer, Harvard succeeded in burying what was far and away the most telling part of the Harvard Russia scandal: With the nondisclosure agreement, the flesh-and-blood victim had quietly disappeared from the story – along with his motivation, his reputation, his experience and the experiences of his employees. Extremely capable lawyering by Harvard's attorneys, to be sure. What actually happened in the Harvard Russia scandal was obscured.

Even Keffer's single best character reference was effaced. Paul Steiger, Hun School valedictorian in the class of 1960, Keffer's boyhood friend, had become executive editor of the *WSJ* in 1991, retiring in 2007. Steiger played no part in the legal proceedings but, after 50 years of enduring friendship, a better guide to Keffer's character could not be found. The university's attorneys had successfully finagled the most interesting character out of the story, leaving only the government's more abstract case.

13.

Summers left his White House job as economic adviser to the president in 2010, but he hadn't abandoned his ambition for a top job in government. In 2012, he campaigned to be named president of the World Bank. By now I had come to think of the story of the overlooked Forum lawsuit as a column to be held in reserve – one last thing I knew that others didn't, a way to remind readers of how questions arising from the Harvard Russia scandal related to Summers's suitability to high public office. In the summer of 2013, as Summers vied with Janet Yellen for President Obama's nomination to chair the Fed, I expected to write it up if Summers got the nod.

As the president's decision loomed, there came a story in *The Wall Street Journal*, "A Close Bond and a Shared Love for 'Dismal Science': Correspondence between Famously Brash Summers and his Uncle, a Nobel Economist, Reveals Flashes of Humility and Tenderness." Jon Hilsenrath, the paper's senior economics reporter had found, in the archives of the Center for the History of Political Economy, of Duke University, a letter from Paul Samuelson to his friend, Stanley Fischer.

In it, Samuelson blamed Rubin for his nephew's failure to disassociate himself from Shleifer: "Rubin should have compelled Larry to stay out of the Andrei Shleifer Moscow matter." It was the first time the Harvard-Russia scandal had been mentioned in the mainstream press in seven years. A few days later, Summers withdrew. I concluded that his famous uncle's opprobrium had been sufficient to knock Summers out of the race. The full story of the Harvard scandal no longer seemed germane. Once again I put away the files.

14.

It all came back to me with a wallop during the presidential campaign of 2016, this time in connection with NATO expansion. Suddenly Russia was back in the news. The aftermath of the Ukraine crisis had brought US-Russian relations to their lowest point since the Cuban missile crisis. But Talbott and Summers, who had served as understudies in her husband's administration, might be running the Treasury and State departments if Hillary Clinton were elected.

Looking back, I felt I could understand the various temptations of the leaders of the team Harvard sent to Russia and their partners. Shleifer was on a dream mission, putting into practice what he had learned about market systems at Harvard, MIT, and the University of Chicago, talking to those who understood best what he had to say. His parents were happily settled in nearby Brookline. He had had made an exceptionally good marriage, and especially loved his infant son. What about his extracurricular investing? What did he know about faculty rules and American law? What about his brazen lying once he was caught? Under pressure, he had reverted to an earlier Soviet self (chapter 13, "Andrei and [the Baseball Star]).

Zimmerman? Shleifer's wife was a trader, and traders just want to be rich. In 2016, *Bloomberg News* wrote up Bracebridge Capital Management as "The Secretive Hedge Fund That's Generating Huge Profits for Yale." Renamed for the street in Newton where she and Shleifer still lived, Zimmerman's firm had become the biggest US hedge fund to be run by a woman, with assets of $10.3 billion, according to the article. The next year *Forbes* estimated her wealth to be $800 million. Steyer had severed their relationship after 1997 and insisted she change the name, but Swenson at Yale remained a satisfied customer – and a close friend. "We took a hard look and found no reason to modify our relationship," Swenson told *Bloomberg*. Yale's initial investment, which had been $25 million, was now worth something like $1 billion, making it one of the university's most profitable. Bracebridge had just booked a gain of 952 percent on a bet Zimmerman had made a decade before on Argentine debt – a $1 billion return on $120 million in principal. In 2005, she had joined Paul Singer's Elliott Management Corp. and two other funds in refusing to settle, unlike nearly all other lenders, for 30 cents on the dollar, when the floating rate of the bonds froze at 101.5 percent a year.

What about Hay? He was an idealist, eager to make his mark, his father a physician, his brother a professor of molecular biology at California Institute of Technology, his sister a broker for Morgan Stanley in Boise. He had earned a master's degree in economics and philosophy at Harvard as well as his law degree. At some point, he added a PhD in mathematics as well, from the Steklov Mathematica Institute of the Russian Academy of Sciences. Mostly, from 1996 on, he was in love with Hebert.

And Hebert, who impressed everyone she met, with her businesslike mien and her openness? She already had the EBRD fund's business – wasn't she entitled to take the next step in the gold rush? Moscow in 1995. Hay suffered greatly in the aftermath of the scandal, the last to be deposed in the government case for having suffered a severe bout of hemorrhagic pancreatitis at Thanksgiving 2002 and subsequent complications. Hay and Hebert settled down to mundane lives, living in London. Hay is said to have eventually become a partner in Delin Capital, a private investment company that discloses little about itself. Hebert disappeared from my ken.

What about Harvard? As would most non-profit enterprises, the university naturally sought to downplay the charges. Shleifer's colleagues in the economics department routinely made light of the government case. The consensus was, at least as Summers described it in his deposition, that Andrei had somehow been "screwed." The university's administration? Albert Carnesale, a nuclear engineer, was provost for only a few weeks at the very beginning of the affair, but physician Harvey Fineberg served as Harvard's number-two administrator from 1997 until 2001, when the outsider Summers edged him out for the presidency of the university. General Counsel Ann Taylor seems to have done her job; her advice was apparently disregarded. The Faculty Committee on Professional Conduct, a rotating panel of seven senior professors, had been sidelined by the government investigation and subsequent trial. After it finally reported in July 2006, interim dean Jeremy Knowles deprived Shleifer of the endowed chair he had been awarded as an inducement to remain at Harvard, but otherwise sealed the report.

There was considerable turbulence among the governing fellows meeting regularly in Loeb House during Summers' presidency. Shipping executive Robert Stone, of Kirby Corp., retired in 2002 after 27 years on Harvard's seven-member governing corporation, seven of them as its senior fellow. Herbert "Pug" Winokur Jr., of Capricorn Holdings, Inc., an energy investment firm, replaced Richard Smith, of General Cinema, in 2000, but was soon under pressure from alumni to resign for having chaired the finance committee of Enron Corp. Robert Rubin, of Citigroup, who replaced Stone, was conflicted in the Russia matter and presumably recused himself. Attorney Conrad Harper, of Simpson Thacher & Bartlett, resigned in 2005 to protest Summers' stewardship on other grounds. And First Fellow James R. Houghton, of Corning, Inc., was simply not up to the task. The consultancy of Derek Bok, originally sought by Summers to "protect the rights of Shleifer," provided continuity on the matter to the Corporation until Robert Reischauer and Nannerl Keohane replaced Henry Rosovsky and Hanna Holborn Gray on the Corporation.

I could even understand the temptation to Harvard president Neil Rudenstine, who was called upon to make the most important decisions involved in Harvard's defense, to fight the government case instead of capitulating to its demands. Nonprofits, including hospitals, almost reflexively defend themselves when charged with wrongdoing. In this case, people were lying to him. Rudenstine was unfailingly discreet in public, but when Clinton campaign manager John Podesta's personal e-mails turned up on WikiLeaks in 2016, among the more salacious items was a note from corporate law chieftain Robert Pirie warning about Summers's desire to return to the Treasury Department. Summers is "an extra bright version of Donald Rumsfeld, arrogantly unpleasant to his subordinates, dismissive to his equals and pandering to his superiors," wrote Pirie. "I spent some time with Neil Rudenstine on Wednesday, and he would use even stronger terms and would be happy to talk to anyone on the subject." (It occurred to me that message might have revealed as much about his predecessor at Harvard as about Summers.)

## 15.

What I couldn't understand was what Summers had been thinking at each stage along the way. I had first met him in 1983. In our first serious conversation, he had exhorted me to write about "the Trio" – Kevin Murphy, Shleifer, and Robert Vishny – three young University of Chicago professors with a paper on the top-down "big push" approach to economic development that was making waves at the time. I admired him for many reasons. He was a contrarian of sorts, a hard-headed policy-oriented liberal who had served, along with Paul Krugman, on the staff of the Council of Economic Advisers under Martin Feldstein during the first Reagan administration. He was witty, agile, crafty, and possessed a zest for argument that reflected his high school debating days; he was also something

I recognized as fundamentally good-hearted. He knew his limitations as an economist and was relatively candid about them. He had survived an episode of non-Hodgkin's lymphoma. He knew what he wanted to do with his life, joining the Dukakis campaign early on. Summers could clearly be sarcastic to those whom he didn't know, but treated with respect those within his circle of trust who disagreed with him. Many years later, his Treasury subordinate and frequent sparring partner Timothy Geithner would go on to become his most successful sponsee.

I saw Summers less often after he went to Washington. After I praised his appointment to the World Bank by George H. W. Bush, *The Washington Post* stopped running my column; I gathered that dissenting Republicans involved in the decision had complained they hadn't been consulted. As late as 2001, I celebrated his candidacy for the Harvard presidency; I expected that Summers would part company with Shleifer and that in the end Harvard and Shleifer would cop a plea. I was startled when I learned that Summers had stayed with the Shleifer family in Newton when interviewing for the job. McClintick reported that Shleifer and Zimmerman had campaigned for his candidacy.

When pressed in his deposition whether he considered that Shleifer and Hay had done anything wrong, Summers replied that he didn't know enough about contract law and the facts of the matter to have an opinion. He didn't know about USAID, he said, but the Treasury view had been that the crucial test for foreign assistance was whether it was valued by officials to whom it was directed. Summers added:

> I had enough knowledge of Russian mores and Russian practices and Russian views from the conversations I had had with Chubais and Vasiliev to be confident that the set of issues contained in the allegation were not issues that were consequential for them; and indeed, that they would have, in part, valued advisers more extensively if they were more involved in actual private-sector activities.

So Chubais and Vasiliev didn't mind if their American counterparts sought to get rich, muscling in on the mutual fund business and enlisting the Russians to block their legitimate competition. What did the rest of Russia think about that? When in Moscow, Shleifer's wife had been running her hedge fund out of Hay's headquarters. What must Harvard think about that? Nearly 2 percent of the

Harvard endowment was invested in Russia at one point in Summers' Treasury tenure. Was that seemly?

Why did Summers not distance himself from Shleifer after he began interviewing for the Harvard presidency? Had Shleifer lied to him, as he lied to Provost Carnesale? Or did Summers really believe Shleifer was free to invest in Russia while he huddled with its leaders? Might Shleifer possess some coercive secret about his friend? Whatever the case, the cabinet officer-turned-university-president man faced a terrible choice: cut his protégé loose; defend him; or button up. He chose the last option. That didn't mean Summers remained passive. Early in his presidency – he testified that he didn't remember when – he urged Jeremy Knowles, then dean of Arts and Sciences, to make sure that Shleifer remained at Harvard "because I felt he made a great contribution to the economics department."

Paul Samuelson, who presumably enjoyed his nephew's confidence, had, in his letter to Stanley Fischer, blamed Treasury Secretary Rubin for failing to "compel Larry to stay out of the Andrei Shleifer Moscow business." When I thought about it I was inclined to agree. I had often been told that Summers had been deeply impressed early on by Rubin's practical instincts. Then again, I wondered how much Samuelson knew about the course of events. Though he and I spoke occasionally and remained friendly throughout, Summers's troubles never came up.

What did Summers's other famous uncle think? Kenneth Arrow, his mother's brother, angered his nephew by signing a letter on the eve of the Russian election in 1996, along with a group of pre-*perestroika*, pre-*glasnost* Soviet economists, condemning the economic policies of the Yeltsin administration. Summers recalled:

> It got enormous play in Russia. I thought it was an irresponsible and politically naïve act to intervene in a way that would predictably favor the communist [candidate] without checking with the US government. He thought that I was losing my proper focus on what the right economic policy should be, in order to serve the political objective of the government. My poor mother [Selma Summers] had to hear my view of Kenneth's actions and Kenneth's view of my views. Fortunately, there were months that passed before [the traditional family gathering at] Thanksgiving.

In the more prosaic matter of ambition, both Summers and Shleifer were truly committed to the economics profession in their youth, and to Harvard's place at or near its pinnacle. They were its department's leaders, and a strong department often develops self-righteous and intolerant tendencies along with the good. Summers and Shleifer had each been recognized by the Clark Medal, as, earlier, had been their Harvard colleagues Zvi Griliches, Dale Jorgenson, Martin Feldstein, and, for the years they were in Cambridge, Kenneth Arrow and Michael Spence. Even today Shleifer remains the economics department's single most influential teacher within the profession. The lengths to which Summers went to keep him at Harvard could best be understood, I thought, by his devotion to the economics department – much as you'd expect from a nephew of its two most honored living citizens.

In the end, I concluded that the nature of Summers' and Shleifer's friendship was the heart of the matter: a modern-day version of Damon and Pythias. Summers is an excellent debater, a shrewd diagnostician, a thought leader who has promoted a particular style of empirical economics, but from graduate school on few expected that he would one day win a Nobel Prize. Shleifer, on the other hand, was almost instantly recognized as possessing that special brilliance that economists call "depth."

From the beginning, the two men were said to have possessed a nearly seamless bond. Summers might not have been able to compete with either uncle as a deep thinker, but he had made his way in public life in ways they never could. All the while, Shleifer was his other half, a portal, not just to Russia, but to empyreal realms of theory. Whatever the case, Summers paid an enormous price for his loyalty: as his antagonist, former Harvard College dean Harry Lewis later observed, he forfeited his honor. But Summers never betrayed his friend.

Shleifer and Zimmerman through their deceptions, and their refusal to face up to them, destroyed their mentor's career as an educator and public servant. He remains an excellent economist. But Shleifer didn't protect Summers as Summers protected Shleifer.

16.

When I finally caught up with Keffer, in 2011, on the way back from hearing

Summers speak in New Hampshire, he was preparing to travel to Panama. He had sold Forum to Citigroup, in 2003, for an undisclosed sum, presumably tens of millions of dollars, at a time when Citi was hoping to dramatically grow its mutual fund service business. The giant bank didn't succeed, and five years later, on the eve of the financial crisis, Citi sold much of the business back to Keffer for a fraction of the earlier price. (Citi had left the unit in Portland after Keffer split his gains with Forum's employees there.) He changed the name on the door but little else. Atlantic Fund Services mostly runs itself, keeping track of around $10 billion in assets.

In 2009, with time on his hands and money in the bank, Keffer had returned to Panama for a celebration of 40 years of the Peace Corps presence there. He had remained in touch with several fellow team members over the years. One of them, Janet Robinson, joined him and, for two days before the party, they traveled around their old haunts in the mountains of Coclé province. They stopped in Caimito, where the storekeeper Keffer had known 40 years before was still the most civic-minded man in town. The storekeeper convened a town meeting. Keffer asked, what did villagers most need that they lacked? The answer seemed to be schooling – a way to move up in the world. The hamlet possessed only an elementary school and a junior high, grades 7 to 9. The head of the junior high became their adviser. Before the end of the year, Keffer and Robinson had obtained permission from Panama City to open a high school. The former minister of agriculture, who forty years before had lent Keffer the truck, was the first to join his board of directors.

Over the next eight years, Keffer and Robinson reached out to public schools in other small mountain towns, donating computers, seeking out English-language training for students, and encouraging enrollment in various district high schools in Coclé province, wherever they found potential students. After a couple of years they arranged with the Hun School in Princeton to annually enroll two or three of the best graduates to see if they were ready for college. The answer turned out to be no: bright and industrious they were, but fundamentally unprepared by government schools to go on to the next level. Keffer and Robinson decided to start a boarding school, incorporating the International Baccalaureate curriculum, in the expectation that its examinations would be a reliable gauge of results. Panamanians would do all the administration and teaching.

A Panamanian friend offered to rent to Keffer a struggling eco-hotel in a scenic location, not far from a famous waterfall. Forum Academy opened in 2014, free, to 30 students Keffer had carefully chosen. By the time 19 of them graduated, in December 2016, he had spent several million dollars supporting the school; Robinson administered its affairs from her home in Kerrville, Texas. Between them, the two had built something resembling the Hun School – not for jocks aiming for Princeton and other elite colleges but for kids from the central mountains headed to college in Panama City. Keffer began seeking Panamanian funders to take it over.

The better I got to know him, the more exemplary Keffer seemed. He was, I thought, exactly the kind of businessman that USAID, under the Clinton administration, should have found a way to send to Russia and keep involved there, with the full faith and credit of the government of the United States behind him.

Instead, the Clinton team sent an unsupervised 31-year old Russian émigré who, however well he understood Russian ways, possessed so little understanding of fundamental tenets of US fair play that he and his associates soon began breaking the laws they had been sent to Moscow to teach. After Shleifer and Hay and their wives were caught, Harvard lawyers successfully obscured what they had done – confusing even the men and women who governed the university, probably including Summers himself.

It may seem a minor matter at this late date, but Harvard University owes it to the world to unseal that settlement in the Forum case, in order to permit the parties to finally come clean about what actually happened to its advisory mission to Moscow. The Harvard Russia scandal was a small but revealing vignette embedded in a much larger and more serious drama. What went wrong should be thoroughly understood.

THE BROKEN PROMISE

CHAPTER THIRTY-ONE

# Two Roads Diverged

So much, then, for the Harvard Russia scandal. What about the context in which it occurred – the history of US-Russia relations since 1989? In these last five chapters, I return to the frame in which the Harvard story should be understood – to American foreign policy since the dissolution of the Soviet empire. No aspect looms larger in these 25 years than the story of NATO enlargement.

The North Atlantic Treaty Organization was formed as a mutual defense pact in 1949, after the first major crisis of the Cold War – the Berlin Blockade. The 12 original signatories of the treaty included the United States, Britain, Belgium, Canada, France, Iceland, Italy, Luxembourg, the Netherlands, Norway, and Portugal. Why Portugal, which had been neutral in World War II? US military planners considered its Atlantic islands would be crucial in the event of war with the Soviet Union.

Forty years later, when the Berlin Wall was torn down, NATO membership stood at 16: Greece and Turkey had joined the alliance in 1952; West Germany in 1955; and Spain in 1982. East Germany was assimilated as part of the reunification of Germany in 1991. The Soviet Union agreed to the treaty with the understanding – but no written assurance – that there would be no further expansion.

Since then, led by US presidents, NATO has enlarged its membership three more times and contemplated a fourth expansion. Poland, Hungary, and the Czech Republic joined in 1997; Estonia, Latvia, Lithuania, Macedonia, Bulgaria, Romania, Slovakia, and Slovenia in 2004; and Albania and Croatia in 2009, as part of the "Adriatic Charter" (and Montenegro in 2017). Former Soviet republics Georgia and Ukraine were named as prospective members in 2008, but no formal plan was adopted. Russia objected to each expansion with increasing vehemence, claiming that the United States had broken its original promise not to expand further east.

To understand the central place that NATO has come to occupy in the politics of the present day, you need to start with what it was invented to contain – a powerful Soviet Union, bent on domination of Europe (at least) in the aftermath of World War II. Herewith, then, a short history of that competition, prefatory to an account of how it has evolved since 1992.

1.

It is all but impossible to recall now the powerful appeal of the gospel of class struggle that Marx and Engels conjured in 1847, when they wrote *The Communist Manifesto*. Arguments about religious belief had been at the center of Marx's family life and university experiences, and the fervor and certainty of the "dialectical materialism" that came to be associated with his name resembles in many respects the Christianity it sought to replace.

Communism was "modern," it was "scientific" (in the spirit of the age), it was said to be inevitable. An international class of workers ("the proletariat") would vanquish and supplant a middle class labeled "bourgeois." This "final crisis" of global capitalism would commence in the most highly developed centers, Germany or Great Britain. Private property would be abolished. Centrally administered planning would replace markets. "History" would end and a glorious future of new and improved humankind would commence.

Instead, Marxism established itself in Europe's most backward nation. Russia, Lenin announced in *The State and Revolution,* a galvanizing pamphlet, would vault over the socialist phase and establish the world's first communist state. A certain amount of state terror would be required to hound the upper classes into submission. The Bolsheviks took over and, for the next 75 years, the Communist Party governed the Soviet Union by a series of decrees.

The US contest with the Soviet Union dominated the second half of the 20th century, but for young people today the plot points of the drama are little more than questions on the advanced-placement high school history exam. Once-furious controversies have been reduced to search terms. Test yourself on these:

> Bolsheviks and Mensheviks, *The State and Revolution*, Winter Palace, Brest-Litovsk Treaty, Whites and Reds, New Economic Policy, Constructivists, Oswald Spengler, Leon Trotsky, Ukrainian famine, *Homage to Catalonia*, Nikolai Bukharin, Molotov-Ribbentrop Pact, Katyn Forest, Operation Barbarossa, Stalingrad, Yalta Conference, Captive Nations, Long Telegram, Berlin Blockade, Chinese Civil War, Chosin Reservoir, Doctors' Plot, Pumpkin Papers, Dien Bien Phu, Army-McCarthy Hearings, Hungarian Revolution, Khrushchev's Thaw, Sputnik, *Doctor Zhivago*, U2 Incident, Cuban Missile Crisis, Tonkin Gulf Incident, Prague Spring, Tet Offensive, Cultural Revolution, Detente, *The Gulag Archipelago*, Solidarity, Pope John Paul II, KAL 007, Reykjavik, Belovezha Forest Accord.

All are part of the arc of the same story. October 1917 may seem like a long time ago, but it's crucial to remember that the Cold War grew out of the Bolshevik Revolution a century ago. The form communism took in China after 1949 developed differently, but its foundations rested on texts Marx and Lenin wrote. Jonathan Haslam, Kennan Professor at the Institute for Advanced Studies, has described the founding impulse:

> The Cold War stemmed from a thoroughgoing revolt against Western values established since the enlightenment, a wholesale rejection of an entire way of life and its economic underpinnings increasingly dominant since the seventeenth century, and the substitution of something new and entirely alien in terms of culture and experience.

All that is over now. As an experiment on a grand scale – whether the "fundamental breakthrough" to "a better world" portrayed by Edmund Wilson in 1940 in *To the Finland Station*, or the nightmare version depicted by George Orwell in *Animal Farm* in 1945, and *Nineteen Eighty-Four* in 1949 – Soviet communism is now recognized to have been a failure as an economic system. On that much, virtually everyone can agree.

The extent to which it achieved at least some of its lofty social ambitions is still fiercely argued. Vladimir Putin famously put his view this way: "Whoever does not miss the Soviet Union has no heart. Whoever wants it back has no brain." Russia is coming to grips with its history in one way, the United States in another. The really interesting questions now have to do with the 25 years that have passed since the USSR dissolved itself in favor of what it called a Commonwealth of Independent States.

2.

How, then, did the Cold War end? To an extent greater than almost anyone understood at the time, the Soviet Union was already stagnating when Mikhail Gorbachev was designated party chairman in 1985 with a mandate to somehow restructure the economy. The burden of Soviet defense spending was too high. Its industrial-style farming was inefficient and could no longer produce enough food to feed the nation. Declining oil prices, the result of Federal Reserve Chair Paul Volcker's war on inflation in the West, were depleting its gold reserves. Whether Gorbachev jumped or was pushed into loosening the USSR's grip on its empire remains very much an open question. The importance of his role as an agent of change is still as disputed as Reagan's place in American history.

What is clear is that Ronald Reagan and Mikhail Gorbachev and their seconds – Secretary of State George Shultz and Foreign Secretary Eduard Shevardnadze – forged an extraordinary working relationship, took advantage of a series of opportunities at an especially perilous time, and, against all expectations, brought the Cold War to an end. So rapid and complete was the change that almost the first thing George H. W. Bush did on succeeding the rapidly aging Reagan as president was to ask Secretary of State James Baker and National Security Adviser Brent Scowcroft to undertake a full-scale review of US policy towards Russia. Had Reagan and Shultz, charmed by Gorbachev, been taken in?

That Reagan might have become a patsy would have seemed laughable to most people at the time. Americans still argue about the strong anti-government rhetoric of Reagan's campaigns – whether he meant it or not. As president, his domestic policy largely followed from his New Deal beginnings. He backed Volcker's campaign to restore monetary stability, saved the Social Security system, embraced Medicare, broke up the telephone company, and deregulated the computer industry. But on foreign policy Reagan was a venturesome hawk. After taking office he had declared the USSR an evil empire, ramped up military spending, and put in motion development of a vast new "Star Wars" system of space-based missile defense.

Yet Reagan was also deeply interested in nuclear arms limitation talks. He called for a 50 percent cut in strategic missiles and the elimination of intermediate-range weapons. "I think I'm hardline and will never appease," he told George Shultz, "but I do want to try and let them see there is a better world if they'll show *by deed* they want to get along with the Free World." Advertised as "trust, but verify," the approach dramatically reduced tensions in a few years. Yet Reagan's core ambition of ridding the world of nuclear weapons was clearly a pipe dream. No wonder, then, that Bush undertook a reality check.

When Gorbachev refused the pleas of East Germany's communist leaders to crack down on their restive citizenry, and the Berlin Wall came down, Bush, Baker and Scowcroft concluded that Soviet leaders were sincere. Suddenly German reunification, a central goal of US policy for 40 years, seemed within reach.

3.

Bush took over, in January 1989, after defeating former Massachusetts governor. Michael Dukakis in a hard-fought campaign, having vowed to lead "a kinder, gentler nation." He had plenty else abroad to worry about his first year. The United States invaded Panama to disrupt its drug trade, then stood by as pro-democracy demonstrations in Beijing's Tiananmen Square were brutally suppressed. A savings-and-loan crisis reached its bailout phase at home. But turmoil in Eastern Europe dominated the news.

Washington and Bonn preferred that Germany remain in NATO. That meant that the armed forces of East Germany, for 40 years dependable units of the Warsaw Pact, would switch sides. German chancellor Helmut Kohl took leadership of what would be known as the "2 + 4 talks," assuaging doubts, securing agreements among the two Germanys and the four once-allied powers that had governed Berlin since 1945 – Britain, France, the USSR and the United States. Behind the scenes, Baker and Shevardnadze talked about the future of NATO.

Debate has continued ever since about what went on behind the scenes. Baker had promised Gorbachev in February 1990 that NATO's jurisdiction would "not shift one inch eastward" from its present position, and Gorbachev considered he had a deal, but, for one reason or another, he failed to get it in writing. Since the mid-90's, Russians have claimed that the United States violated Baker's pledge not to expand. Many US policymakers and analysts deny it. The ins and out of what went on are tricky.

In "Deal or no Deal? The End of the Cold War and the US Offer to Limit NATO Expansion," Joshua Shifrinson, of Texas A&M University, concludes on the basis of much archival work that the "Russian assertions of a 'broken promise' regarding NATO expansion have merit." Even before the Reunification Treaty was signed in September 1990 in Moscow, NATO was pushing the limits.

That summer had been especially difficult for President Bush. Iraqi dictator Saddam Hussein's forces invaded and occupied Kuwait in August, threatening to reduce oil exports from the Persian Gulf. Bush resolved to remove the occupiers. He thus spent that summer and autumn preparing to go to war with a long-time Soviet ally. He met Gorbachev in Helsinki in September. He conducted closed-door negotiations with congressional leaders to raise gasoline and other taxes to pay for the war, violating a pledge he had made to the Republican convention ("Read my lips: No new taxes!"), only to have liberal Democrats and conservative Republicans sabotage the deal. To secure the Democrats' cooperation, he agreed to raise income taxes on the well-to-do instead.

After a build-up lasting several months, the war started in January 1991; it lasted 96 hours. Iraqi forces, with their Soviet weaponry, were decisively defeated, heightening the turmoil within the Soviet Union and its satellites.

By mid-1991, the Soviet empire was coming apart. All sides scrambled for advantage. Urgent US-Soviet negotiations began, aimed at buying back (with funds appropriated by the US Congress) and returning to Russia nuclear weapons and fissile material from Belarus, Ukraine, and Kazakhstan. The climax came in August, when the head of the KGB and a handful of other high-ranking Communist leaders attempted to arrest Gorbachev and Boris Yeltsin in a *coup d'etat*. They failed, and Gorbachev's government survived, but only because Yeltsin took over.

The final act unfolded in November, when Yeltsin and the leaders of Belarus and Ukraine met at a government hunting lodge in Belovezha Forest, a national park, and, over the course of a weekend, agreed that the three main constituents of the Soviet Union would become independent nations. The USSR formally dissolved a month later. Citing the Germany case as precedent, Poland, Czechoslovakia and Hungary began quietly pressing Washington for admission to NATO. Baker was noncommittal. A North Atlantic Cooperation Council was established. There would be time enough to sort out matters in the second term.

When the 1992 US presidential campaign began, Bush knew he was facing a difficult task. Reagan had been elected in 1980; the White House usually changed parties after three terms. Sure enough, "supply-siders," led by Republican congressman Newt Gingrich, turned on Bush for having agreed to raise taxes. Federal Reserve chairman Alan Greenspan was slow to ease interest rates. Bush's choice of Dan Quayle as running mate didn't work out as he had hoped. And the president himself suffered from mild ill-health.

With billionaire businessman H. Ross Perot pulling 19 percent of the popular vote as a third-party populist candidate, Bill Clinton, the little-known 43-year-old governor of Arkansas, won the presidency.

4.

The United States had arrived at a fork in the road without anyone taking much notice. A new generation was about to take control. Bush (b. 1924) had been a navy pilot in the Pacific in the closing days of World War II; his closest advisers (Baker (b. 1930), Scowcroft (b. 1925), and Treasury Secretary Nicholas Brady (b. 1930)), had come of age in the early days of the Cold War. They served in the military and worked on Cold War policy throughout the '70s and '80s. Former secretary of state Shultz (b. 1920), who continued to exercise great influence, had been a marine during World War II.

Clinton (b. 1946), on the other hand, had suffered the dilemmas of the Vietnam War. He avoided the draft in 1969 with a high lottery number, but not before employing various delaying tactics. His closest advisers – his wife, Hillary Rodham Clinton (b. 1947), Vice President Al Gore (b. 1948), Assistant to the President for Economic Policy Robert Rubin (b. 1938), Deputy Secretary of

State Strobe Talbott (b. 1946), Deputy Treasury Secretary Roger Altman (b. 1946), Labor Secretary Robert Reich (b. 1946) – were formed in the same crucible. Only Gore had served in the military.

Where the Bush team were steeped in the tradition of unsentimental power politics in foreign relations known as realism, the Clinton administration would pursue what came to be called (depending on who did the calling) liberal internationalism or international liberalism – deep-seated convictions about human rights and progress. Now, suddenly, the world had become a different place. The United States had become the world's predominant power. It no longer had a rival.

Clinton had campaigned on a promise to do something about the slow recovery: "It's the economy, stupid!" was written on his campaign war room wall. For the first year of his presidency most of his attention was focused on the passage of a stimulus bill that included a new top income tax-bracket. *The Agenda*, Bob Woodward's book about Clinton's first year, mentions Russia only once, to say that, with the Cold War ended, Clinton concluded that managing Congress would replace the longstanding contest with the Soviet Union as the "threshold test" by which his presidency would be judged.

That didn't mean that the new president didn't harbor some strong ideas about Russia's problems. He had spent the first week of 1970 in Moscow, part of a five-week vacation from Oxford, during his second academic year as a Rhodes Scholar. Afterwards he wrote an 18-page paper for his expatriate Polish tutor, "Political Pluralism in the Soviet Union."

Another Rhodes Scholar, Strobe Talbott, was Clinton's housemate in those days. It was he who had urged Clinton to travel to the Soviet Union; he himself had visited for the first time the year before. An Ohio native (Dayton), Talbott studied Russian at Hotchkiss, majored in Russian literature at Yale (where he was chairman of the *Yale Daily News*), and worked in Moscow as an intern for *Time-Life* in the summer of 1969. In the spring of 1970, he was translating the smuggled diaries of Nikita Khrushchev, which had come into the hands of *Time*.

Clinton began his studies at Yale Law School, where he met and married Hillary

Rodham, before returning to Arkansas politics. Talbott went to work for *Time*, eventually becoming the magazine's Washington bureau chief. Twenty years later Clinton was president of the United States. Talbott became architect of his Russia policy.

Talbott's views had been enriched by keeping company with his friend Richard Holbrooke, with whom Talbott had toured Eastern Europe in the late '80s. An old Vietnam hand who turned to investment banking after a decade as editor of *Foreign Policy*, Holbrooke was scathing about the passivity of the Bush administration as Yugoslavia, for nearly 50 years a USSR satellite, began to break apart. Already in '93, Holbrooke told Talbott that NATO eventually would be required to intervene in the Balkans to keep peace. Holbrooke's core consideration, according to his friend Roger Cohen, a future columnist for *The New York Times*: "the West had a responsibility to ensure the freedom and security of the nations that had been cast into the Soviet totalitarian nightmare at Yalta, in 1945."

Talbott and Holbrooke worked to make certain that NATO expansion would become "one of the pillars" of the Clinton administration's foreign policy. Holbrooke would become Clinton's ambassador to Germany and, later, assistant secretary of state for Europe and Eurasian affairs. Talbott would become deputy secretary of state. Within the Clinton administration, Defense Secretary Les Aspin, and his deputy, William Perry, opposed expansion. So did most senior American military commanders, predicting a "train wreck" in relations with Russia if it were to go ahead. There were plenty of outside critics as well, including many former officials in the Bush administration.

But with National Security Adviser Anthony Lake leading the charge, and Talbott heading an interagency committee, Russia's protests were ignored. Expansion would make Russian internal politics more difficult, Talbott acknowledged in his memoir, and would strain Russia's relationship with the West. "Don't do this!" warned his opposite number in the Russian Foreign Ministry. "Nevertheless, it was the right thing to do," wrote Talbott.

5.

The '90s were Russia's toughest years. Privatization began, but inflation reduced savings to sawdust and joblessness soared. Old-line Communists regained influence in elections. In September 1993, Yeltsin forced a showdown, dissolving the old Supreme Soviet once and for all, ordering elections of a new parliament to retroactively affirm a new constitution. Rebel lawmakers attempted a coup but failed ignominiously. Yeltsin's government persevered, supported at every turn by the Clinton administration.

Behind the scenes, NATO expansion had become a policy objective. In mid-'93 Secretary of State Warren Christopher had stated that it was "not on the agenda." By the end of the year it was. Lech Walesa of Poland, Vaclav Havel of Czechoslovakia, and Arpad Goncz of Hungary met with Clinton in Washington to press for admission. Even Yeltsin seemed to entertain the possibility in an off-hand comment on a visit to Poland in August.

At a NATO conference in Prague in January '94 Clinton made it official: expansion would take place, "not whether but when." He notified Yeltsin beforehand, but didn't consult him. Yeltsin countered with a proposal, first privately to Clinton, then publicly, that post-communist states should enter NATO, or a successor organization, as a bloc, "at an appropriate time" – in 10 to 20 years, in the timetable that Prime Minister Viktor Chernomyrdin suggested. The Clinton team went ahead without further consultation. Yeltsin's biographer Timothy Colton wrote later: "A ticking time bomb had been set."

Meanwhile, in the Balkans – where wars in 1911 and 1912 had lit the fuse that led to World War I – ethnic antagonisms were boiling over. In April 1992, the Serbian army laid siege to Sarajevo, capital of secessionist Bosnia and Herzegovina. European diplomacy failed to halt the conflict. Holbrooke's and Talbott's fears were realized: Yugoslavia was falling apart. After the Srebrenica massacre of Bosnian Muslims, in July '95, NATO forces bombed Bosnian Serb positions at the insistence of the Clinton administration. Yeltsin fumed, but was powerless to stop either the conflict itself or the intervention.

The Bosnian War ended in November '95 when Holbrooke and former Swedish prime minister Carl Bild brokered the Dayton Accords. Russian troops were included in the peace-keeping arrangements, but subordinated to NATO commanders. News of the intervention played no better in Russia than did the loans-for-shares sleight-of-hand privatization occurring at the same time. Communist and ultranationalist candidates scored big gains in Russia's parliamentary elections. Yeltsin seemed certain to be defeated for a second term.

Against all odds, Yeltsin was re-elected in July. Clinton had promised Yeltsin that NATO would postpone the vote on Polish, Hungarian and Czech Republic membership until after both presidents were reelected. (Czechoslovakia had dissolved itself in 1993 and Slovakia remained on the sidelines.) Russian diplomats sounded out Talbott on conditions that might make expansion acceptable: no nuclear weapons in new member states; "co-decision-making" on issues involving European security; and a formal treaty to enshrine both provisions. The United States ruled out all three: no treaty, no veto, and no promise: "NATO wasn't going to consign new members to second-class status by promising never, under any circumstances to put nuclear weapons on their territory," wrote Talbott a few years later.

6.

With the November 1996 election approaching in the United States, opposition to NATO expansion stiffened among experts. Talbott remembered, "It seemed virtually everyone I knew from the world of academe, journalism, and the foreign-policy think-tanks was against enlargement." Diplomat George Kennan denounced the measure as "a strategic blunder of potentially epic proportions." Fifty prominent foreign policy experts signed an open letter opposing enlargement the following June, including Democratic stalwarts Bill Bradley, Sam Nunn, Gary Hart; arms control expert Paul Nitze; and former defense secretary Robert McNamara. John Lewis Gaddis, of Yale University, a prominent historian of the Cold War, described the policy as "ill-conceived, ill-timed, and above all ill-suited to the realities of the post-Cold War world." Indeed, he continued,

> I can recall no other moment in my experience as a practicing historian at which there was less support, within the community of historians, for an announced policy position.

Clinton was undeterred. They were not, of course, polling Russians. Talbott assured him that polls showed only the foreign policy elite objected. Meeting in Helsinki in March, Yeltsin asked Clinton to exclude Baltic nations from membership, at least any time soon. Clinton simply waltzed him around. About the same time, Senator Richard Lugar published a report of a study group assembled by the Council on Foreign Relations: "Russia, Its Neighbors, and an Enlarging NATO" (the project was overseen by an up-and-comer named Victoria Nuland). With prestige derived from the success of the nuclear buy-in he had sponsored a few years before, Lugar argued in favor of continued enlargement. Stability in central Europe was "just as much in Russia's interests as our own," he wrote. Membership should soon be offered to the Baltic states and Ukraine, the task force concluded. Only one of the 29 members disagreed: Scowcroft. "The kind of unlimited expansion implicit in the report would be a disaster," he wrote in a stinging dissent.

By now Clinton was preoccupied by Russia's aid to Iran's ballistic missile program and its program to develop nuclear weapons. Israel was furious about the situation, and the US Congress was threatening sanctions against Russia. Soon the American president had a problem of his own making: revelations of the Lewinski affair surfaced in January 1998. By March, it was clear the Russian economy was headed for serious trouble; the crisis came to a head in August. Meanwhile, Serbian president Slobodan Milosevic had begun another ethnic cleansing campaign, this time aiming to drive ethnic Albanians out of a region where they had lived for decades.

Once again Talbott and Holbrooke – the latter now Clinton's nominee to become US ambassador to the UN – pressed NATO to prepare to intervene, under the doctrine of "responsibility to protect" that had been fashioned throughout the '90s by political scientists, philosophers, historians, legal scholars and commentators. China opposed intervention, even on these humanitarian grounds, as did Russia. In a stormy phone call to Clinton in October, Yeltsin described the use of force as something more than unacceptable. It was "forbidden," he said, hanging up. The bombing began in March.

This time Russian resentment boiled over – Foreign Minister Yvgeny Primakov, headed for talks in Washington, ordered his airplane to turn around in mid-air. Barely a thousand bombs dropped on Serbian targets in the course of a month had sufficed to end the Bosnian War in 1995. The war in Kosovo required much more force – 44 days of bombing, with hundreds of sorties a day. Soon

NATO forces began bombing military targets in Belgrade itself. A truce took hold, and Yeltsin dispatched a column of troops to serve as peace-keepers. A tense confrontation between the American commander of NATO forces and a detachment of Russian paratroopers in control of the Pristina airport was defused.

The Kosovo intervention left an especially bitter taste among ordinary Russians. The treatment of its old ally was viewed as irrefutable evidence that the United States believed it could do whatever it pleased. Clinton admitted privately that "something pretty basic is broken." Yeltsin narrowly staved off a second impeachment attempt in the spring. In August, with the end of his second term approaching, he chose as prime minister, his presumptive successor, a former foreign intelligence officer named Vladimir Putin. Why Putin? Timothy Colton found a clue in *Presidential Marathon*, Yeltsin's final memoir. Of an earlier decision, to hire a new chief of staff the year before, he wrote:

> I was already coming to feel that society needed some new quality in the state, a steel backbone that would strengthen the political structure of authority. We needed a person who was thinking, democratic, and innovative, yet steadfast in the military manner. The next year, such a person did appear... Putin.

7.

The Clinton administration had set out the pattern of NATO expansion. The next two administrations largely followed suit. There was a short-lived enthusiasm for a change of direction after George W. Bush was elected, generated by his father's advisers. Putin had come into office talking about Russia joining NATO. James Baker wrote about the advantages of having a partner, instead of a rival. "One sad lesson of the twentieth century is that refusing to form alliances with defeated adversaries is more dangerous than forming such alliances." The proposal went nowhere.

Six months after taking office, Bush met Putin for the first time, in Slovenia. He looked the Russian president in the eye, he said, and saw "an honest, straightforward man." By most accounts, the two genuinely liked each other. Vice President Dick Cheney, on the other hand, told friends that whenever he saw Putin, announced, "I think KGB, KGB, KGB."

Then came 9/11. The Al Qaeda raids were only the third time in history that America had been attacked on its own soil: the British expedition to burn the Capitol and the White House, in 1814, was the first; Pearl Harbor, in 1941, was second. The effect on Bush was transformative. Two weeks later he asked Defense Secretary Donald Rumsfeld to secretly develop plans to invade Iraq. The Russian president had been the first to call Bush to offer aid; their friendship was genuine. Putin visited Bush at home in Crawford, Texas, in November 2001. To that point, Bush was hoping to keep him "inside the tent," he later explained, expecting that both the United States and Russia would soon be dealing with the Chinese. Gradually the darker Cheney view of Putin gained the upper hand.

By the end of 2002, Bush had abandoned his attempt to chart a new course with Russia. He traveled to Prague in November for the NATO summit, where he pressed for a "big bang" admission of Estonia, Latvia, and Lithuania, plus Romania, Bulgaria, Slovakia and Slovenia. That was divisive enough, but far more so were his plans to invade Iraq. Bush sought to gather a coalition, as his father had in 1991, but German chancellor Gerhard Schröder opposed the invasion, as did French president Jacques Chirac. Rumsfeld replied to their objections with a dismissive distinction between "Old Europe" and "New Europe."

After Colin Powell reassured the UN about the presence of "weapons of mass destruction," Putin flew first to Berlin, then to Paris, to align himself with the Germans and the French in opposition to the war. High-level last-minute talks with the Russians failed completely – when the Russians warned of jihad, the United States offered to compensate them for the loss of their oil contracts. So the United States went to war in March 2003 with only the British among their major allies. About the same time as Bush's "mission accomplished" landing on a US aircraft carrier, Putin called him to warn about what might happen next. "This is going to be awfully difficult for you," he said. "I feel bad for you." The war in Iraq quickly bogged down. Still, Bush was re-elected.

That fall, Chechen terrorists seized a school in Beslan in the Caucasus and held it until negotiations broke down. Nearly 400 people were killed, most of them children, in the rescue attempt. Previously the United States and Russia had cooperated successfully in dealing with Islamic extremists. That autumn the United States had refused to work closely with Russia against the Chechen rebels

– some of them were moderates in Washington's eyes, their secessionist grievances legitimate. According to Thomas Graham, who served as senior director for Russia on the US National Security Council from 2004 to 2007, the Beslan terror was a turning point in US-Russia relations. Then came the Orange Revolution.

In Moscow's reading, the United States had master-minded the protests and streets scenes in Ukraine in order to install a pro-Western figure as president instead of Yanukovych, the candidate Putin had endorsed – perhaps a dress-rehearsal for regime change in Russia itself. Soon after Viktor Yushchenko was installed, Putin spoke obliquely to a television audience about the United States and what he considered its long-range plans:

> Some want to tear off a big chunk of our country. Others help them do it. They help because they think that Russia, one of the greatest nuclear powers of the world, is still a threat, and this threat has to be eliminated. And terrorism is only an instrument to achieve these goals.

Bush ignored Putin's complaints. In his second inaugural address, in January 2005, the American president escalated his ambitions, expositing a new "Freedom Agenda." Henceforth the mission of the United States, said Bush, would be "to seek and support the growth of democratic movements and institutions in every nation and culture, with the ultimate goal of ending tyranny in our world." The supporting role Washington had played in Ukraine's "Orange Revolution," in 2004, and Georgia's "Rose Revolution," in 2005, would continue. The next year, in a speech that especially infuriated the Russians, Cheney asserted in Vilnius, Lithuania, that "no one can justify actions that interfere with democratic movements."

A pair of high-visibility Russian political assassinations provided counterpoint – journalist Anna Politkovskaya in Moscow, former FSB agent Alexander Litvinenko in London. Both were routinely blamed on Putin. Who could doubt that the United States had been wise to expand NATO? Putin countered: "It is extremely dangerous to attempt to rebuild modern civilization, which God had created to be diverse and multifaceted, according to the barracks principles of a unipolar world."

8.

As he neared the end of his second term as president, Putin was riding high. In 1999, just before taking office, he had published an unusual broadside. In

"Russia at the Turn of the Millennium," Putin had sounded an alarm: "Russia is in the midst of one of the most difficult periods in its history, For the first time in the past 200-300 years, it is facing a real threat of sliding to the second, and possibly even third echelon of states in the world. We are running out of time for removing this threat," he had written. Now he had been in office for seven years. Russia was more prosperous than it had ever been. Oil prices were nearing $100 a barrel, and Putin had begun using its pipelines to extract political concessions from neighboring governments. He had groomed a pair of aides as successors to the presidency in 2008 – Chief of Staff Dimitry Medvedev and Minister of Defense Sergei Ivanov.

In February 2007, Putin adopted a new public posture. In a strong speech to the Munich Security Conference, he accused the United States of having become a global bully since the end of the Cold War. The United States had plunged the Mideast into turmoil with its invasion if Iraq. It had begun an unnecessary new arms race with its pursuit of space weapons and systems of missile defense. It had moved NATO to the borders of Russia. Putin didn't mention the Guantanamo prison, rendition of suspects to secret interrogation centers in nations around the world, and the torture and prisoner abuse at Abu Ghraib in Iraq, but he didn't have to. It had all been in the headlines for two years.

> Today, we are witnessing an almost uncontained hyper use of force – military force – in international relations, force that is plunging the world into an abyss of permanent conflicts.... We are seeing a greater and greater disdain for basic principles of international law... the United States has overstepped its national borders in every way... in the economic, political, cultural, and educational policies it imposes on other nations. Well, who likes this?

Putin had chosen his venue carefully. German chancellor Angela Merkel, US Defense Secretary Robert Gates, Senators John McCain and Lindsey Graham sat stony-faced in the audience. Gates replied mildly in his address the next day: "One Cold War was quite enough." Russia, he said, "is a partner in our endeavors."

Putin's speech was part of a broad change in Russian self-presentation. The mild-mannered Medvedev had been a hit at Davos the month before. Russia Today, a new government-owned television channel, had begun broadcasting in English in 2005, with a 25-year-old editor-in-chief, Margarita Simonyan (who had spent a student year in New Hampshire), and snappy new look. Originally dismissed as just so much propaganda, like the Munich speech, Simonyan's appointment signaled that Russia was embracing Western standards of case-making. RT would have many Bill O'Reillys of its own, but its coverage of the world through Russian eyes would be not much worse than that of Fox News, and sometimes better.

Most Americans scarcely noticed Russia's new stance. Bush had announced his surge in Iraq the month before Putin spoke; he still hoped to be seen to have "won." Otherwise his presidency had been hobbled by a series of reversals, culminating in devastating midterm elections, in which Democrats gained control of both houses of Congress. He had appointed Henry Paulson treasury secretary and Ben Bernanke chairman of the Federal Reserve Board; within a year they would be dealing with a looming sub-prime lending crisis. The president was heading for the sidelines.

But Bush had time to visit Putin in Sochi, on his way to the fractious NATO summit in Bucharest, where membership for Ukraine and Georgia was to be discussed. The Eastern European nations, NATO's newest members, clamored for their admission; Germany and France voiced their doubts. No formal "action plans" were prepared; instead, there was strong language in the communique: "We agreed today that these countries will become members of NATO."

There was no long wait for a reaction. In August, Russia bloodied Georgia's nose in a short-lived war over the fate of the breakaway republics of South Ossetia and Abkhazia in the southern Caucasus. Forty thousand Russian soldiers set the Georgian army on its heels and, after five days, stopped just short of Tbilisi before turning around and going home. The breakaways were recognized as newly independent nations. Russia's reply to NATO was relatively little-noticed by the public in the run-up to the global financial crisis. Only presidential candidate John McCain raised a ruckus. Ten years later, South Ossetia continues to hope that Russia will annex it; Abkhazia, which simply wanted to be free of Georgia, is an economic basket case.

9.

Senator Barack Obama outpolled Senator John McCain in 2008, 53-46 percent. He began his term as president with another round of hopes for a "reset" of relations with Russia. He had defeated Hillary Clinton in the primaries largely on the strength of his opposition to the war in Iraq (although he had not been elected to the Senate in time to cast a vote against it). So it was a surprise when he asked Clinton to serve as secretary of state and she accepted.

Clinton had often scorned Putin in her campaign. George W. Bush might have claimed he had looked into Putin's eyes and gotten "a sense of his soul," but she knew better. "He was a KGB agent – he doesn't have a soul," she told a fund-raising crowd. And from the beginning, Clinton sought to differentiate her views from those of the president, according to Mark Landler, White House correspondent for *The New York Times*. "Avidly, if discreetly, Clinton played the house Hawk in Obama's war cabinet," Landler wrote in *Alter Egos: Hillary Clinton, Barack Obama, and the Twilight Struggle over American Power*.

Clinton was close to Talbott and to Holbrooke (who died, at 69, in 2010). In Landler's account, she took a special pleasure in baiting Putin. After Russia's parliamentary elections of 2012, at a meeting of European leaders in Lithuania, Clinton reproached Russia for fraud and intimidation – on the eve of Putin's campaign for a third presidential term. "Putin was livid," wrote Landler; he considered that Clinton had deliberately sent "a signal" to "some actors in our country," sending protesters into to the streets in Russia's first major demonstrations since the 1990s. US enthusiasts of regime change hopefully dubbed it "the Snow Revolution."

All this was in the distant background of the news. Obama's first two years in office were devoted to coping with a deep recession, and to the passage of the Affordable Care Act. The midterm Tea Party election and budget impasses dominated the two years after that. The Arab Spring had begun in December 2010 – ostensibly democratic revolutions in North Africa and the Middle East – at least there was more good news on the international front, or so it seemed. As secretary of state, Clinton pushed for intervention in Libya, over the objections of Defense Secretary Robert Gates. Not until September 2012, when Clinton's ambassador to Libya and three other Americans were killed in an attack on the American consulate in Benghazi, did foreign policy begin to return to center stage. Qaddafi himself was hunted down and killed in October, but by then congressional Republicans had begun the investigation that would hound Clinton for the next four years.

Practically unnoticed as Obama defeated Mitt Romney in 2012 was Putin's pursuit of the trade zone he was seeking to form among several former Soviet republics, including Ukraine and Belarus: the Eurasian Economic Community (EAEC). Its creation was among the chief planks of his return to power. It was this, perhaps, that Romney had in mind when, during the campaign, he pronounced Russia "without question our number-one geopolitical foe." In December, Hillary Clinton described Putin's plan as an effort to "re-Sovietize" the region and said, "We are trying to figure out effective ways to slow it down or prevent it."

Turbulence continued throughout 2013. Moscow first tried to browbeat Ukraine with a trade war to make its case; it then sought to entice its neighbor to join the EAEC with a large package of economic aid. When President Viktor Yanukovych wobbled in November, demonstrators favoring membership in the European Union instead began gathering in Kiev's main square, the Maidan, site of the Orange Revolution in 2004.

The Sochi Olympics eclipsed the crisis in the United States, but in Kiev it continued to build. A hastily contrived diplomatic agreement in February sought to halt the demonstrations by promising new elections in December. But when the protests turned violent, the promise was quickly forgotten. Yanukovych, who had been democratically elected, fled to Moscow.

The single most intriguing mystery of the Ukrainian crisis has to do with Victoria Nuland, by now assistant secretary of state for European and Eurasian affairs, who was seen passing out cookies to demonstrators in Maidan Square days before Yanukovych's flight. In the '90s, she had been chief of staff to Talbott. She became deputy national security advisor to Vice President Dick Cheney on the eve of the war in Iraq. After four years as ambassador to NATO, she spent two years in the private sector before returning to government as spokesperson for Secretary of State Clinton. By 2013 Nuland was the Obama administration's point person on Russia. It was Nuland who in February was secretly taped, probably by the Russians, saying "F— the EU" for dragging its feet in supporting the demonstrators. The conversation was anonymously posted to the Internet. That was, of course, Russia's first hack.

Putin responded to what he called the Ukraine "coup" with another speech, this one given in an ornate room in the Kremlin to an audience of parliamentarians and political grandees. Like his Munich address seven years before, the speech was designed to be read in the West. Russia was, Putin said, bound to act.

> [O]ur Western partners crossed the line, conducting themselves crudely, irresponsibly, and unprofessionally. After all, they were fully aware that millions of Russians live in Ukraine and Crimea. They must have lost all their political instincts and even common sense. Not to foresee the consequences of their actions Russia was pushed to a point beyond which it could no longer retreat. If you compress a spring as tightly as possibly, eventually it will snap back hard....

Of Western policies since the end of the Cold War, Putin said,

> They have deceived us many times, made decisions behind our backs, placed before us *faits accomplis*. This happened with NATO's expansion to the east, as well as the deployment of military infrastructure near our borders. They kept telling us the same thing, "Well, this does not concern you." Easy for them to say. ...They are constantly trying to force us into a corner because we have independent policies, because we stand up for ourselves, because we call things like we see them and do not engage in hypocrisy.

Ukraine formed a government, dominated by ministers drawn from the pro-Europe regions of the country. The US government announced its "strong support." Whereupon Putin played the card he had left. He moved Russian troops to the border and sent well-armed special forces into Crimea to take over Ukrainian government buildings, insignia removed from their uniforms. Two weeks of uncertainty followed; back-channel negotiations went nowhere; and, in March, a plebiscite hastily organized by the Russian-speaking population (its polls supervised by Russian soldiers) approved annexation by the improbable margin of 97 percent. Local militias began a civil war, and Russia took over the peninsula. Nikita Khrushchev had ceded Russian jurisdiction in the Crimea to the Ukrainian Soviet Socialist Republic in 1954. Now its "reunification" with Russia was complete.

The civil war in eastern Ukraine escalated, and threatened to spread. In

September 2014, Obama convened a meeting of outside foreign policy experts and asked, "Will somebody tell me: what's the American stake in Ukraine?" In Landler's account:

> Strobe Talbott, who had spent much of his professional career studying the Soviet threat during the Cold War, was slack-jawed. Preserving the territorial integrity of states liberated from the Soviet Union was an article of faith in Washington, at least for those of Clinton's generation, who had watched the Soviets invade Hungary in 1956. Talbott argued that the West couldn't simply stand by while the East had its way with one of its neighbors…Stephen Hadley, who had been George W. Bush's National Security adviser, echoed him. "Well, I see it somewhat differently than you do," Obama replied. "My concern is that it will be a provocation, it'll trigger a Russian escalation that we're not prepared to match."

A year later, Hillary Clinton was publicly advocating providing defensive missiles to the Ukrainian army – anti-tank missiles and the like. The Russians, she told a fund-raiser, were behaving like the old Soviets, seeking "to stymie and to confront and to undermine American power wherever and whenever they can." She continued,

> We all wish that Putin would choose to modernize his country and move toward the West instead of sinking himself deeper into the historical roots of czar-like behavior and intimidation along borders and projecting Russian power in places like Syria and elsewhere.

And there matters stood when the presidential campaign of 2016 raised the temperature sharply without adding any clarity to the debate.

10.

A few months after the annexation of Crimea, *Foreign Affairs* conducted an illuminating exchange of views. It is as good a place as any to assess the current situation. John Mearsheimer, of the University of Chicago, wrote "Why the Ukraine Crisis Is the West's Fault." Mearsheimer is, after Henry Kissinger, the leading expositor of the realist view in international affairs, and described a triple package of encroachment: NATO enlargement, European Union expansion, and aggressive democracy promotion. Of these, NATO was the "taproot" of the trouble. Putin's actions should be easy to comprehend, he wrote, especially for those who remembered Russian experiences with Napoleonic France (in 1812), imperial Germany (in World War I) and Nazi Germany (in World War II). He continued,

> No Russian leader would tolerate [NATO], a military alliance that was Moscow's mortal enemy until recently, moving into Ukraine. Nor would any Russian leader stand idly by while the West helped install a government there that was determined to integrate Ukraine into the West.... After all, the United States does not tolerate distant great powers deploying military forces anywhere in the Western hemisphere, much less on its borders. Imagine the outrage in Washington if China built an impressive military alliance and tried to include Canada and Mexico in it.

Michael McFaul, 53, Obama's in-house Russia expert and, later, ambassador to Moscow, took the opposite view. Back at Stanford University after his government service, he argued that if Russia was really opposed to NATO expansion, he asked, why didn't Yeltsin raises a stink after 1999, when NATO expansion began? Hadn't Russian president Dimitry Medvedev permitted the United States to continue to operate its airbase in Kyrgyzstan? Hadn't he tacitly acquiesced to NATO intervention in Libya?

> In the five years that I served in the Obama administration, I attended almost every meeting Obama held with Putin and Medvedev, and, for three of those years, while working at the While House, I listened in on every phone conversation, and I cannot remember NATO expansion ever coming up.

The real reason for the annexation, McFaul contended, had to do with internal Russian politics. Putin needed to cast the United States as an enemy in order to discredit those who opposed his election to a third presidential term. He feared a "color revolution," like the Orange Revolution in Ukraine in 2004, might force him from power.

Meanwhile, Alexander Lukin, vice president of the Diplomatic Academy of the Russian Ministry of Foreign Affairs, described "What the Kremlin Is Thinking:

Putin's Vision for Eurasia." Western leaders who wished to resolve the Ukraine crisis and prevent similar ones from occurring in the future, "had better get at putting themselves in Moscow's shoes," he wrote. He described the Eurasian Union Putin was seeking to create, linking the economies of Armenia, Belarus, Georgia, Kazakhstan, Kyrgyzstan, Russia, Tajikistan, and Ukraine. It would, he said, be similar to the European Union but not particularly a rival to it.

Russian Slavophiles had long spoken of the special nature of Russian civilization, Lukin observed. They contrasted the collectivism of Russian peasant communities with traditions of European individualism, emphasizing Russian singularity and "togetherness." Now the nationalists were identifying commonalities with those who spoke the family of Turkic languages, or "Turanians," of the Central Asian Steppe, where culture and values also differed markedly from standards prevailing in the West. Religious fundamentalism had maintained (or, in Russia, reasserted) the upper hand across the spectrum of religions –orthodox Christianity, Islam, Judaism, and Buddhism. Western permisssiveness was rejected in favor of strong stands against homosexuality, abortions, and euthanasia. In this view, the present-day Russian Federation could be said to have much in common with Iran.

11.

This much is background. Where do the underlying matters stand today? NATO enlargement has yet to become a familiar topic, much less the Clintons' long-running commitment to it. The election of Donald Trump has confused the issue. What will it take to get discussion going? A lot more than this little book.

A fair amount of scholarship is already in the works. Keep an eye on historians Andrew Bacevich, of Boston University, and Mary Elise Sarotte, of the University of Southern California; and on strategists Mearsheimer and Stephen Walt, of Harvard's Kennedy School of Government. Expect an avalanche of argumentation in the next few years. I will continue to track it periodically on *Economic Principals.com*, consistent with whatever else is going on. In the meantime, I feel as though I owe the reader a few more licks.

CHAPTER THIRTY-TWO

# The Generation of '91

I met an old friend in the library one afternoon, a sharp old hand who had done time in Moscow many years before. It was the autumn of 2016; I had an armful of books. "What are you reading?" she asked. "Russia," I replied, with some enthusiasm. "Oh, Russia! Who cares?" Relations between the two countries are the worst since in 1963. How did we get so far off the track? The US press must bear a certain portion of the blame.

1.

The Soviet Union had been a forbidding place for journalists during the Cold War, because it was so expensive of money and grit to maintain a bureau there – a plum assignment for up-and-comers, a haven for those passionate or curious enough to abide year after year. Like many others of my generation, I first learned about the country from *The Russians*, by Robert Kaiser of *The Washington Post*, and *Russia: The People and the Power*, by Hedrick Smith of *The New York Times*, both books published in the Watergate year of 1976. By the end of the decade, a somber mood had set in. *Russia: Broken Idols, Solemn Dreams* (Times Books, 1983), by David Shipler, a *Times* correspondent in Moscow from 1975 to 1979, reflected the developing Soviet sclerosis. The book was regularly confiscated from travelers entering the USSR.

After Gorbachev became party secretary in 1985, Moscow slowly came alive. A talented press corps assembled to cover the demise of the Soviet Union. By the early '90s, Moscow became an open city, a magnet for talented young journalists of all sorts. Representatives of the big papers still ruled the roost. A series of successful books shaped public perceptions: *Lenin's Tomb: The Last Days of the Soviet Empire*, by David Remnick of *The Washington Post*, won a Pulitzer Prize in 1993. *Down with Big Brother: The Fall of the Soviet Empire*, by Michael Dobbs, appeared in 1997, after its author served successive terms in Yugoslavia, Poland and Russia for the *Post*. Serge Schmemann, of *The New York Times*, a highly influential Moscow reporter in those years, published his prescient *Echoes of a Native Land: Two Centuries of a Russian Village* (Knopf), also in 1997.

By then, a second generation had arrived to tell the story of the transition, of "shock therapy" and privatization. You can get a vivid feeling for the times from David Hoffman, of the *Post*, who published *The Oligarchs: Wealth and Power in the New Russia* in 2002; or from *Sale of the Century: Russia's Wild Ride from Communism to Capitalism* (2000), by Chrystia Freeland, then of the *Financial Times* (today she is Canada's foreign minister). A third excellent book – *Rebirth of a Nation, An Anatomy of Russia*, by John Lloyd, of the *Financial Times* – didn't get nearly the attention it deserved when it appeared, only in Great Britain, in 1998, a harbinger of the disappointment that would set in.

By the time the husband-and-wife team of Peter Baker and Susan Glaser arrived for the *Post*, in late 2000, the narrative of disappointment was taking hold. *Kremlin Rising: Vladimir Putin's Russia and the End of Revolution* appeared in 2005; scorn for Putin is palpable throughout. Baker took over the White House beat for the *Post*, where he wrote the excellent *Days of Fire*, about the administration of George W. Bush, before moving to the *Times*. Steven Lee Myers spent seven years in Moscow for the *Times* and produced the very useful *The New Tsar: The Rise and Reign of Vladimir Putin* in 2015. The next year, *Times* White House correspondent Mark Landler published *Alter Egos: Hillary Clinton, Barack Obama, and the Twilight Struggle over American Power*, a revealing account of the foreign policy differences between the president and his would-be successor. Taken together, these 10 books constitute the spine of the narrative of the mainstream press since Gorbachev.

None of the three authors who concentrated on the years of the transition – Freeland, Hoffman, Lloyd – had anything to say about the Harvard Russia scandal, but that's not the issue here. Perhaps a special place in journalism hell might be found for Strobe Talbott who, for more than a decade, was *Time* magazine's reigning expert on US-Russia affairs. Whatever history makes of Talbott as an architect of NATO enlargement during the seven years he served as deputy secretary of state – he described his experiences in detail in *The Russia Hand: A Memoir of Presidential Diplomacy* – surely the one-time newsman is to be condemned for the fact that, for all its pretensions to faithful reproduction of the inside track, *The Russia Hand* doesn't mention the Harvard Russia scandal. That's *my* idea of corruption.

It is the collective mood swing, euphoria to hostility, that interests me here. Many North Americans, in particular, believed they were witnessing a Second Russian Revolution, equal and opposite to the first. They took the revolution's success for granted and made little or no attempt to report the way it looked to Russian eyes. (They didn't say much about NATO expansion, either.) When it didn't turn out that way, they were profoundly disappointed.

To be sure, the Moscow press corps in the '90s was large, brilliant, and various – it produced a biweekly free tabloid, *The eXile*, aimed at the expatriate community, which added to the ferment – and it is easy to find counterexamples. Matt Taibbi, of *Rolling Stone* magazine, comes to mind. But, with the exception of the *FT*'s John Lloyd, the more prominent journalists in Moscow in the late '80s and early '90s were liberal internationalists. I think of them as the Generation of '91, and David Remnick, editor of *The New Yorker*, as their foremost exemplar. His influence spans those 30 years, from 1988 to the present day.

2.

Remnick, born in 1958, grew up in Hillsdale, New Jersey, a suburb northwest of New York, his father a dentist, his mother an art teacher. He studied Russian in high school, and majored in comparative literature at Princeton University, where he met the writer John McPhee. Instead of waiting on tables as an undergraduate, Remnick worked as a stringer for newspapers and, summers, painted houses. After graduating, he taught English for a six months in a Japanese university. *The Washington Post* hired him in 1982, and, after he advanced swiftly through the paper's sports, style, and metro sections, posted him to Moscow in 1988. He was 29 years old.

During the next four years, Remnick distinguished himself in an especially talented press corps, writing three or four hundred stories a year. It wasn't easy for Remnick to move to Russia, still less easy for his wife, Esther Fein, previously a reporter for *The New York Times*. Remnick's grandfathers had successfully left Vilnius and Kiev for the United States after 1905. Fein's mother and her family had a far rougher escape from Siberia after World War II. Admiration for any part of what the Soviets had achieved did not run in either family. Now in Moscow they were "witnesses to a singular triumphant moment in a tragic century," Remnick wrote. "It was Oz, the world's longest-running and most colossal mistake, and the only way to endure it all was the perfection of irony." The inefficiency of the Soviet system is the lesser part of the story – grain harvests rotting in rain, coal miners sucking their "oxygen cocktails." The regime of repression – of speech, of memory, of life itself – is the heart of Remnick's story of its gradual collapse.

*Lenin's Tomb* is a profoundly literary book, cool, personal, ironic, consistently novelistic in the manner of its telling. The book is constructed as a five-act drama recapitulating events of Remnick's tour. Against the background of a recapitualation of the monstrous cruelty of Stalin, is counter posed an account of the rise of Mikhail Gorbachev, 1985-89; followed by a chronicle of the wondrous year of 1990-91, when Lithuania began to cast off its Soviet occupation and Russians, for the first time in their thousand-year history, elected a president. The climax is an exhilarating first-person report of the August '91 coup attempt, when hardliners sought to arrest Yeltsin and Gorbachev; followed by an antic denouement, including the rise of Yeltsin, the disestablishment of the Communist Party, the dismissal of Gorbachev, and the trial of the plotters. The book ends just as "shock therapy" begins. *Lenin's Tomb* is all the more remarkable for being spun out of the testimony of hundreds of living Russians. As Remnick wrote, "The last generation of reporters in the Soviet Union was the luckiest. We were witnesses to a singular triumphant moment in a tragic century. What's more, we could describe it, we could talk to the players, major and minor, with relatively little fear of jeopardizing anyone's freedom."

Reviewing *Lenin's Tomb* for *The New York Times*, the *FT*'s John Lloyd wrote, "An extraordinary confluence of observation, hard work, knowledge and reflection, a better book on the withdrawing roar of the Soviet Union is hard to imagine."

His major reservation concerned "the absence of any but the implicit recognition of an economic infrastructure: the increasingly revealed calamity of the collapse of the command-administrative system and its partial replacement by a wolfish capitalism and the vast criminality that seems inevitably to attend the attainment of market relations." Remnick, he says, "was clearly not interested."

Tired of chasing those daily stories, newly aware of his ability to weave longer and more complex narratives, Remnick left the *Post* for *The New Yorker* in 1992. He continued travelling to Russia, beginning in late '93, for an afterword for the paperback edition of *Lenin's Tomb* ("[E]verywhere I went... there was a sense of drift, even hopelessness, about political life...."). In 1997, he published a second book, *Resurrection: The Struggle for a New Russia*, not nearly so compelling as Hoffman's or Freeland's accounts of the rise of the oligarchs. The book includes an account of Yeltsin's victorious reelection campaign, and concludes on a note of cautious optimism about the prospects. "I see no reason that Russia cannot make a break with its absolutist past much in the way that Germany and Japan did after the war," Remnick writes.

> The almost uniformly rosy predictions for China and the almost uniformly gloomy one for Russia seem wrong to me. Political reform, literacy rate, natural resource base. Richard Layard, of the London School of Economics, and John Parker, a former Moscow correspondent for *The Economist*, have recently predicted that Russia; "may well have outstripped countries like Poland, Hungary, Brazil, and Mexico by the year 2020, with China far behind."

Layard and Parker were somewhat more optimistic about Russia's future than he was, wrote Remnick, "but it is not an unreasonable view."

Remnick was named editor of *The New Yorker* in 1998, replacing Tina Brown. He published books on Muhammad Ali, in 1998, and Barack Obama, in 2010, and between times, edited several anthologies of *New Yorker* pieces and started a popular radio interview show. He continued writing about Russia: about Putin (2000 and 2003); chess grand master Garry Kasparov (2007); the opposition to Putin (2011); and Ambassador Michael McFaul (2014). He was especially energetic before and after the Sochi Olympics, when he published short pieces about the punk-rock collective Pussy Riot, homophobia in Russia, preparations for the Olympics, and Putin's re-moralization campaign ("Putin's Four Dirty Words"). None of it could be construed as sympathetic. A 2014 cover during the Olympics featured a figure-skating Vladimir Putin leaping while five little Putin lookalikes feign disinterest from the judges' stand.

3.

After the Ukraine crisis, *The New Yorker*'s antipathy for Putin escalated sharply – as did that of *The New York Times* and the editorial page of *The Washington Post*. Putin's speech on the annexation of the Crimean peninsula – "the spring snaps back hard" – was of little interest. The downing of Malaysian Airlines Flight 17 fanned flames of indignation. So did the brutal civil war in Syria, with Russia backing Assad. The editorial board of *The New York Times* wrote, "Vladimir Putin is fast turning Russia into an outlaw nation."

The 2016 election of Donald Trump complicated matters. That the Russian government sponsored interference in the US presidential election, with a view to damaging the Clinton candidacy, now seems beyond doubt, though few believe it was decisive. The possibility of collusion and subsequent obstruction has become the focus of Special Counsel Robert Mueller's investigation. A substantial segment of the electorate equates Putin with Trump. In "Trump and Putin: A Love Story," in August 2016, Remnick wrote, "Putin's affinity for Trump is clear."

In "Active Measures," in March 2017, Remnick, staffer Evan Osnos, and Moscow stringer Joshua Yaffa, brought the matter to a boil, spelling out the case that, with the Democratic National Committee (DNC) hacks, Putin had begun "a larger war against Western institutions and alliances."

> Posted to one of the grayest of the Soviet satellites [East Germany], Putin entirely missed the sense of awakening and opportunity that accompanied perestroika, and experiences only the state's growing fecklessness. [Putin] rarely mentions any sense of liberation after the fall of Communism and the Soviet Union,… [H]e recalls the 1990s as a period of unremitting chaos., in which Western partners tried to force their advantages, demanding that Russia swallow everything from the eastward expansion of NATO to the invasion of its Slavic allies in

the former Yugoslavia. This is a common narrative, but it ignores some stubborn facts. The West welcomed Russia into the G-8 economic alliance. The violence in the Balkans was the worst in Europe since the end of the Second World War and without intervention would likely have dragged on. And Russian security concerns were hardly the only issue at stake with respect to the expansion of NATO; Poland, Czechoslovakia, and other countries in the region were now sovereign and wanted protection.

"It just felt to me grotesquely unfair, if that word can be used in geopolitics, that yet again the Central Europeans were going to be screwed," Strobe Talbott, Bill Clinton's leading adviser on Russia and the region, said. "To tell them they had to live in a security limbo because the Russians would have hurt feelings and be frightened just didn't hold water."

Eventually Remnick will assemble his pieces into another book. He will have the chance then to expand on the history of the decades since Gorbachev took over, to make the case for liberal internationalism, and to respond to criticism. Dissertation writers will go to work. Remnick has had an extraordinary career as a latter-day Orwell, a critic of authoritarian ways, denouncing doublethink and oppression wherever they exist. His core conviction, the inalienable right of self-expression, is largely undisputed in the United States. Expansion to class, race, creed, gender, sexual orientation has been argued through with considerable success in America. But Remnick is still not interested in economic infrastructure and the conditions of material life.

It is time to pay less attention to the Generation of '91. Bring on the generation of '06, realists formed on the anvil of Iraq, Iran, Afghanistan, those who are more than a little skeptical of America's self-conception as the shining city on the hill, forever eager to make the rest of the world safe for democracy. Pay more attention to the internal strains on NATO, to the new-found ambivalence of Turkey in particular. And, if you're really interested, subscribe to *Johnson's Russia List*, the invaluable compendium of news, for $50 a year.

CHAPTER THIRTY-THREE

# Toward a New History of Russia

We need a good history of Russia in the couple hundred years since 1812 – or, if you like, the three centuries since Peter the Great – a broad narrative whose handful of plot-points are familiar and make sense to Russians and Americans alike. We do not have one yet. Plenty has been published in this centenary year of the October Revolution, the one that brought the Bolsheviks to power, but relatively little about the years before the experiment with communism began – or after it shut down. This is more complicated than it sounds.

1.

It's a commonplace that the press writes the first draft of history, but correspondents only write within the confines of the history that they know. Long before they go abroad, their convictions have been shaped by families and friends. Thus John Reed wrote *Ten Days That Shook the World* about the Bolshevik Revolution. But long before he did, he had read *The Communist Manifesto*, attended meetings of the Socialist Club at Harvard, travelled widely, interviewed Marxist theoretician Karl Liebknecht in Berlin, and heard all about Lenin's *The State and Revolution*.

These days, correspondents are informed by a large community of historians, social scientists, and strategists. An extraordinarily useful book in this regard is *Know Your Enemy: The Rise and Fall of America's Soviet Experts*, by David Engerman, a biography of the academic field known as Russian studies – its rapid growth in the years of the Cold War, fracture in the '70s, and ultimate collapse in a heap of disagreements. Today the community of Russian studies is starting over again, this time to be located in a new top-down approach (see, for instance, Odd Arne Westad, *The Cold War: A World History* [Basic, 2017]). Meanwhile, we are once again looking for a bottom-up; account of Russian history – not just the history of the last few years, but history over the long haul – since 1825, say, when 3,000 officers and soldiers in St. Petersburg brought the first blush of democratic revolution to Russian cheeks in the civil disobedience known as the Decembrist Revolt.

John Reed's first draft, which appeared in 1919, was enormously influential in shaping perceptions of the Russian Revolution; *Ten Days that Shook the World* has been in print ever since. Who among Moscow correspondents has written an eye-witness account of events of these last 25 years that will fundamentally shape the way the history of Russia is written going forward? My candidate is Fred Weir, long-serving correspondent of the *Christian Science Monitor*. Like John Lloyd, of the *Financial Times*, who wrote the best book on the transition of the '90s, Weir has special advantage. He was for many years a member of the Communist Party – Canada's, in his case. (Lloyd is a Scot.) As an apostate, Weir, like Lloyd, writes about Russia with a degree of sympathy.

2.

A Canadian citizen, born in 1951, Weir was a third-generation "red diaper baby," nephew of an influential Comintern agent, and a member of the Party himself. He studied Russia as a graduate student but not with a view to living in the Soviet Union. After Gorbachev had come to power, the first general secretary born after the 1917 revolution, Weir decided he wanted to see the situation close up. He moved to Moscow in 1986 as a correspondent for the *Canadian Tribune*, a weekly newspaper published by Canada's Communist Party, now defunct.

He travelled widely in the late '80s for the *Tribune*, as the Soviet empire began to come apart. He wrote a book on Gorbachev's reforms, conducted two cross-country tours of Canada as well, promoting his work and sampling opinion. He witnessed the optimism of *perestroika*, the enthusiasm for open elections, the surfacing of ancient ethnic hatreds, as the Soviet regime loosened its grip. By the '90s, the economy was falling apart, all but the "cooperatives," the private firms

Gorbachev had permitted to be formed. His friends, members of the educated elite, had begun complaining of "the theater of democracy."

In an account of his experience in Russia that he published in 2009, Weir wrote,

> Sometime in the spring of 1991, I realized how far they had taken this. I was invited to a garden party at the country home of Andrei Brezhnev, nephew of former Soviet leader Leonid Brezhnev, in Zhukovna, an elite dacha settlement outside of Moscow. One of the guests, whom I had known for years as a functionary of the Komsomol (the Young Communist League) rolled up in a shiny white Volvo and told me he was now president of an export-import firm Another, whom I'd often dealt with as an official of the *Tribune's* fraternal newspaper, the Soviet Communist Party organ *Pravda*, boasted that he'd just been hired at a private bank. A third, even more surprising because he was the son of renowned Soviet dissident Andrei Sakharov, leaned over the table and handed me a card that announced him as an "international business consultant."

Over the next few years, Weir worked on a book with David Kotz, a professor of economics at the University of Massachusetts. *Revolution from Above: The Demise of the Soviet System and the New Russia* (Routledge), appeared in 1997. The authors' thesis – that the Soviet system had been overthrown by its own ruling elite – was novel and controversial when first proposed, but has come to be more widely accepted for having been borne out by events. *The Tragedy of Russia's Reforms: Market Bolshevism against Democracy*, by Peter Reddaway and Dmitri Glinski, made many of the same points when it appeared four years later.

Central to Weir's account are the events of 1993, which he witnessed first-hand. The Russian parliament that had come to power in democratic elections in 1993 – the Supreme Soviet – had institutional power rivalling that of the president; it reflected the interests of many diverse groups that had been harmed by "shock therapy." It became "an obstacle in the process of rapidly building capitalism," he wrote in his memoir, "and Yeltsin swept it aside." People think it was Putin who restored autocracy to Russia, Weir continued, but in fact it was Yeltsin. "Russia's best hope for democracy in our time died, and was buried in an unmarked grave, after a two-day wave of political violence in the streets of downtown Moscow in October 1993."

Instead of morphing into a businessman like his friends, Weir became a journalist. He pieced together a living writing for the *Hindustan Times, The Independent, South China Morning Post* and, since 1998, as the *Monitor*'s correspondent. (The venerable Boston-based daily discontinued its print editions in 2008, but maintains a string of excellent correspondents around the world for its digital operations.) Kotz and Weir added four chapters in 2007, and reissued it as *Russia's Path from Gorbachev to Putin*. Kotz's own book about the United States, *The Rise and Fall of Neoliberal Capitalism* (Harvard, 2015) fared less well. The fundamental point was lost. The transition had been a revolution from above.

Married, with two children, Weir lives in a small village near Moscow. He is a latter John Reed who has lived to tell the story. To read through his *Monitor* clips over the years is to glimpse the present-day in the making.

3.

In March 2017, in a dispatch headlined "A Revolution Forsaken? Why Is Russia Ignoring Its First Flirtation with Liberalism?" Weir engaged in a little historiography, suggesting a very different periodization than the one usually given.

Most Russians knew that two revolutions occurred in Russia in 1917, not just one, he wrote. The first, the February Revolution (designated by Marxist historians as the Bourgeois Revolution), led to the, abdication of the czar and the creation of a pro-Western government. The second, the October Revolution eight months later, brought the Communists to power. Yet, the government was not paying much more than pro forma attention to either in the centenary year of both.

A little background: The events of 1917 stemmed directly from the European war that began in August 1914, after an assassination in the Balkans triggered battle plans among the major powers that had been many years in the making – the Great War, it would soon be called. Russia was then allied with Britain and France against the Central Powers – Germany, Austria-Hungary, and the Ottoman Empire.

Like nearly everybody else involved, Russians first reacted with enthusiasm, expecting quick resolution. Six months later, with a third of the German Army pressing forward through Poland on the Eastern Front, and the Austro-Hungarian army attacking from the south, it had become clear that the war was a disaster.

Czar Nicholas II took command of the army in the field in the summer of 1915, which immediately made matters worse. Nicholas was, Weir wrote, "more of a family man than a national leader, appeared indecisive and out of touch, and even members of his own family were plotting against him." His wife's adviser, the monk Rasputin, was assassinated in December 1916. By then, army mutinies were widespread, refugees from the fighting were flooding into the cities, and famine compounded the problems. Confronted at a remote outpost near the front with news of mass demonstrations and armed clashes in St. Petersburg, the czar simply agreed to quit.

The February Revolution was the end of the three-hundred-year-old Romanov dynasty. The provisional government that came to power consisted of a mix of pro-Western liberals and center-leftists committed to democracy, Weir wrote, and, "For the first time in Russian history, they declared freedom of speech, the press, and public assembly, and pledged to transform Russia into a 'normal' European country." The government vowed to continue the war, determined to respect its predecessor's commitments. "[N]o one saw the second revolution coming," wrote Weir. "The possibilities seemed vast." The czar and his family were evacuated to Tobolsk, in the Urals, in the expectation that they would continue a journey to Japan in the spring. Instead they were executed by the Bolsheviks in July 1918." (You can see a pretty faithful dramatization of all this from the three-hour Hollywood biopic "Nicholas and Alexandra," made in 1971.)

The German High Command soon recognized the opportunity. In April, Germany sent Nikolai Lenin home from exile in Zurich, along with a trainful of other Bolsheviks. Lenin spent a few months organizing in St. Petersburg while the Duma debated, reluctant to crash the Bolsheviks and other left-wing forces.

> "As liberals, they believed they were a temporary government, and didn't want to give in to revolutionary impulses," Nikolai Smirnov, director of the official Institute of History in St. Petersburg [told Weir]. "They thought they had time and were very concerned that

any major reforms should be enacted by the constitutional assembly, so they would have proper legal underpinnings. They hoped to create the institutions of democracy, which would then resolve the main issues like peace, land reform, and workers' rights. But in a time of revolution, it's fatal to fall behind events."

In October, Lenin and the Bolsheviks slammed shut the window. They took over the government, dissolved the Duma, and enlisted as much of the Imperial Army as they could. They expropriated crown lands, occupied churches and gentry estates, took over the banks, and put workers in charge of factories. This second revolution was essentially a coup, order imposed from above by a relative handful of uncommonly confident leaders.

An armistice was declared in December; a treaty with the Axis powers signed in March. Ukraine, Georgia, and Finland gained their independence. Poland and the Baltic Republics were ceded to Germany. Russia lost as much as a third of its population and much of its industrial base. There followed a five-year civil war, the Red Army battling the Whites, in which British, French and, later, the American armies sought to intervene, without success.

The communist forces consolidated their power, and, in 1923, proclaimed the Union of Soviet Socialist Republics. The winners began to write their history, in terms of the string of dominant personalities we have known ever since: Lenin, Stalin, Khrushchev, Brezhnev, Andropov, Chernenko, and, in 1985, Gorbachev.

4.

Why was so little attention paid to the February Revolution in present-day St. Petersburg? A one-room exhibit at the Museum of Political History was one of the few official notices taken of the centenary of the event. Weir polled a series of Russian historians and politicians. All seemed at least a little reluctant to engage. "There's a bit of interest… now that the anniversary is upon us, but not very much," Lev Lurye, a specialist in the history of St. Petersburg told him, "This is a story with a very bad ending, and nobody likes that."

Weir speculated that deeper reasons for ignoring the short-lived crossroads existed – namely, the parallels with the events that followed the collapse of the

USSR under Gorbachev, "which remain sharply controversial to this day." Pro-Western liberals had again been quick to assert power after 1989, he wrote, "but that did not last very long." The same situation of dueling powers had developed, this time between Yeltsin and his conservative-dominated parliament. And, once again, the better-organized party had clamped down. Yeltsin had written a new authoritarian constitution and created a class of powerful oligarchs. Putin had simply picked up where he left off, extending a new style of autocracy.

Still, Weir wrote, no civil war ensued in the '90s; nothing like the terrible excesses of communist rule. Russia might have returned to its traditional pattern of top-down, one-man rule, "but it also had personal freedoms, a consumer economy, and at least a formal – though tamed – multiparty parliamentary system." The historians he interviewed buttressed the argument.

Lurye, the historian who organized the exhibit in St. Petersburg, stressed the long-run change that had taken place. "In 1917, we had 85 percent of the population living as illiterate peasants in the countryside. By 1991, the urban population was 85 percent, and they were educated people with a very different mind-set," "However things may look, Russia is richer and more liberal than at any time in its past. Today there is no 1917 on the horizon, and the chances for gradual, evolutionary change look good."

Boris Kolonitsky, a historian at the European University at St. Petersburg, mentioned fear of chaos and civil war. "The majority of Russians will pay a big price to avoid revolution; they crave stability above all," says "We have over-fulfilled our quota of revolutions. This feeling is a huge source of support for the present regime."

Vitaly Milonov, an ultra-conservative parliamentarian who is one of the few to favor a national holiday to commemorate the February Revolution (as a day of national tragedy) told Wier, "The February Revolution brought only incomprehensible chaos that the Russian people could not bear. They may have suffered from the czar, but they suffered more from the lack of a czar."

Nikolai Smirnov, director of the official Institute of History in St. Petersburg, said, "The past has definitely made Russians wiser. We went through those terrible events after 1917, and 70 years of Soviet life, and they have amply demonstrated to us that to destroy is always easier than to build. We didn't repeat the worst aspects of that history after the Soviet Union fell apart because we had learned those lessons, and we knew better."

Daniil Kotsyubinsky, author of several books about St. Petersburg, said, "We live today in the softest variant of the traditional Russian state. And we can probably thank the memory of those terrible events a century ago for enduring that everyone was careful not to repeat them after the Soviet Union collapsed."

Moreover, Weir, wrote, many conservatives claim that Russia is a separate civilization, more collectively minded than the West, and most people therefore naturally prefer more authoritarian forms of government. Advocates of Putin's plans for the Eurasian Economic Union (EAEU) cite his high public approval ratings to buttress their case. Czarism without the dynasty is the system appropriate to the diverse cultures and vast spaces between Europe and Asia, they say.

As for Putin, in the summer of 2017 Weir posted this assessment on the Facebook page he uses as a blog:

> Putin's "popularity," as expressed in opinion polls, is certainly a complex subject. I personally [almost] never hear anyone expressing "ardent love" for him. On the other hand, you seldom hear the kind of vicious rejection that one constantly heard about Soviet leaders [in private conversations] or Boris Yeltsin [out in the open]. It's true that Putin's rating is manipulated, by media coverage, and also by the conditioned sense that 'there is no alternative.' It's don't talk about him at all. Russians are more apolitical these days than I've ever seen them; most just seem to be getting on with their own lives. As for the USSR, you don't need to read the polls to know there is widespread nostalgia for those days. Again, not a simple thing. But, again, hard to get an anti-Soviet rise in conversation with most Russians these days.

Weir's blueprint is, I think, the right one for the next history of Russia: A sudden enthusiasm for Western ways that was quickly reined in. After Yeltsin's October 1993 crackdown on the democratically elected parliament, a new chapter in Russian history had begun. The privatization that began slowly under Gorbachev and accelerated sharply under Yeltsin did indeed create something like a vital bourgeoisie. But the emergence of the oligarchs and, a short time after, the muscular *siloviki*, were its more important creation.

The Harvard advisers who, for a time, sought to portray themselves as somewhere near the center of the story, in fact were simply among its collateral damage. It was not silly to have been hopeful about Russia in the early '90s – to have hoped that Yeltsin might choose Boris Nemtsov as his successor instead of Putin. The idea that things might have turned out differently is an old theme in Russian history. But it is their country, not ours. It is time to pay closer attention to what they are doing with it.

CHAPTER THIRTY-FOUR

# Sympathy for the Devil

It was May 2017, the 21st St. Petersburg International Economic Forum, "the Russian Davos," and Vladimir Putin was in an upbeat mood. Indian prime minister Narendra Modi was there; so was UN Secretary General Antonio Guitteres. Megyn Kelly, of NBC, served as interlocutor-in-chief, putting tough questions to the Russian president about the extent of Russian hacking.

A secret offer that Putin had made to Donald Trump in March, via diplomatic channels, of an across-the-board re-set in Russia-US relations, including digital arms-control talks, was sitting on the American president's desk. The recognition of what had happened to US politics in the interval since the election had yet to sink in. So Putin spoke to a plenary session of the conference, outlining Russian hopes for "unconventional solutions, new formats of cooperation between states, regional integration associations, business and the scientific community."

1.

At every opportunity that day Putin stressed Russia's participation in digital technology, not as a separate industry but as the foundation of all else, a "new paradigm for the development of the state, the economy, and society as a whole." He promised a revised regulatory environment, state support for companies, infrastructure projects, and increases in education and training, "many times over."

> Owing to our excellent schools of mathematics and theoretical physics, we are capable of taking the lead in a number of areas of the so-called new economy, primarily the digital economy. Russian information technology companies are certainly competitive on a global scale. Our specialists are not just coming up with the best, unique software solutions but are also creating a new area of knowledge, a new environment for developing the economy and life.

A few months later, Kaspersky Lab, perhaps Russia's single best-known global brand, suffered when a story described Israeli intelligence officers peering over the shoulders of Russian government hackers in real time as the Russians searched computers running Kaspersky software around the world for the code names of American intelligence programs. "It was a case of spies watching spies watching spies," wrote Nicole Perlroth and Scott Shane in *The New York Times*.

Was it true? Probably. *The Times* vouched for its story, and *The Washington Post* followed it up and added details. Never mind that US and Israeli companies are among Russia's foremost competitors in global software markets. Never mind, as the article noted, that the US National Security Agency had exploited unnamed antivirus software for its own foreign hacking operations. Because they do the same, the NSA had long avoided Kaspersky software. Now the US Department of Homeland Security had already ordered Kaspersky software to be removed from all federal computers.

Reports of Russian meddling continued to flood throughout the summer. In September, John Hudson, foreign affairs specialist at the online news site *Buzzfeed*, broke the most under-covered story of the year. Putin, in that secret offer, had proposed an across-the-board re-set of relations – diplomatic, military and intelligence, including a "sweeping non-interference agreement" beginning with measures to prevent election meddling. *The Wall Street Journal* confirmed the offer had been made, but neither the *Times* nor the *Post* followed up.

A few weeks later, in October, at another annual conference, Putin was more somber. Western and domestic Russia-watchers had met for three days behind closed doors with Russian policy-makers at the annual meeting of the Valdai Club in Sochi. Marc Champion, an editorial writer for *Bloomberg News*, summed up the sense of the meeting: "Russia's ability to influence the debate in

Washington, let alone reset a damaged relationship, has vanished, according to current and former policy makers...."

As usual, Putin spoke on the last day of the meetings and took questions. When Sabine Fischer, an analyst for a Berlin foundation, noted his criticisms of the West and asked what he considered had been Russia's most significant political misstep of the past 15 years, he replied, "Our most serious mistake in relations with the West is that we trusted you too much. And your mistake is that you took that trust as weakness and abused it." A little later he added, "Two-and-a-half decades gone to waste, a lot of missed opportunities, and a heavy burden of mutual distrust."

2.

William Safire, the well-connected conservative commentator for *The New York Times*, first gave the shrewd Punch-and-Judy interpretation of Russian affairs, in a column headlined "*Siloviki* versus Oligarchs," way back in 2003. At least it was from him I first learned the word. These "men of power" – the former KGB colleagues and military officers whom Putin had thrust into high positions – had sidelined old-time Soviets and democratic reformers of all sorts. Now they were locked in a battle with the handful of bold young opportunists who had become super-rich by ripping off the nation's natural resources.

These new Russian robber-barons had been up-and-comers in the old university-based administrative class, the *nomenklatura*. Putin had offered them a deal, wrote Safire: the *siloviki* would run the country and the oligarchs could keep their ill-gotten gains – as long as they stayed out of politics and cut the rulers in on some of the money. Some oligarchs had already capitulated; others had left the country.

The instant case was that of Mikhail Khodorkovsky. The photogenic young banker had gained control of Yukos Oil, the nation's largest petroleum exporter. Now Khodorkovsky planned to merge the company with Exxon-Mobil, thereby becoming perhaps the richest man in the world, a rival to Bill Gates. He had begun doling out contributions to political parties across the political spectrum, extolling the virtues of democracy. This was more than the boss was willing to tolerate, Safire wrote:

Putin ordered the arrest, trial, conviction and jailing of Khodorkovsky and the seizure of his billions of stock. All this was to be done legally by the *siloviki's* men in black robes [judges], of course, with Putin pretending to have no part in it.

Khodorkovsky talked about running for office from jail, wrote Safire, but that was ridiculous in present-day Russia, where Putin had reasserted control of the media. His "power-hungry mafia [had] the nation by the throat." Which faction to prefer? The contest between the oligarchs and *siloviki* reminded Safire of the 10-year war between Iran and Iraq. "We can only root for both sides to lose."

3.

Safire didn't have much sympathy for the problems Putin faces. I have more. Of the various ways I've tried to think about the problems of the Russian transition, the most helpful is a lens fashioned late in life by Jane Jacobs, the Canadian-American social philosopher and economic journalist.

Jacobs' first book, *Death and Life of Great American Cities*, made her famous. It appeared in 1961 and, as an attack on then-dominant ideas about city planning, presaged in many ways the complicated taste change that has led to a vast reshaping of the urban landscape in the 60 years since she wrote. Her second book, *The Economy of Cities*, made more direct impression on me. I read it only after Robert Lucas cited it in connection with an abstruse argument among economists about the nature of economic growth.

Sharp observation and clear writing, I discovered, had led Jacobs to the same conclusion that the economists I covered were gradually reaching via their own methods of mathematical description and formal logic: the recognition that the creation of new knowledge was central to growth, in ways that mere capital accumulation never could be. I had never heard such striking example of the power of journalism to augment expertise – especially in the case of blind spots acquired through professional education that Thorsten Veblen had described as cases of "trained incapacity." A third book, mostly about currency matters, appeared in 1985. Between times Jacobs beat back plans to drive a superhighway across lower Manhattan, where she lived. In 1968 she and her husband left New York City for Toronto to save a son from the Vietnam draft.

Her fourth book, *Systems of Survival: A Dialogue on the Moral Foundations of Commerce and Politics* (Random House, 1992), has been especially helpful in thinking about Russia and its problems. It is not an easy book to assimilate. Jacobs was 76 when she published it; she was, I suspect, tired of seeking to influence technical economics from outside the field. Rather than employ her own authoritative voice, as she had in the past, she wrote the book in the manner of a Platonic dialogue, a series of didactic conversations among six bookish New Yorkers conducted over a series of meals. She chose the form, she said, because this kind of informal discussion was precisely what she considered was most needed in the present day by those dealing with "moral and ethical conflicts that spring up in surprising ways." If it weren't for Jacobs's demonstrated knack for seeing things that experts somehow didn't understand, I wouldn't have stayed with the book.

Jacobs was interested in codes of conduct – subjective understandings of personal responsibility that render possible the vast webs of trust in individuals and institutions that characterize the modern division of labor. (She had conceived her project one day 40 years before when she had deposited a speaking fee paid in D-marks in a German bank, which would reappear a few days later as dollars in her New York bank account.) What were the norms that held together economic life and made it work so smoothly? She tackled the subject in her usual manner, scouring biographies, business histories, and scandals; dipping into sociology and anthropology; clipping newspapers; talking to friends.

Whenever she came across behavior described as admirable, she reformulated it as a precept, a rule of moral conduct. When she was done, and ready to write, she found she had identified not one great system of moral imperatives, but two. One code governed professions associated with the maintenance of a particular territory, whether an ancient city or a modern state; the other, with commercial life. She called these loose pairings "syndromes," meaning "things that run together." Often they were contradictory.

Guardians of society – she took the term from Plato – were expected to display many of the virtues of ancient Greek rulers or medieval knights or religious orders. They include police, soldiers, policy-makers, rulers. Jacobs prepared a table of the relevant commandments she had collected: guardians were expected to shun trading favors for money, to exert prowess, to cherish obedience and discipline, to adhere to tradition, respect hierarchy, prize loyalty, take vengeance, deceive for the sake of the task, embrace leisure, dispense largesse, behave ostentatiously, remain exclusive, show fortitude, respond fatalistically, and treasure honor.

Those who make their livings in marketplace behave very differently – not just merchants and entrepreneurs, but all those who engage in free exchange, including scientists, publishers and newspaper folk. In Jacobs' tabulation, they were expected to shun force, to compete, do deals, respect contracts, work hard, prize efficiency, initiative and enterprise, invent things, dissent freely, collaborate easily with strangers and aliens, promote comfort and convenience, practice thrift, invest carefully, and are both optimistic and honest.

There are anomalies and ambiguities in her classification, she admitted. Problems arise when one moral code or another gets too much of an upper hand in society; or when values are commingled. Jacobs wrote, "Former Marxist societies desperately need to clarify right and wrong in business and politics. But so do we."

She was right about that! No other distinction so helpfully disambiguates the mysteries of Donald Trump's presidency, for example – a lifelong commercial operator thrust suddenly into the position of guardian-in-chief. Or consider Putin's challenge – a consummate guardian of Russian interests, tasked with nurturing a developing commercial sector.

By flatly asserting the existence of two fundamentally different moral systems, Jacobs goes to the heart of the world in which we live, a world of governance and a world of enterprise – or so it seems to me. Both systems evolved over millennia. Each is necessary to the well-being of the whole, and each is populated (in the main) by very different sorts of people.

Jacobs's ideas about the nature of economic growth have mostly been confirmed by what at first was called "new" growth theory. Corroboration of her insights about and the norms associated with institutions of governance will take considerably longer. In the meantime, we must rely on common sense.

4.

Having invested heavily in re-establishing some of his nation's coarse governance formations, what chance is there that Putin will improve them? That he will recognize the necessity of furthering a rising business class? That he will identify a suitable successor by the time his fourth presidential term ends in 2024? A market economy typically grows itself. Its institutional framework, though, cannot be assembled in a day – or even 20 years.

Stories of predatory law enforcement officials and abusive regulators abound. How to tell whether the Kremlin's puissant anti-corruption initiative is changing expectations and behavior? Putin recently fired 11 of 84 regional governors; most were replaced by managers in their later 30s and early 40s. Meanwhile, the central government is running a widely followed contest to identify promising managers under 50: 300 winners will receive scholarships to continue their managerial education.

Russia's Central Bank chief Elvira Nabiullina, 59, in particular, gets high marks for having avoided a currency crisis despite the steep recession that followed the Western sanctions following the annexation of Crimea. Minister of Economic Development Maxim Oreskin, 35, said to be a Putin favorite, presides over a ministry staffed by alumni of blue-chip Western firms. The economy is growing again, but examples of new export industries are hard to find. To boost the country's shipbuilding industry, Putin recently proposed that only Russian ships be permitted to transport oil and gas along the Northern Sea Route, which halves transport time compared to the Panama and Suez canals.

A particularly interesting commentator on these topics is Leonid Bershidsky, 46, a journalist with a long history of constructive engagement. Bershidsky was the first publisher of the Russian edition of *Forbes*; subsequently founding editor of *Vedomosti*, the Russian business daily owned until last year by the *Financial Times* and *The Wall Street Journal*; a novelist; ands, briefly, a banker. Since 2014, when he left Moscow for Berlin, Bershidsky has written frequent columns for *Bloomberg View*. He is no friend of Putin and his circle, but nobody else I read follows the Russian development story more knowledgeably.

Did Putin seriously believe that such repair, as he secretly proposed in that overture in March, was possible in the first months of the Trump presidency? In that case, he badly misunderstood the situation that had developed in the United States. Bershidsky disparages such "feverish attempts" to repair relations as deliberately misleading. "Russia's capacity to take pain is constantly underestimated," he has written, and "Putin clearly believes it is higher than his

Western adversaries think." A return to the bargaining table to discuss measures, however modest, to dial back tension would be a good start. It is hard to imagine such negotiations proceeding very far while Trump is in office.

CHAPTER THIRTY-FIVE

# The Accidental President

I have often argued in *Economic Principals* that Donald Trump's election should be understood as mostly accidental – not the result of an American realignment or identity crisis, but rather a fluke, a surprising outcome best understood as a delayed reaction to the end of the Cold War.

The strategy of containment that the United States adopted in the late 1940s held the line pretty well. Competition between the rival systems reached the farthest corners of the world. There were military misadventures and shockingly dangerous passages along the way, but the taboo against use of nuclear weapons proved strong. Trade, technological change, and regulatory flexibility did the rest. By the 1980s, the United States had zoomed ahead. After 1979, China, Brazil, India, the Eastern European nations and finally Russia itself entered global markets.

The success of globalization that followed cloaked the butcher's bill of trade and peace – job losses, hollowing out, and vast changes in the political landscape. The end of the Cold War was precipitated by a mostly quiet crash in weapons industries, especially in the USSR and the United States. The 2008 financial crisis, which brought the world to the brink of a second Great Depression, emphasized the risks of global interdependence.

External pressure served to keep the choice of presidential candidates within a relatively narrow band for 70 years. But the appeal of electing an outsider had been growing in the United States since 1992, when software entrepreneur H. Ross Perot won 19 percent of the popular vote. Ralph Nader's less popular but more sophisticated candidacy in 2000 cost Al Gore the election. In 2016, continuing globalization and technology shocks, plus revulsion against the Clinton and Bush dynasties, combined to bring about a result that no one anticipated.

Probably Trump himself never expected to be elected. His campaign began as a brand-building exercise, a lark in which he could not lose, except that he won, and now he's in a world of trouble. His views of Russia may be sensible enough, but they seem to have been formed mainly by talking to wealthy Russian customers who bought into his development projects, especially those who bought apartments in his troubled Trump World Tower, across the street from the United Nations, at the time of the ruble crisis. In any event, Trump has been unable to outline those views in a persuasive manner. Or, for that matter, do anything much else besides tweet.

Whether Trump will serve a full term isn't clear. The shoe-leather reporting of the early days has given way to Special Counsel Robert Mueller's team of investigators. Trump's narcissism, instead of subsiding, has grown more acute. It is too early to speculate as to how his administration will go into the history books. One way or another, the vandalism and ill-will he has generated will be reduced. The unfortunate skew to US-Russia relations imparted by US foreign policy of the last quarter-century was there before Trump arrived. Hoping to repair the relationship, he has made it worse.

The good news is that constraints have led Trump to the appointment of a series of sensible realists, including several who know a thing or two about Russia: Chief of Staff John Kelley and Defense Secretary James Mattis among the generals; Secretary of State Rex Tillerson and Ambassador Jon Huntsman among the diplomats. It is the beginning of a long journey back to common sense.

CHAPTER THIRTY-SIX

# The Broken Promise

Russia's economic transformation after 1985 was its own doing. A military-industrial titan under communism, hard-pressed in its 40-year rivalry with the United States, unable to feed itself or pay its bills, the USSR convulsed, restructured, and, after a dozen years, reemerged as Russia. The Russian government today is as a new kind of autocracy, so far connected to the world economy mainly through petroleum, grain, and threats – less hungry, still powerful, down on its luck, but willing to change. Twenty-five years of careless NATO bullying by three US presidential administrations have left Russia defensive, resentful and a little reckless.

There was nothing fated about NATO expansion. Had George H. W. Bush had won the election in 1992, events would have proceeded differently – how, we'll never know, but differently. Principles of caution and restraint were built into the generation that waged the Cold War. Not so the baby boomers who came to power afterwards. Bill Clinton and Strobe Talbott, who had traveled in Russia during Oxford vacations, began eight years of pressing Russia, rejecting a chorus of advice. George W. Bush, at the urging of Vice President Dick Cheney, followed their lead. Barack Obama only weakly resisted NATO expansion. And Hillary Clinton, with her contempt for Putin and enthusiasm for arming Ukraine, might have made matters worse.

In his final press conference, Obama laid out the American version of the story.

At the beginning of his term, he said, "I did what I could to encourage Russia to be a constructive member of the international community and tried to work with the president and the government of Russia in helping them diversify their economy...." Then Putin returned to the presidency, conducting affairs on the premise that "whatever America's trying to do must be bad for Russia." He "hammered home" the adversarial spirit by annexing Crimea and invading portions of Ukraine, whereupon the United States and Europe had no choice but to impose stiff sanctions. And as for the hacking that followed,

> The Russians can't change us or significantly weaken us. They are a smaller country. They are a weaker country. Their economy doesn't produce anything that anybody wants to buy, except oil and gas and arms. They don't innovate. But they can impact us if we lose track of who we are.

In fact, America has lost track of its identity. It has shirked, if not abandoned, its role as a global leader, at least in the sense associated with the Marshall Plan and the formation of the United Nations in the years after World War II. The tradition is probably more durable than is commonly thought. It ruled the day as recently as 2008, when the Federal Reserve Board, supported by the Bush administration, the 110th Congress, and the Obama campaign, provided the global leadership necessary to stem the financial crisis. In its relations with Russia, however, the United States has failed to live up to its ideals: to play fair; to behave, not magnanimously, but with clear-headed respect for the interests of others, in this case, an old foe temporarily disadvantaged. The United States didn't start the Cold War. It did much to end it on peaceful terms. But three presidents played the leading role in re-igniting it, by doing as they pleased with respect to Russia after 1993.

Compared to US foreign policy, the Harvard team leaders' shenanigans in the Russia scandal were small potatoes. Yet the same themes are to be found in the vignette. Taking advantage of a rival in a weakened state, then pretending it didn't happen. Hauteur. Stonewalling. Cover-up. And in this case, outright dishonesty. Striking was the extent to which official Washington was willing to overlook what happened: all but Attorney General Janet Reno and Justice Department prosecutors, and, of course, *The Wall Street Journal*. I might have hesitated to bring the embarrassment up again except for what I had learned about Harvard's success in obscuring matters by sweeping the Keffer lawsuit under the rug. When its professor, his wife and their chums embarrassed the foreign policy of the United States by cheating in full view of the Russians, the Harvard Corporation should have owned up to the deed. Instead it compounded the offense.

A few last exculpatory words about Larry Summers. As a university president, he was out of his milieu. But as a social democrat at the center of economic policy-making, Summers has been a rock-solid pillar of the center-left since he began advising Michael Dukakis in 1986. He has built bridges to the opposition and routinely advanced matters for the common good. Alone among the Clinton team, he has owned up to the administration's greatest mistake. "In retrospect," he told the peripatetic Tyler Cowen, his former student, "there was not enough respect shown to what had once been a proud nation that didn't think of itself as having been defeated." He mentioned the expansion of NATO in particular. Nobody is perfect, but Summers is to the Democratic Party what his teacher Martin Feldstein was to the Republicans – the wisest all-around economic adviser of his generation. As such, he kept faith with his parents and with his famous uncles.

Yet even today Summers professes to know nothing about the USAID case. He should have known better from the day the first *WSJ* article appeared. Striking, too, were the failures of those whom he counted on to set him straight: Shleifer and Zimmerman, his closest friends; his informal advisers; Robert Rubin, his boss; and the leaders of the university that sought him out and named him president. None of those in authority at Harvard – not the economics department, the administration, or the governing Harvard Corporation itself – had the courage to insist Summers choose between his duty and his friends. Only the general counsel, Anne Taylor, tried. Promises were broken at every level.

What next? Russian interference in the 2016 election, didn't change the result. The Democrats and *The New York Times* and *The New Yorker* should stop kidding themselves that it did. The cyberattacks and behind-the-scenes overtures arose from a pique and profound misunderstanding of the American system. The fact that the hacking and the two-way back-channel sweet talk occurred has made it highly unlikely that Trump can do more than stabilize the situation. As the veteran diplomat Jack Matlock told the Russian news agency *Interfax* recently, it would have been easier to persuade President Hillary Clinton to improve relations despite her espoused hawkish positions than to count on Trump to succeed in doing so.

Meanwhile, Vladimir Putin was elected in March 2018 for a fourth term as president. When he completes it, in 2024, he will have ruled Russia longer than Stalin – and will still be only 72. The program director of the Valdai Club, Ivan Timofeev, had some wise words for his fellow Russians, advocating what he called the "stealth approach" to great nationhood, a word surely chosen for domestic consumption. Ratchet down the threats to Western nations. Foster economic growth. Build regional integration in Eurasia. Expand participation in international organizations. Play an increasingly active role in resolving global issues.

> It is time for us to quit constantly complaining about the treachery of the West, and stop dwelling on who cheated us and how in the 1990s. The West is unlikely to have any compunction. However, such rhetoric creates a depressive impression outside the Western world… We need a language of opportunities that we see for ourselves in the world, and which we want to offer the world. Fortunately, Russia has something to work with in this area.

For the United States, plenty of hard work lies ahead, charting a coherent and credible foreign policy. Strategists should now turn their attention to realistic appraisals of Russian energy policy – what Jonathan Haslam, Kennan professor at the Institute for Advanced Study, calls "the endless and frustrating attempts to outflank American power." Putin will exploit leverage where he can – with oil and gas pipelines in Europe, liquefied natural gas in Saudi Arabia, in whatever deals he can make with China, India and Iran; by maintaining a presence in Nicaragua and Venezuela; and with technology, perhaps, in North Korea. Yeltsin might not have cared much about multi-polarity but Putin certainly does. The situation is reversed: Putin's goal, says Haslam, is to contain American power.

The promise that was broken after 1989 had to do with departures from long-professed ideals in the way American power was to be exercised in global affairs – with honesty, civility, dependability, and restraint. There had been deviations – Vietnam was the most dramatic example – yet, for whatever failures of the policies that it produced, the conviction remained that liberal democracy, and some form of the constellation of values surrounding it, would be preferred eventually by those who had a choice. Cooperation, especially in trade, was understood as the way to enhance the prospects for its extension. After 1992, the central pillar of restraint was removed and a succession of American presidents sought to govern as leaders of a hegemonic power. A good deal of resentment was the result, especially in Russia and China.

A quarter-century of discord in America followed the end of the Cold War. If the United States can reason through the sources of its discontent, and devise policies to address the very real injuries that accompanied a different sort of peace, Americans may find their way back to that earlier self-confidence, albeit with a greater sense of humility. In that case, the United States will continue as before, as an exemplar of the best, if not the last, hopes of democracy. In any event, 25 years after "the unipolar moment," the giddy triumphalism of "the end of History" has become history itself.

It is time to sober up.

APPENDIX I

# Andrei Shleifer's Letter to Provost Albert Carnesale

# HARVARD UNIVERSITY
## DEPARTMENT OF ECONOMICS

ANDREI SHLEIFER
Professor of Economics

325 LITTAUER CENTER
CAMBRIDGE, MASSACHUSETTS 02138
(617) 495-5046

Exhibit 816
Witness SHLEIFER
Date 4·8·02
S. O'Connell

Dr. Albert Carnesale
Provost
Harvard University
Massachusetts Hall

May 9, 1997

Dear Al,

In light of the current investigation of Harvard's and my work in Russia by USAID, as well as of developments inside Harvard, I decided to put down on paper for your attention my views on the subject and on the best way to proceed from here.

## The Projects

Harvard has been assisting Russian economic reformers through projects financed by USAID since 1992. These projects dealt with the issues of privatization, legal reform, restructuring of privatized firms, development of securities markets, tax reform, land reform, and several other matters of economic reform. I have been the Principal Investigator on these projects, and Jonathan Hay has managed them from Moscow. Some elements of the projects, such as tax and land, have been more autonomous, but in general the projects have required close supervision -- intellectual and financial -- from both of us over the last five years. The projects have been initiated, expanded, and -- in the case of the most recent one -- won to a significant extent on the strength of our reputations and relationships with the Russian officials.

By most accounts, the projects have been successful. Even the last year's GAO report, which started as an attempt to find fault with the projects, has acknowledged the many accomplishments of these projects. Financially, the projects have brought in about $50 million in activity to HIID, and probably about $6 or 7 million in overhead for Harvard and HIID. More important, these projects brought Harvard a good deal of recognition as the world center of advisory work and research on transition and reform in non-market economies. As a small indication of that, all the top Russian graduate students in Economics, some of whom are quite brilliant, now come to Harvard for their Ph.D. studies.

## The Investigations

Historically, the projects enjoyed a superb relationship with the US government. A year ago, senior officials at USAID publicly referred to USAID's "special relationship with Harvard." Unfortunately, this relationship has completely deteriorated in the last year.

Last spring, the General Accounting Office, on the request of Congressman Gilman, initiated an investigation of Harvard's projects. While we cannot prove what prompted this investigation, there is a lot of evidence that an important reason was the Congressman's, or his assistant's, antagonism toward Jeff Sachs. The GAO investigators proved to be highly professional and, in my opinion, fair. We have cooperated with them fully, and eventually -- together with many people at USAID -- convinced them that ours was an important and successful project. In the end, the investigation -- having taken up an enormous amount of everyone's time -- has produced a very positive evaluation of these projects with some nit picking on the periphery. And of course, no wrongdoing of any sort has been found. I also note that USAID did not fare nearly as well in the report as Harvard did.

In the United States, the GAO audit has been largely forgotten. Unfortunately, not so in Russia. Several months after the report's publication, a communist newspaper in Russia printed an article falsely alleging that, according to the GAO report, Chubais and Boycko -- the Chairman and the CEO of the Russian Privatization Center, respectively -- have stolen $116 million of World Bank money. [Chubais, as you probably know, is now first Deputy Prime Minister of Russia and the architect of Russia's economic reforms, whereas Boycko is Deputy Head of the Administration of the President of Russia. I have worked with both of them since 1991, and have actually brought Boycko into the work on reforms.] As a consequence of this false newspaper account, the Russian Interior Ministry and the Russian counterpart of the GAO are starting their own investigations into the affairs of the RPC. I will return to the issue of the consequences of US government investigations in Russia later.

Following the GAO audit, Harvard's relationship with USAID deteriorated rapidly. USAID dramatically stepped up interference in the projects, attempted on several occasions to move funds from Harvard, and sharply cut the budget. During the last two months -- a key point to which I return later -- USAID demanded the renegotiation of our contract if it is to continue funding. Their argument is that the nature of Harvard's activities in Russia has changed so much that a renegotiation is called for. In particular, our involvement with the RPC has declined sharply because Boycko left the RPC, and I have been extremely reluctant to take responsibility for that organizations activities. We have attempted to renegotiate the agreement, but without success since USAID keeps imposing new demands every time the old ones are addressed. At the moment, the project does not have funding beyond the end of this month.

A couple of weeks ago, we have learned that the Inspector General's Office of USAID has started an investigation of Jonathan Hay and myself. We do not know what started this investigation, though we have a lot of circumstantial evidence that Credit Suisse First Boston had something to do with it. Several months ago, a CSFB employee was caught in a blatant attempt to bribe a Russian customs official by including two watches in a sealed envelope containing a license application. CSFB has been informed of the bribery attempt, and the employee resigned. Although Harvard employees were not involved in this scandal, the Moscow office of CSFB has taken the position that Harvard is behind the treatment they received. We also have evidence that USAID is trying to cover up the CSFB episode. I would not be surprised if USAID has been threatened by CSFB that, unless they "get" Shleifer and Hay, CSFB will create a scandal and expose USAID incompetence in "overseeing" Harvard, which might explain USAID's zealotry. In addition, there have always been rumors circulating in the communist press about Hay, -- e.g., Hay is a well-known CIA agent, a KGB agent, has acquired an aeronautics company, has secret interests in the securities industry, etc. -- and investigators seem to be giving this nonsense some credibility.

It is now patently clear that, unlike the GAO audit, the current investigation has the objective of "getting" Hay and Shleifer, and possibly Harvard, rather than of discovering the truth. The strategies that USAID has utilized have been outrageous, as well as possibly in violation of US laws. Mark Ward of USAID has lied to Hay, and evidently misled you as well, on several issues, including the CSFB story and my wife's relationship with ILBE, another institute we work with (I come back to this below). Hay's e-mail was copied, and actually erased, either by USAID or by someone who showed it to USAID investigators. Vicious rumors have been spread by the investigators about both Hay and myself in Moscow. I am not sure what exactly the next steps by these investigators are going to be.

With respect to ILBE, I want to be very clear about the relationship between my wife's company and ILBE-Consulting, a commercial affiliate of ILBE. As background, the Institute for Law Based Economy ("ILBE") was set up as a non-profit Russian corporation, and is a sub-contractor to HIID in the legal reform project. It has been staffed by approximately fifty Russian lawyers committed to the development of a market economy in Russia, who are among the best and the brightest in their generation. It provides drafting services for the office of President Yeltsin, the relevant Russian executive branch offices, and the relevant committees of the Duma on legislation and implementing regulations in the commercial law area. It is the only entity of its kind in Russia, with a superb reputation even with the communists. In US terms, it acts as a sort of combination legislative drafting office of the relevant executive branch agencies, the office of legislative affairs at OMB, the drafting staff of the relevant congressional committees, and the legislative references service of the library of Congress. In addition, ILBE now acts as the outside counsel to the Russian SEC on a wide range of regulatory matters.

To help make ILBE self-supporting, it has set up a profit-making entity, ILBE-Consulting, that acts as a private law firm doing legal work for a fee for private clients. This was also done so that ILBE lawyers, who have had little experience in the "real world" of an ongoing market economy, could get practical experience in the legal areas where they were drafting laws. A careful policy requirement was put in place so as to avoid any conflict of interest between the work done by ILBE and the work done by ILBE-Consulting. -- e.g., ILBE-Consulting is not permitted to take on an engagement to seek a license, or an administrative approval, or a change in regulation at an agency where ILBE has or will provide legislative drafting service; or to represent anyone before the Russian SEC; etc. Every engagement undertaken by ILBE-Consulting must be approved by the general director of ILBE to make sure that these policies are adhered to. Lawyers are required to keep daily time records to keep track of the various projects they may work on -- whether it be ILBE work (which may be charged to different donors) or ILBE-Consulting work. The establishment of ILBE-Consulting, the policy provisions concerning its engagements, and the procedures for approving its engagements were all reviewed and approved by the USAID project director and by the USAID contracting officer in Moscow. This type of profit-making subsidiary is common in the US, and the RPC in Russia has also established such a subsidiary with USAID approval and encouragement.

When ILBE-Consulting was established, I understood my role to be to help them, and for this reason I introduced them to my wife, who did some business with them and paid for it. Again, as background, my wife is the general partner in a $400 million hedge fund, called Farallon Fixed Income Associates, that invests in fixed income securities (bonds, as opposed to stocks) in the US and in the emerging markets. Its clients are wealthy individuals and university endowments, including Yale, Princeton, and many others. Some of the fund's investments are in Russian bonds and in Russian foreign debt. I want to stress to you, incidentally, that I have never kept my wife's activities secret from any of my colleagues in the Economics Department -- or for that matter from the US and Russian government officials that I have dealt with -- and I have never considered there to be any potential conflict of interest between her and my activities. Moreover, the USAID restrictions are not applicable to spouses, nor do they apply to investments in government debt; they only apply to investments in "a business, profession, or occupation."

My understanding is that my wife used ILBE-Consulting for some translation, as well as legal intermediaries in executing some of her trades on the Russian bond market. For your information, it is very common in Russia to use lawyers for such activities. This business is entirely legal, and if anything USAID should be pleased that their own goal vis a vis ILBE-Consulting was being pursued. Instead, they appear to be taking the position that my wife's relationship with ILBE-Consulting was improper. I am genuinely disgusted with this position, as well as with Mark Ward's obviously deliberate attempt to ignore the clear distinction between ILBE and ILBE-Consulting in referring to my wife's relationship with ILBE-Consulting.

In any event, it is now obvious that this investigation will attempt to humiliate Jonathan, myself, and Harvard at all costs.

Relationship with HIID

During the Perkins regime, this project enjoyed a truly fantastic relationship with HIID. HIID provided technical support, helped me recruit and retain personnel, and in return received the overhead. The substantive involvement of HIID in the project was minimal. When Perkins retired from HIID, the project's Russian counterparts expressed concern about the new regime, which is the reason that I asked Dwight Perkins to speak to you. Following your conversation, Dwight assured me that I will have control over the project, and insisted that your discussions with him need not be put in writing as I originally requested.

Unfortunately, in the last year, the relationship between the project and HIID has deteriorated. I will not get into all the details, but will give you two illustrative examples.

a) Despite my requests, and in a stark contrast to Perkins policies, HIID has refused to give raises to key employees in Russia, some of whom have quit as a result. The last person who is quitting is the expatriate accountant at ILBE, which as you might imagine creates enormous problems for the integrity of ILBE's financial systems, as well as possibly for Harvard.

b) In the last two weeks, I have learned that HIID literally raided the project for $100,000 – completely legally but in my opinion inappropriately. Dwight Perkins has established the precedent that HIID does not collect overhead on office rents paid in Russia, since HIID does not do anything for these rents. HIID actually has the right to collect this overhead, but Dwight simply thought it was inappropriate. In fact, we made a big deal out of telling GAO that we do not collect overhead on rents, as evidence of our good intentions, and they were receptive to this point. This policy was just reversed, retroactively, against my wishes. The money, I should say, has been already promised to ILBE, and so we now have to violate our agreement.

You might interpret this evidence as suggesting only that Sachs and Shleifer do not get along, and that perhaps Sachs, or a person he designates, should be given an opportunity to run this project. It seems relevant to me in this regard that it was Hay and Shleifer who got this contract, and that everyone at Harvard understands how little HIID has to do with these projects intellectually. (As an example, Jeff did not seem to be aware in his first conversation with me after the investigation started that the project was working with the Russian SEC, a major component of the project.) But there is a far more important point here, namely that Jeff in charge would simply not be acceptable to the Russian government. Jeff burned his bridges with the Russian reformers in 1993, when he publicly resigned and condemned the policies of the government, which at the time was going through a difficult period. These people (the principal of which are Prime Minister Chernomyrdin and Chubais, but including several other reformers as well) have not forgotten about his conduct, and not surprisingly would oppose the situation in which such a public and severe critic gets control of funds intended to help the government to implement reforms. I cannot project exactly how much of a problem Harvard would get into with the Government of Russia if Sachs was put in charge, but it would be substantial. It was precisely this concern that prompted me to ask Dwight Perkins to speak to you in the first place.

I conclude that it is infeasible to continue this project in a way that allows HIID to exercise so much control over resource allocation, and the relationship with USAID and the investigators.

## World Bank Contract

At the moment, Harvard is competing for a World Bank contract for technical assistance to the Russian SEC. This contract is likely to be awarded in the next few weeks, and Harvard is in a strong position to win it. The money in this contract would come from the Russian Federation's World Bank loan. The proposal was submitted to the Russian SEC by Harvard on behalf of HIID. The proposal was based to a significant extent on the work that Hay and Shleifer have done in Russia. I can assure you that it will not be acceptable to the Russian government to have this project managed by parties other than the Principal Investigators designated on the proposal. In fact, Mr. Vasiliev, the Chairman of the Russian SEC, has indicated his willingness to come to Cambridge to inform you about this personally.

During my meeting with Jeff and Greg Poppe, I specifically asked Jeff whether he would oppose the transfer of the project from HIID to other places at Harvard should Harvard win this contract. He specifically stated that he would not oppose such a transfer. I think that it is absolutely essential for Harvard to decide how this proposal could be managed. If the USAID investigation ends to everyone's satisfaction, and Harvard wins the World Bank contract, it might be possible to have the contract run out of some place at Harvard such as the Kennedy School or even the Economics Department, but with HIID providing accounting and other support and receiving some overhead in return. HIID would not have any control over the personnel or budgetary decisions of the project, but would be paid for its technical services.

For this to work out, we need to put the USAID investigation behind us. I cannot manage the World Bank project with the investigation underway. I also firmly believe that Harvard

## World Bank Contract

At the moment, Harvard is competing for a World Bank contract for technical assistance to the Russian SEC. This contract is likely to be awarded in the next few weeks, and Harvard is in a strong position to win it. The money in this contract would come from the Russian Federation's World Bank loan. The proposal was submitted to the Russian SEC by Harvard on behalf of HIID. The proposal was based to a significant extent on the work that Hay and Shleifer have done in Russia. I can assure you that it will not be acceptable to the Russian government to have this project managed by parties other than the Principal Investigators designated on the proposal. In fact, Mr. Vasiliev, the Chairman of the Russian SEC, has indicated his willingness to come to Cambridge to inform you about this personally.

During my meeting with Jeff and Greg Poppe, I specifically asked Jeff whether he would oppose the transfer of the project from HIID to other places at Harvard should Harvard win this contract. He specifically stated that he would not oppose such a transfer. I think that it is absolutely essential for Harvard to decide how this proposal could be managed. If the USAID investigation ends to everyone's satisfaction, and Harvard wins the World Bank contract, it might be possible to have the contract run out of some place at Harvard such as the Kennedy School or even the Economics Department, but with HIID providing accounting and other support and receiving some overhead in return. HIID would not have any control over the personnel or budgetary decisions of the project, but would be paid for its technical services.

For this to work out, we need to put the USAID investigation behind us. I cannot manage the World Bank project with the investigation underway. I also firmly believe that Harvard should drop out of the competition if it cannot resolve its internal differences, and notify the Russians of that immediately. The issue, in my opinion, is urgent.

## Four Options

I believe that Harvard has four options on how to proceed from here. These options are:

a) To move along with the investigation.

b) To resist the investigation on legal grounds.

c) To have Hay and Shleifer resign.

d) To terminate the USAID project.

I would like to make a few comments about these options, and to ask you to make a decision.

7

*Option a).*

Option a) would require my disclosing my financial information to investigators. In this regard, you should be aware of the following two points. First, I do not have any investments in Russia, and have not violated any conflict of interest rules in this contract. I have told Greg Poppe, and repeat to you, that I will be pleased to disclose my financial records and show my tax returns to the Harvard legal office. Second, my wife and I do have substantial investments in private companies and partnerships in several countries, and I believe the investigators' attempts to investigate these partnerships will be an utter disaster for my family as well as for our business associates. The investigators will not understand what these partnerships and companies do and will attempt to get to their records. Even worse, they have indicated that they will produce a publicly available report of their investigation, which means that my family's financial affairs will become a matter of public record. For these reasons, it is entirely unacceptable to me — and I believe should be unacceptable to Harvard — to pursue option a). I also remind you that I am not an HIID employee, and that the contract on its face pertains to HIID employees only, and applies only to individual employees and not their spouses. It is particularly upsetting to me, in this regard, that USAID is trying to change the contract and to involve me in its conflict of interest investigation.

*Option b).*

Harvard can take the hard line with the investigators and contest their attempts to get access to my financial records on the grounds that I am not subject to conflict of interest rules (which is true). My guess is that this is a bad strategy for several reasons. First, Harvard might lose. Second, USAID will make the most of this challenge, since they desperately want some satisfaction in this investigation. Third, the World Bank contract could not proceed under the circumstances of a continued investigation. For these reasons, I do not find option b) attractive.

*Option c).*

Hay and Shleifer may resign to terminate this investigation. This option seems attractive, since the investigation will end and Harvard will keep the overhead. However, I want to alert you to several problems, some of which I believe are extremely severe.

First, you should be aware that, with Hay's resignation, the project loses all its intellectual and financial controls in Russia. The fact that the GAO audit has not identified any inappropriate use of funds despite a very aggressive effort is a striking testimony to Hay's managerial ability. I do not believe that with Hay's, as well as ILBE expatriate accountant's, resignation, such financial integrity can be guaranteed.

Second, I want to just warn you that the turnover of control over this project to Sachs is likely to cause a problem with the Russians. Whether you want to face this problem is up to you, but I do not in my capacity as the PI, recommend it. Senior Russian officials are prepared to make this case to you personally if necessary.

Third, if Hay and I resign, Harvard should inform the Russian government and the World Bank immediately that it is dropping out of the competition on the World Bank project.

Fourth, and very importantly, I do not believe that even if this investigation ends, it will be the last investigation of the project. I am sure that Congressman Gilman will step up to the plate after USAID is done, and so may others.

Fifth, and most important to me, I, as the PI, find this option genuinely embarassing and unattractive. It shows Harvard's willingness to cave in to pressure and to the awful tactics by USAID despite there being no evidence of wrongdoing by myself and Hay.

*Option d).*

The last option is to terminate the project, and to inform USAID about this decision. Having considered several alternatives, I believe this to be the most attractive option. I firmly believe that the benefits of such termination outweigh the costs. Moreover, given USAID's refusal to finance the contract unless it is renegotiated, Harvard is in perfect position to terminate this agreement now.

The benefits of the termination are several fold:

1) At the moment, the project is impossible to run from both the substantive and financial perspectives. If the project ends, so will the potential risks.

2) USAID will get its pound of flesh and terminate the investigation.

3) As importantly, with no project, further investigations are much less likely.

4) Jonathan Hay and myself will be spared a totally unacceptable interference by the government in our and our families lives.

5) USAid will find ways to finance the valuable activities of the project, including most importantly the tax component, from the saved resources. I am now reasonably confident that these components will find alternative ways of financing themselves, including from USAID.

6) The road will open for the World Bank contract should Harvard win it.

7) Last but not least, the Russian government officials we are working with will be protected against the likely consequences of a prolonged confrontation between Harvard and USAID.

There are two costs of termination:

9

1) Embarrassment for Harvard. I personally believe that this embarrassment is not significant, and is less than will occur with the other alternatives, especially given USAID's tactics and the possibility of a significant escalation in the future. In fact, a decisive action in response to the pressure tactics is most principled way to proceed

2) Lost overhead. I can only remind you that HIID has already collected several million dollars in overhead, and is not in any way entitled to more. Besides, it is not in my opinion appropriate for Harvard to do projects solely to collect overhead.

**Urgent Action is Needed**

I urge you to make this decision rapidly for several reasons:

First, we want to terminate this investigation now, before subpoenas are issued and the legal battle gets out of control. I have been asked by the investigators to meet with them next week, and my attorney advises me against doing so.

Second, Jonathan Hay is fed up, and is ready to quit immediately: without him I cannot vouchsafe for financial integrity of the project in Moscow -- let alone its substantive quality.

Third, Harvard needs to take a position on the World Bank.

Finally, USAID insists on renegotiation and has stopped all funding: it is a great time for Harvard to send them to hell.

In sum, as the Principal Investigator of this project, as well as the person who has raised the funds for the project in the first place, I urge you to terminate the project now. I eagerly await your response and am ready to meet at your earliest convenience.

Sincerely,

Professor of Economics

cc: Mr. Greg Poppe
    Ms. Anne Taylor

APPENDIX II

# The Steyer Memo

MAY-20-1996 17:02 FROM ILBE TO 8101617349537

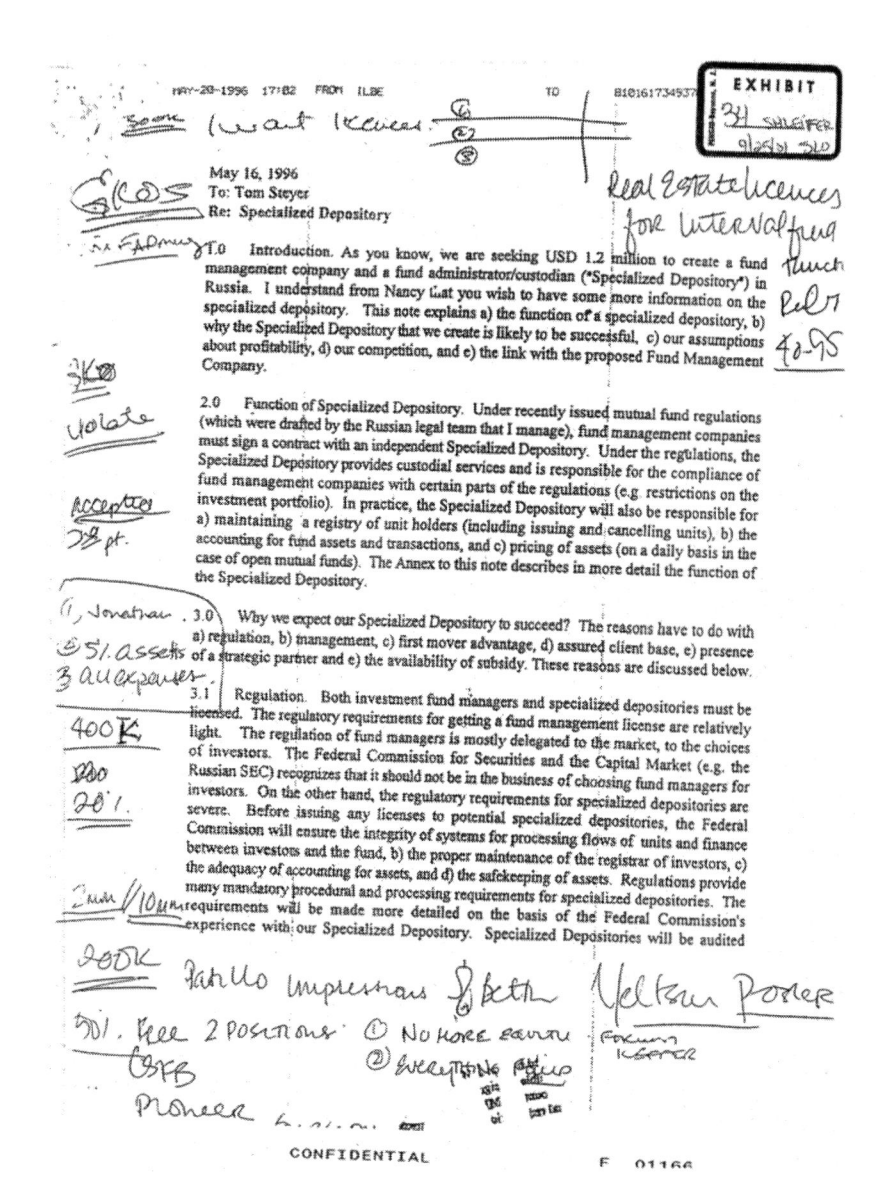

May 16, 1996
To: Tom Steyer
Re: Specialized Depository

1.0 Introduction. As you know, we are seeking USD 1.2 million to create a fund management company and a fund administrator/custodian ("Specialized Depository") in Russia. I understand from Nancy that you wish to have some more information on the specialized depository. This note explains a) the function of a specialized depository, b) why the Specialized Depository that we create is likely to be successful, c) our assumptions about profitability, d) our competition, and e) the link with the proposed Fund Management Company.

2.0 Function of Specialized Depository. Under recently issued mutual fund regulations (which were drafted by the Russian legal team that I manage), fund management companies must sign a contract with an independent Specialized Depository. Under the regulations, the Specialized Depository provides custodial services and is responsible for the compliance of fund management companies with certain parts of the regulations (e.g. restrictions on the investment portfolio). In practice, the Specialized Depository will also be responsible for a) maintaining a registry of unit holders (including issuing and cancelling units), b) the accounting for fund assets and transactions, and c) pricing of assets (on a daily basis in the case of open mutual funds). The Annex to this note describes in more detail the function of the Specialized Depository.

3.0 Why we expect our Specialized Depository to succeed? The reasons have to do with a) regulation, b) management, c) first mover advantage, d) assured client base, e) presence of a strategic partner and f) the availability of subsidy. These reasons are discussed below.

3.1 Regulation. Both investment fund managers and specialized depositories must be licensed. The regulatory requirements for getting a fund management license are relatively light. The regulation of fund managers is mostly delegated to the market, to the choices of investors. The Federal Commission for Securities and the Capital Market (e.g. the Russian SEC) recognizes that it should not be in the business of choosing fund managers for investors. On the other hand, the regulatory requirements for specialized depositories are severe. Before issuing any licenses to potential specialized depositories, the Federal Commission will ensure the integrity of systems for processing flows of units and finance between investors and the fund, b) the proper maintenance of the registrar of investors, c) the adequacy of accounting for assets, and d) the safekeeping of assets. Regulations provide many mandatory procedural and processing requirements for specialized depositories. The requirements will be made more detailed on the basis of the Federal Commission's experience with our Specialized Depository. Specialized Depositories will be audited

CONFIDENTIAL

F 01166

frequently by the Federal Commission. The Federal Commission expects to issue few licenses to specialized depositories which means that a) the market for these services will be divided between few organizations (in the short to medium term we expect to capture most of the market) and b) pricing is likely to be less than perfectly competitive.

Our project stands to benefit more than any other from the Federal Commission's approach to regulation. This is for three reasons. First, we have the best probability of receiving a license. Our project is the flagship Specialized Depository of the Federal Commission designed to set the standard for the market place and to be used to define the operational and procedural thresholds that must be met by others to enter the business. Every decision we make about design, systems and procedures will be taken in close cooperation with the Federal Commission. Our project will be established with the active involvement of the Russian legal team that the Federal Commission entrusted with the drafting of the original mutual fund regulations. Second, we are likely to get a license before anyone else which will give a significant first mover advantage (discussed below). Third, our project will set the market standard. Given this project's relationship to the Federal Commission, any other attempts by definition will be in a catch up mode.

3.2 Management. We have the best management team. The ability of management is proven in Russia and has an exceptional reputation for honesty and competence which is unique in the Russian market place. The president, Julia Zagachin, is one of a few professionals who have successfully built large infrastructure operations, earned the confidence of the Federal Commission, every major western institutional investor active in the Russian equity markets, the Russian brokerage and banking community. She is completely bi-lingual and bi-cultural. The future head of operations, Nadezhda Masenkova is currently Chief Operating Officer of the DCC. She developed procedures and controls currently in use by the DCC. The strategic partner (discussed below) brings a first rate management team with similar western expertise that will be involved in the set up of the Specialised Depository.

3.3 First mover advantage. The economics of the Specialised Depository business give the advantage to the first group that gets established and attracts clients. In Russia, we are that group. In the early phase while no one else is set up we can be profitable with lower volumes of processing and high margins. As the business progresses, we can lower margins and maintain profitability with higher volumes of processing. Any other competitor that wishes to beat our prices must be able to immediately get the higher volumes that make it possible to live with the lower margins. The need for high volumes for profitability should be a significant barrier to entry for new competitors. This is also the case in the West where this business tends to be concentrated with a very few providers such as State Street/DST in the United States or Hexagon and Premier Trust in the United Kingdom. In the short to medium term our advantage comes from the fact that the regulator wants us to be first. In the future we can keep our dominant position through a quality service at low prices where profitability is maintained by the fact that we built up higher volumes in the early years.

3.4 Assured client base. We have an assured client base for two reasons. First, we are establishing the Specialised Depository simultaneously with the establishment of a fund management company. The fund management company will be managed by Elizabeth Hebert who has managed the best performing fund publicly traded Russia fund for the last two years. Her commitment to use the Specialised Depository will be an important signal to other potential clients. When Elizabeth chose to use the DCC as her custodian in Russia (at that time managed by Julia Zagachin), other market participants followed. We expect that the similar pattern will occur with the Specialised Depository. Second, the Federal Commission will direct potential fund managers to use the Specialised Depository that we are establishing. This is natural since the Federal Commission has an interest in ensuring that its flagship project sets the standard for the market place, and it has an interest in ensuring that fund managers that are licensed use the Specialised Depository that best meets regulatory standards.

3.5 Presence of strategic partner. Forum Financial is the strategic partner. The company is a Portland, Maine based fund administrator/distributor for commercial banks managing funds in the US but restricted by banking regulations from distributing funds directly to the public. Forum currently provides fund administration, transfer agency and valuation services to clients with $14 billion under management. They also have a start-up operation in Poland. Forum won a tender conducted by the World Bank and the Russian Commission to establish the procedures and design the systems to be used by the model depository. Forum will contribute technical know-how of operations and systems. They will also contribute senior management expertise and systems specialists to shadow the local management team. The presence of a strategic partner should ensure that we are protected from making mistakes in the selection of systems and the development of procedures.

3.6 Subsidy from World Bank Funds. The Federal Commission has awarded Forum Financial $2.5 million to develop systems and procedures for a model Specialised Depository. The Federal Commission has indicated that the Specialized Depository that we propose to create will be the Russian beneficiary of this work. This money will be used to pay consultancy fees, rent, translation of software, systems development, write procedures, and advise the Commission on regulatory issues. We also expect that the proposed Specialized Depository will be hired by Forum Financial as a sub-contractor, and that, as a result, the company will immediately generate revenue with should fund some of the start up costs. As a result the investment is significantly reduced, as operations of this type tend to require a high up front investment.

4.0 Assumptions About Profitability. The key variables that determine profitability of the Specialized Depository are a) the fixed cost of establishing the Specialized Depository, b) the marginal cost of processing a client account, c) the price that can be charged for processing a client account, and d) the number of client accounts that the Specialized Depository will process. The assumptions that we have made are illustrated in the table entitled "Administration Bureau."

While we believe that we have all the pieces in place to make the Specialized Depository successful, we never established such a business and do have some uncertainty about the precision of the numbers reflected in the business plan. For example, while we have the advantage that many of the fixed costs will be covered by the technical assistance funds, we are uncertain about the fixed costs associated with the establishment of a custodial service. Like many other issues, the issue of whether or not it is necessary to establish a custodial service (or whether for some assets we can or should use services provided by others) is one that will have to be addressed with our strategic partner in the implementation of this project.

Due to such uncertainties, we have used very conservative figures in the business plan. The business plan shows that the Specialized Depository will charge between $15 and $12 per year per client account per year (i.e between 1% and 1.5% on an average investment of $1000). We have been told that a comparative figure in the United States or the United Kingdom is $30. The low price reflects i) our lack of knowledge about the number of transactions per account per year, and ii) sensible caution about the ability to charge monopoly prices. Even if we are the dominant player in the market, we think it is possible that there would be pressure from regulators to keep prices down. Our foreign ownership and management structure also makes us reluctant to assume that we can "charge through the nose" for our services. Our assumptions about price and cost are illustrated below:

| Year of operation | 1996 | 1997 | 1998 | 1999 | 2000 |
|---|---|---|---|---|---|
| Price charged for processing a single client account | $12 | $12 | $12 | $12 | $12 |

| Cost of processing a single client account | $9 | $8.8 | $6.5 | $5.5 | $5.0 |
|---|---|---|---|---|---|
| Profit per account | $3 | $3.2 | $5.5 | $6.5 | $7.0 |

The falling marginal cost relates primarily to the efficiency of operators in processing accounts. We assume that operators reach a western level of efficiency (2000 accounts per operator) only in the year 2000. In our assumptions, in the first 18 months of operation operators process accounts at only 40% the efficiency of their western counterparts.

The key variable that is likely to determine the success of the venture is the number of client accounts. Here again we want to be conservative in our representations to you and Nancy. We assume that we go from processing 31,000 accounts in the beginning of 1996 to 238,000 accounts in the beginning of the year 2000. Under these assumptions, the Specialized Depository becomes cash flow positive in the third quarter of its operation and gives profit net of Russian tax of about $600,000 after 3.5 years of operation. Of course, if we were to assume that this Specialized Depository has a large market share and that it were to process millions of accounts, it would be an extremely profitable operation! We are certainly well positioned to achieve such success if Yeltsin wins the election and the mutual fund industry booms in Russia (and we expect both of these things to happen). However, the only scenario that we wish to present to you and Nancy is the conservative scenario that has been presented to you in the original business plan and that is summarized in the table above.

5.0 Our competition. There are two potential sources of competition to this project. They are i) Russian banks and ii) Credit Suisse. We do not think that Russian banks are serious competitors because they are not trusted by the market place. Domestic banks, have a reputation for unbridled opportunism particularly where inside information is available. They also are extremely slow to develop anything new in the way of services. We think that they will watch and wait. Credit Suisse is a more serious threat since it has indicated that it would be interested in this fund administration business and because it is the furthest advanced in custody of any insitution in Russia. We think our position is superior to that of Credit Suisse for the following reasons. First, Credit Suise will not offer clients the registrar (transfer agent) service. Instead they will farm out their customers' register of unitholders to a Russian holder of corporate registers. The company that they have chosen has a dubious reputation in the market place and very Russian concept of client service and confidentiality.

Second, Credit Suisse has explicitly stated that they will not offer the service to clients until they have launched their own fund in order to create/maintain a barrier to entry (remember without a depository a fund can't be licensed). The Federal Commission will resist any attempt by a fund manager to block entry of competing funds in this way (Pioneer in Poland is a perfect example of what the Federal Commission intends not to happen in Russia). Finally, Credit Suisse will not have access to the technical assistance nor to the inside track afforded by the technical assistance to the Federal Commission.

6.0 Connection with the Fund Management Company. You have received a business plan from Elizabeth Hebert for investment in a fund management company. The Specialised Depository and the Fund Management Company are being offered to you as a package. We are not interested in your investment in the Specialised Depository unless this is helpful to raise the funds needed to start the Fund Management Company. This is for several reasons. First, the success of the Specialised Depository will be increased if we have a lead respected client to start things off. A fund managed by Elizabeth Hebert would have this effect as discussed above. Second, the Federal Commission will not license the Specialised Depository except as a package with its first client. For this reason we think that it is important to have control over the first client to ensure that there are no problems or friction in the set up stage. Third, we frankly want to start both of these things at the same time and are tying our futures to this strategy. We would like our backers to do the same with their investment.

7.0 I hope that this is a helpful summary of the Specialized Depository project. This work is on a short fuse. If you are interested in participating in the initial investment, it is important to block out some time to focus on this project. The Specialized Depository already has financing in place. If worse comes to worse it can be financed by the strategic partner. He has already indicated his willingness to do so (under this scenario we would still get 51% of it). If you are willing to participate in the financing of the Fund Management Company (even on a modest scale), we are ready to offer you an opportunity to invest in the Specialized Depository.

8.0 I look forward to talking with you about the proposal.

## Annex 1: Functions of the Specialized Depository

Under the current regulations the Specialized Depository plays both a traditional custodial role and a compliance function.

*Custody*

As the custodian of the mutual fund the specialized depository's functions include:

holding of assets and accompanying ownership records
cash control accounting, where separate payment and disbursement accounts are maintained by the specialized depository on behalf of the fund and reconciled on a regular basis with fund accounting
recording and accounting for capital and income received by the fund through investment of fund assets
- processing corporate actions notifications from investee issuers and acting on the instructions of the fund manager with regard to such actions
documenting authorisations on fund transactions
receipt of payments from subscriptions and payment for unit redemptions upon appropriate instructions
payment for fund expenses at the direction of the fund manager
- settling all securities transactions with the market

*Specialised Registrar and Unitholder administration*

The specialised registrar function requires the specialised depository to control various aspects of the relationship between the unit holder and the fund manager including:

maintaining the register of unitholders,
processing unit purchases and redemptions, order verification and data entry, processing, verification and reconciliation of transactions of unit sales and redemptions as reported,
documenting all changes to the register unrelated to creation or cancellation of units (i.e. change of address),
responding to customer service inquiries,
- mailing informational materials upon instruction of the fund manager.

*Fund Accounting and Valuation*

The Specialized Depository would also hope be offer the following (in fact this requires certain modification to existing regs, but we expect this to be achievable):

securities valuation, which must be conducted daily using price quotes obtained from reputable sources (e.g., The Russian Trading System),
processing of corporate actions, including stock splits and dividend payments, which can effect the total value of the funds assets,
accounting and accruing of Fund expenses and income in compliance with the applicable regulations,
calculation of the net asset value (NAV) of the fund based on daily reports received.

In addition to the traditional role of a fund administrator the current regulations require that the the specialised depository assumes a regulatory function on behalf of the Commission and is responsible for reporting all improprieties of the fund manager to the Commission.

① Real Estate License
② 5% of ~~assets~~ assets based fee.
③ 5% of ~~assets~~ Depository
Revenues.

Want Real Estate
① Nancy
② Jonath
③ Real Estate License
100 for 5%
Renegotiate first —
mutual fund (?)
partial license & dept.
full interest
modified plan.

# Notes

I began this book with no good idea of how much original work it would entail. Now that it is finished, I have no time left to create a section of endnotes for the printed edition. Newspaper journalism aspires to a provisional kind of truth, the best that can be said quickly. And 15 years of writing online have left me in the habit of attributing or linking my sources, rather than identifying them in footnotes or endnotes.

I have resorted instead to a relatively new tradition of documentation. I have established a website, www.becausetheycould.com, where I will add end-notes as needed, responding mainly to requests for clarification, correction, etc. Links to the online columns can be found there as well; in each case, they contain the original links. A bibliography of my main sources can be found there, and a handful of useful links. I will actively maintain the site as long as there is interest in it and preserve it for at least a dozen years. I can be reached at warsh@economicprincipals.com.

# Index

## A

Abernathy, Fredrick, 97
Abkhazia, 219
Admati, Anat, 149
Aldrich, Peter, 84, 179 *ff*, 180
Allison, Graham, 169
Alternative Dispute Resolution (ADR), failure of, 18, 99
Arrow, Kenneth, 155, 198
Andropov, Yuri, 239
Aslund, Anders, 130, 133, 141, 172
Aspin, Les, 211
"Assigned-to" trial, 35-39, 40-48
Atlantic Fund Services, 200

## B

Bacevich, Andre, 225
Baker, James III, 123, 169, 206-8
Baker, Peter, 228
Ballantyne, Janet, xiii, 185
Baltic Republics, 166, 204, 214, 216, 239
Bank Handlowy, 166
Beam, Alex, 63
Becker Center on Chicago Price Theory, 110
Belovezha Forest Accord, 205, 209
Bentsen, Lloyd, 61
Bernanke, Ben, 137
Bershidsky, Leonid, 249
Beslan, 31, 216-7
Besley, Tim, 116
Blanchard, Olivier, 103-4
Blavatnik, Leonard, 175
Blinder, Alan, *The Fabulous Decade*, x, 154
Bloom, Sara Miron, 6, 8, 44, 46
Bok, Derek, 67-70, 100, 196
Bolshevik Biscuit Company, 25, 106, 171-2
Bolsheviks, 204, 205, 235, 238-9
Bombardieri, Marcella, 22
Bosnian War, 212-3
"Boss," 112
*Boston Globe*, ix, 3, 22, 61, 63, 72, 77, 116, 119, 170
Boycko, Maxim, 43, 170
Bracebridge Capital Management, 194
Bracebridge Road, Newton, 130
Bradley, Bill, 213
Bradley, Richard, 57, 101
Brainard, Lael, 154
Brady, Nicholas, 135, 209
Brandenburger, Adam, 14
Brezhnev, Leonid, 236
Brody, Kenneth, 189
Brosens, Frank, 189
Bullard, James, 152
Bush, George H. W., 109, 168-72 *ff*, 206-9, 252
Bush, George W., 219, 220, 223, 228 *ff*, 252
Butler, Michael, 23

## C

Cambanis, Thanassis, 3
*Canadian Tribune*, 235
Cape Cod, 24, 26, 85, 182
Carnesale, Albert, 87, 114, 185; letter from Shleifer, 258
Casper, Gerhard, 60
Carroll, Michael J., xiii
Champion, Marc, 244
"Charlie's Angels," 5, 12, 47
Chase Bank, 139, 177
Checks and balances, 89
Cheney, Dick, 215-7, 221, 253
Chernenko, Konstantin, 239
Chernomyrdin, Viktor, viii, 173, 212
Christopher, Warren, 173, 212
*Chronicle of Higher Education*, 13
Chubais, Anatoly, 4, 25, 29, 32, 36, 44, 82-84, 105-9, 121, 143, 167, 170, 174-8, 185, 197
Citigroup, ix, 9, 69, 146, 161, 188-9, 195, 199
Clay, Lucius, 28
Clinton, Bill, 83, 105, 119, 128-9, 138, 200, 210 *ff*; biography of, 171-3, 252
Clinton, Hillary, 126, 192, 210, 220-3, 253, 255
Cohen, David, 175, 181
Cohen, Rodgin, 189
Cold War, 205, 206; ended, 210 *ff*, 237
*Cold War: A World History, The*, 235
Colton, Timothy, 143, 188, 212, 215
*Communist Manifesto*, 204, 235
Corrigan, E. Gerald, 148 *ff*
Cowen, Tyler, 255

Credit Suisse First Boston, 85, 106 *ff*, 160, 170, 191
Custer, George Armstrong, 15

## D

Damon and Pythias myth, 199
Daniel, D. Ronald, Harvard Treasurer, 9, 54
Darman, Richard, 135
Davos, Russian version, 243
"Deadwood," 108
Decembrist Revolt, 235
D. E. Shaw, 134
DeLong, J. Bradford, 103
Dimand, Robert, 154
Dobbs, Michael, 228
Dornbusch, Rudiger, 104
Dukakis, Michael, 104, 146, 207

## E

Easterly, William, 14
*Economic Principals*, xiii, 57, 62; bulldog edition, xiii, 76, 189, 225, 251; not a blog, 76 *ff*
*Economist, The,* 57, 128, 175, 231
Eliot, Charles, 59
Elliott Management Corp., 194
Engels, Friedrich, 204
Engerman, David, 234
Enron Corp., ii, 9, 54, 69, 195
Eurasian Economic Community, 221

## F

False Claims Act, ix, 4, 17 *ff*, 40, 86, 187
Farallon Capital Management, 175, 180

*ff*; and "Steyer memo," 189 *ff*
Farallon Fixed Income Associates, 181, 184
February Revolution, 237
Feeney, Mark, xiii
Ferguson, Niall, 14
Feynman, Richard, 66
Feldstein, Martin, 25, 104, 114, 138, 158, 169, 175, 186, 196, 199, 255
Fineberg, Harvey, 61, 69, 75, 87, 114
Fischer, Sabine, 245
Fischer, Stanley, 101, 147, 155, 193, 198
Flemings Bank, 177, 179, 182
Ford, Henry II, iv
*Foreign Affairs* symposium on Ukraine, 224 *ff*
*Foreign Policy*, 211
Foreign policy, US, iv, 81 *ff*, 160 *ff*, 204 *ff*, 211, 214, 220
Forum Financial, xii, 84, 159, 164, 191
Franklin Templeton Fund, 160, 177
Frayn, Michael, 28
"Freedom Agenda," 217
Freedom Support Act, 169, 172
Freeland, Chrystia, 128, 228, 231
Fujimori, Alberto, 90 *ff*

## G

Gaddis, John Lewis, 213
Gaidar, Yegor, 83, 105; biography of, 167-8, 169, 173, 174
Gates, Robert, 218, 220
Geithner, Timothy, 135-7
"Generation of '91," vii, 227 *ff*
Georgia war, 219
Gilman, Martin, 140 *ff*
Gingrich, Newt, 209

Glaser, Susan, 228
Glass-Steagall Act, 137
Glinski, Dmitri, 236
Goldin, Claudia, 94, 103, 115, 132
Goldman, Marshall, 128, 169, 188
Gorbachev, 206-8, 229-30, 235,
Goncz, Arpad, 212
Gorbachev, Mikhail, xi, 82, 104, 123, 128, 166, 167, 168, 169, 173, 206 *ff*, 228, 230, 235, 239, 240, 242
Gore, Al, 69, 98, 99, 210, 252
Graduate (Booth) School of Business, University of Chicago, 9-13, 27, 110
Graham, Lindsey, 217
Graham, Thomas, 217
Gray, Hanna Holborn, 9, 54, 196
Greenspan, Alan, viii, 61, 120, 149, 150, 151, 154, 170, 171, 209
Griliches, Zvi, 175, 199
Guitteres, Antonio, 242
Guzman, Abimael, 90

## H

Harper, Conrad, 9, 54, 69, 195
Hart, Oliver, 104
Harvard Corporation, 8, 29, 53, 98, 100, 111, 255
*Harvard Crimson*, xiii, 115, 116
Harvard economics department, 14, 53, 84; defense of Shleifer, 112
Harvard Institute for International Development, 35, 43, 46, 51, 55, 97, 114, 172, 188,
*Harvard Magazine*, xiii
Harvard Management Company, 50, 114
Harvard Russia scandal, vii, 161, 192,

193, 203, 229; as a story about the US, iii; compared to NATO enlargement, xi, 68; as described by David McClintick, 78 *ff*
Hart, Gary, 213
Haslam, Jonathan, 205, 256
Havel, Vaclav, 212
Hay, Jonathan, vii, viii, ix, 3, 5-7, 10, 12, 17 *ff*, 28, 36, 41, 44, 51, 63, 71, *ff*, 80 *ff*, 92, 94, 107, 111, 120, 160, 170, 177 *ff*, 201; settlement, 68; and "Steyer memo," 189 *ff*, text, 268 *ff*
Hay, Dr. Robert, 20, 179, 181, 183
HealthSouth, 92
Hebert, Elizabeth, vii, ix, 21 *ff*, 81 *ff*, 107, 177 *ff*, 194; and "Steyer memo," 189 *ff*, text, 269 *ff*; dismissed as defendant from government suit, ix
Hellwig, Martin, 149
Hilsenrath, Jonathan, xiii, 146, 155, 193
Hirsch, Michael, 157
Hoffman, David, *The Oligarchs*, 4, 10, 105 *ff*, 175, 228, 231
Holbrooke, Richard, 211, 213-4, 220
Horse manure, 117
Houghton, James, 9, 54, 69, 97, 196
Hoxby, Caroline, 58
Hudson, John, 244
Hun School, 162, 192, 200-201
Huntsman, John, 252

## I

*Institutional Investor*, xii, xiii, 81, 82, 89, 96, 113, 178, 183
Iran, iii, 214, 233, 246, 256
Iuliano, Robert, 54, 97, 100

Ivry, Sara, 111, 187

## J

Jacobs, Jane, 246-8
Jakubski, Adam, 165-6
Jennings, Steven, 106-7
Johnson, David, 126-8
*Johnson's Russia List*, 126, 128, 233
Jones Professorship, Whipple V. N., 110
Jordan, Boris, 106-7, 109, 113
Jorgenson, Dale, 113-5, 175, 199
*Journal of Economic Perspectives*, 9, 12, 52, 66, 89, 94, 103, 116, 131
Jowett, Benjamin, iv
Judt, Tony, i

## K

Kaiser, Robert, 227
Kann, Peter, xiii
Kaplan, Fred, 170
Kasparov, Gary, 231
Kaspersky Lab, 244
Keffer, John, xii, 84-87, 160 *ff*, 253; career of, 160-201; squeezed out, 181 *ff*, 269 *ff*; life story, 187; in Panama, 160-1, 199-200
Kelley, John, 252
Kelly, Megyn, 243
Kennedy, Donald, 62
Kennan, George, 213, 256
Keohane, Nannerl, 54, 69, 196
Khodorkovsky, Mikhail, 33, 176, 245-6
Kindleberger, Charles P., 150
Klein, Ezra, 153
*Know Your Enemy: The Rise and Fall of*

*American Soviet Experts*, 234
Knowles, Jeremy, 8, 29, 53, 100, 113, 116, 117, 181, 195, 198
Kolonitsky, Boris, 240
Kosovo War, xi, 215
Kotz, David, 236-7
Krugman, Paul, 196
Khrushchev, Nikita, 172, 205, 211, 222, 239
Kumins, Roseanne, 39

## L

Lake, Anthony, 211
Landes, David, 151, 175
Landler, Mark, 220, 223, 228
Layard, Richard, 141, 172, 231
Lenin, 127, 204, 205, 235, 238, 239
Leonhardt, David, 136
Lewis, Harry, 199
Liebknecht, Karl, 234
Liesman, Steve, vii, xiii, 26
Litvinenko, Alexander, 217
Livshits, Alexander, 179
Lloyd, John, 174, 176, 228-231, 235
Loans-for-shares, 109, 176, 213
Longbrake, John, 188
López-de-Silanes, Florencio, 50-52, 68, 115, 132
LSV Asset Management, 22, 133
Lucas, Robert, 163, 246
Lugar, Ricard, 214
Lukens, Dana, 190, 192
Lukin, Alexander, 224-5
Lurye, Lev, 239-40

## M

Marshall Plan, 28, 123, 254
Marx, Karl, 204-5
Mason, Edward, 17, 35
Matlock, Jack, 255
Mattis, James, 251-2
"Mattress cash," 175
Matthews, Owen, 128
Mazzone, Judge David, 18, 22, 87, 98, 99, 186
McCain, John, 137, 219
McClintick, David, xii, xiii, 63-66, 81-87, 96, 113, 179-81, 183, 187, 197
McCloy, John, 28
McClung, Nellie, iv
McFaul, Michael, 224
McMillan, John, 89, 91, 94
McNamara, Robert, 213
Mearsheimer, John, 223, 225
Mercier, Kathleen, Harvard Office of Sponsored Research, 46
Merkley, Senator Jeff, 157
Meyer, Jack, 50, 52, 53, 55, 136
Milonov, Vitaly, 240
Milosovic, Slobodan, 90
Money market mutual funds, 163
Monrad Professorship, Ernest E., 116
Montesinos Torres, Vladimiro, 90
Moral syndromes, 247
Murphy, Kevin, 196
Myers, Steven Lee, 228

## N

Nabiullina, Elvira, 249
Nader, Ralph, 252

Nemser, Earl, 22
Nemtsov, Boris, 127, 242
*New York Times* editor's note on Shleifer, 85
Nicholas II, 238
Nicholas and Alexandra, 238
Nielsen, Holly, 185
*Nineteen Eighty-Four*, 205
Nitze, Paul, 172, 213
*No Precedent, No Plan*, 140-143
*Nomenklatura*, 167, 176, 245
Non-disclosure agreement, iii, 161, 189, 192
*Normal Country, A,* 55
Norris, James, USAID Moscow, 43
North Atlantic Treaty Organization, ii, 124, 203
Nuland, Victoria, 214, 221
Nunn-Lugar Threat Reduction Act, 172
Nunn, Sam, 213

## O

Obama, Barack, iii, 129, 136, 137, 141, 146, 147, 150, 152, 153, 158, 189, 193, 219-224, 228, 231, 254
O'Connor and Associates, 180
O'Neill, Louis, 85, 107, 108, 184
O'Reilly, Bill, 219
"Orange Revolution," 217, 221, 224
Oreskin, Maxim, 249
Orwell, George, 205, 233
Owen, Stephen, 58
Owens, John, USAID, 46

## P

Paletta, Damian, 146

Pallada Asset Management Company, 22, 179
Palmeiro, Rafael, 74
Panama, iii, xi, 162, 188, 199-201, 207, 249
Parker, John, 231
Perkins, Dwight, 39, 46
Perlroth, Nicole, 244
Perot, H. Ross, 171, 209, 252
Perry, William, 211
Peru, corruption in, 89
Pfaff, William, 124
Pioneer Investments, 177
Pirie, Robert, 196
Podesta, John, 196
Poland, privatization in, 164-170, 182
Politkovskaya, Anna, 217
Portland, Maine, xii, 84, 160, 164, 184, 186, 189, 204
"Post-Communist revolution," 170
Primakov, Yvgeny, 214
Pussy Riot, 231
Putin, Vladimir, 31, 34, 108, 122, 124, 127, 216, 231-2, 236, 256,
Munich speech, 219; on Ukraine crisis, 220-5, 228; problem of governing, 243 *ff*
Putnam, Robert, 111, 188

## Q

*Quarterly Journal of Economics*, 115
Quayle, Dan, 209

## R

Reagan, Ronald, 15, 104, 168, 169, 198,

206-9
Reddaway, Peter, 32-34, 127, 236
Reed, John, ix, 234, 235, 237
Reich and Tang, 163, 164
Reich, Robert, 210
Reischauer, Robert, 54, 69, 196
Remnick, David, 228-33
Reno, Janet, 122, 254
*Revolution from Above: The Demise of the Soviet System and the New Russia*, 236
Riesman, David, 59
Robbins, Carla Anne, vii, xiii, 26, 53, 65, 72, 88
Robinson, Janet, 200-201
Rogers, William Barton, 59
Romer, Christina, 189
Romney, Mitt, 221
"Rose Revolution," 217
Rosenberg, John, 101
Rosengren, Eric, 152
Rosovsky, Henry, 69, 196
Rubin, Robert, viii, ix, 9, 24, 29, 53-55, 61, 69, 105, 112, 120, 136, 138, 145-7, 150, 153, 155, 171, 173, 180, 181, 185, 186, 189, 193, 195, 198, 210, 255
Rudenstine, Neil, 54, 60, 62, 69, 75, 87, 99, 114, 196,
Rudloff, Han-Joerg, 106
Rumsfeld, Donald, 196, 216
Ryan, Richard O., 110

**S**

Sachs, Jeffrey, viii, ix, 39, 44, 82, 83, 114, 141, 165, 169, 172, 174, 188
Safire, William, 245, 246
Sakharov, Andrei, 236
Salmon, Felix, 130, 157
Samuelson, Paul, 60, 155, 193, 198
Sarajevo, 212
Sarotte, May Elise, 225
Scheiber, Noam, 135, 136, 139
Schmemann, Serge, 228
Shevardnadze, Eduard, 206, 208
Scowcroft, Brent, 124, 206, 207, 209, 214
Scrushy, Richard, HealthSouth CEO, 92
Seward, Zachary, xiii
Shady Hill School, 182
Shane, Scott, 244
Shleifer, Andrei, vii-x, 3, 5-29, 36-41, 43-47, 49-56, 63, 65-75, 80-88, 92-100, 102-17, 120-2, 130-4, 136, 141, 142, 151, 155, 156, 160-172, 174-99, 201, 255, 258-68; as editor of *Journal of Economic Perspectives*, 9, 89; and Clark Medal, ix, 12, 52, 66, 73, 103; settlement, 68-71; as Nobel nominee, 114; as a "normal professor," 130 *ff*; letter to Carnesale, 185, 195-8; Steyer memo, text, 269 *ff*
Shipler, David, 227
Shultz, George, 110, 206-9
*Siloviki*, 31 *ff*, 108, 242, 245, 246
Simonyan, Margarita, 218, 219
Singer, Paul, 194
Smirno, Nikolai, 238, 240
Smith, Hedrick, 227
Smith, Richard, 195
Sochi Olympics, 221
South Ossetia, 219
"Snow Revolution," 220
Spence, Michael, 199
Sperling, Gene, 153

Srebrenica, 212
Stalin, Josef, 127, 230, 239, 256
*State and Revolution, The,* 204, 205, 235
"Star Wars" missile defense, 207
Steiger, Paul, xiii, 162, 192
Stein, Jeremy, 14, 152
Stern, US Attorney Donald, ix, 21, 27, 119, 120, 122
Stern School of Business, New York University, 13
"Steyer memo," 23, 182, 190; text, 269 *ff*
Stiglitz, Joseph, 9, 131
Stone, Robert, 9, 54, 69, 195
Subchak, Anatoly, 33
Sunshine, Gabriel, 180
Summers, Lawrence, iii, viii, ix-xii, 5-9, 14, 15, 36, 47-57, 60, 61, 65-69, 74-75, 81-88, 92-105, 108, 111-6, 120-2, 133, 135-41, 145-58, 160, 161, 165, 169-73, 182-9, 193-201, 229, 255; deposition, 24-29; and MIT, 53 *ff*; denies interference in Harvard's decision to go to trial, 97; on exclusion of Credit Suisse First Boston from Treasury forum, 105; and Justice Department, 116; Treasury view of USAID, 196; as candidate for treasury secretary, 135 *ff*; as candidate for chairman of the Federal Reserve, 142-4, 145-9; as Obama adviser, 188 *ff*; as candidate for World Bank presidency and Federal Reserve Board chairman, 193; non-Hodgkins lymphoma, 194 *ff*; as a social democrat, 255; betrayed by Shleifer and Zimmerman, 255
Swenson, David, 181, 194

*Systems of Survival: A Dialogue on the Moral Foundations of Commerce and Politics,* 247

## T

Taconic Capital Advisers, 189
Taibbi, Matt, 229
Talbott, Strobe, 156, 171-3, 185; biography of, 210-4, 220, 223, 229, 233, 253; special place in journalism hell, 229
Taylor, Anne, 54, 97, 99, 100, 195, 255
Teichman, Jennifer, xiii
*Ten Days that Shook the World,* 234, 235
Tillerson, Rex, 252
*Time* magazine, viii, 120, 156, 172, 229; "Committee to Save the World," ix, 61
Timofeev, Ivan, 256
*To The Finland Station,* 205
*Tragedy of Russia's Market Reforms: Market Bolshevism against Democracy, The,* 235
Traub, James, 101
Treisman, Daniel, *Without a Map,* 8, 11
Trump, Donald, iii, iv, xiii, 225, 232, 244, 248-52, 255
Trump World Tower, 252

## U

Ullman, Robert, 47
Ukraine crisis, 193, 223, 232
Unipolar, i, 217, 257
US Agency for International Development (USAID), vii-viii, ix-xiii, 6, 19, 21, 26, 28, 37-39, 43, 44, 46, 55, 66, 68, 72, 83, 86, 98, 105-8, 112-5,

120, 121, 131, 161, 170-3, 197, 201, 255 ; Harvard team's view of Moscow office, 171; whistle-blowers, 184-6; rumored call to US director by Summers, 115
US District Court, Portland, 186

## V

Valdai Discussion Club, 244, 256
Vasiliev, Dimitry, 6, 29, 44, 82-86, 121, 161, 167, 170-4, 178-4, 190, 197
Veblen, Thorsten, 246
Vishny, Robert, 11, 22, 27, 133, 196
Volcker, Paul, 139, 149, 154, 206, 207

## W

*Wall Street Journal*, vii, xii, xiii, 26, 50, 53, 64, 65, 72, 77, 88, 89, 92, 100, 128, 146, 154-6, 185, 186, 192, 193, 244, 249, 254, 255
Walt, Stephen, 225
Ware, Paul, 20, 45
Watson, James L., 58
Wayne, Leslie, 165
Wedel, Janine, 94
Weir, Fred, biography of, 235-241
Westad, Odd Arne, 235
Weitzman, Martin, 116, 117
Wilson, Edmund, 205
Winokur, Herbert, 9, 54, 69, 195
Woodlock, Judge Douglas, 7, 13; rulings, 16-23, 26, 27, 31, 34, 37, 40, 41, 43, 48, 49, 51, 55, 66, 72, 88, 98, 122, 186, 190, 191; on Steyer memo, 187
World Bank loan, 181-4, 191

World Economic Forum, Davos, 81, 84, 87, 146, 176, 177

## X

## Y

Yale University, 49-51, 68, 104, 115, 134, 153, 162, 181, 210, 213; endowment fund, 180, 194
Yanukovych, Viktor, 217, 221
Yellen, Janet, *The Fabulous Decade*, x, 146, 147, 152-5, 158, 193
Yeltsin, Boris, ii, vii, 4, 25, 26, 31-34, 66, 72, 83; biography of, 166-70, 173-9, 188, 209, 212-5, 224, 230, 231, 236, 240-2, 215, 236, 240

## Z

Zagachin, Julia, 84-86, 177-179, 181-5, 191
Zients, Jeffrey, 153, 154
Zimmerman, Nancy, vii, ix, 6, 21, 26, 71, 83-87, 130, 141, 172, 175-187, 189-192, 194, 197, 199, 255; settlement, 71; as Summers' adviser, 187; Steyer memo text, 269
Zoido, Pablo, 89
Zyuganov, Gennady, 83, 176, 177

Made in the USA
Middletown, DE
01 June 2018